SECOND EDITION

Machine Learning with Python Cookbook

Practical Solutions from Preprocessing
to Deep Learning

Kyle Gallatin and Chris Albon

Beijing · Boston · Farnham · Sebastopol · Tokyo

Machine Learning with Python Cookbook

by Kyle Gallatin and Chris Albon

Published by O'Reilly Media, Inc., 1005 Gravenstein Highway North, Sebastopol, CA 95472.

O'Reilly books may be purchased for educational, business, or sales promotional use. Online editions are also available for most titles (*http://oreilly.com*). For more information, contact our corporate/institutional sales department: 800-998-9938 or *corporate@oreilly.com*.

Acquisitions Editor: Nicole Butterfield	**Indexer:** Potomac Indexing, LLC
Development Editor: Jeff Bleiel	**Interior Designer:** David Futato
Production Editor: Clare Laylock	**Cover Designer:** Karen Montgomery
Copyeditor: Penelope Perkins	**Illustrator:** Kate Dullea
Proofreader: Piper Editorial Consulting, LLC	

April 2018:	First Edition
July 2023:	Second Edition

Revision History for the Second Edition

2023-07-27:   First Release

See *http://oreilly.com/catalog/errata.csp?isbn=9781098135720* for release details.

978-1-098-13572-0

[LSI]

Table of Contents

Preface

When the first edition of this book was published in 2018, it filled a critical gap in the growing wealth of machine learning (ML) content. By providing well-tested, hands-on Python recipes, it enabled practitioners to copy and paste code before easily adapting it to their use cases. In a short five years, the ML space has continued to explode with advances in deep learning (DL) and the associated DL Python frameworks.

Now, in 2023, there is a need for the same sort of hands-on content that serves the needs of both ML *and* DL practitioners with the latest Python libraries. This book intends to build on the existing (and fantastic) work done by the author of the first edition by:

- Updating existing examples to use the latest Python versions and frameworks
- Incorporating modern practices in data sources, data analysis, ML, and DL
- Expanding the DL content to include tensors, neural networks, and DL for text and vision in PyTorch
- Taking our models one step further by serving them in an API

Like the first edition, this book takes a task-based approach to machine learning, boasting over 200 self-contained solutions (copy, paste, and run) for the most common tasks a data scientist or machine learning engineer building a model will run into.

Conventions Used in This Book

The following typographical conventions are used in this book:

Italic
Indicates new terms, URLs, email addresses, filenames, and file extensions.

Constant width

> Used for program listings, as well as within paragraphs to refer to program elements such as variable or function names, databases, data types, environment variables, statements, and keywords.

Constant width bold

> Shows commands or other text that should be typed literally by the user.

Constant width italic

> Shows text that should be replaced with user-supplied values or by values determined by context.

Using Code Examples

This book is accompanied by a GitHub repository (*https://oreil.ly/MLwPython*) that has instructions for running a Jupyter Notebook in a Docker container with all dependencies used in this book. By replicating the commands from this book in the notebook, you can ensure the examples in this book will be completely reproducible.

If you have a technical question or a problem using the code examples, please send an email to *support@oreilly.com*.

This book is here to help you get your job done. In general, if example code is offered with this book, you may use it in your programs and documentation. You do not need to contact us for permission unless you're reproducing a significant portion of the code. For example, writing a program that uses several chunks of code from this book does not require permission. Selling or distributing examples from O'Reilly books does require permission. Answering a question by citing this book and quoting example code does not require permission. Incorporating a significant amount of example code from this book into your product's documentation does require permission.

We appreciate, but generally do not require, attribution. An attribution usually includes the title, author, publisher, and ISBN. For example: "*Machine Learning with Python Cookbook*, 2nd ed., by Kyle Gallatin and Chris Albon (O'Reilly). Copyright 2023 Kyle Gallatin, 978-1-098-13572-0."

If you feel your use of code examples falls outside fair use or the permission given above, feel free to contact us at *permissions@oreilly.com*.

O'Reilly Online Learning

O'REILLY® For more than 40 years, *O'Reilly Media* has provided technology and business training, knowledge, and insight to help companies succeed.

Our unique network of experts and innovators share their knowledge and expertise through books, articles, and our online learning platform. O'Reilly's online learning platform gives you on-demand access to live training courses, in-depth learning paths, interactive coding environments, and a vast collection of text and video from O'Reilly and 200+ other publishers. For more information, visit *https://oreilly.com*.

How to Contact Us

Please address comments and questions concerning this book to the publisher:

O'Reilly Media, Inc.
1005 Gravenstein Highway North
Sebastopol, CA 95472
800-889-8969 (in the United States or Canada)
707-829-7019 (international or local)
707-829-0104 (fax)
support@oreilly.com
https://www.oreilly.com/about/contact.html

We have a web page for this book, where we list errata, examples, and any additional information. You can access this page at *https://oreil.ly/ml_python_2e*.

For news and information about our books and courses, visit *https://oreilly.com*.

Find us on LinkedIn: *https://linkedin.com/company/oreilly-media*

Follow us on Twitter: *https://twitter.com/oreillymedia*

Watch us on YouTube: *https://youtube.com/oreillymedia*

Acknowledgments

The second edition of this book is clearly only possible because of the fantastic content, structure, and quality laid out in the first edition by the original author, Chris Albon. As the first author of the second edition, I cannot understate the degree to which this made my job way, way easier.

Of course, the machine learning space also evolves rapidly, and the updates included in this second edition could not have been written without the thoughtful feedback of my peers. I'd specifically like to thank my fellow Etsy coworkers Andrea Heyman, Maria Gomez, Alek Maelstrum, and Brian Schmidt for acquiescing to requests for input on various chapters and being unwillingly coaxed into sudden brainstorming sessions that shaped the new content added to this edition. I'd also like to thank the technical reviewers—Jigyasa Grover, Matteus Tanha, and Ganesh Harke—along with the O'Reilly editors: Jeff Bleiel, Nicole Butterfield, and Clare Laylock. That being said, the number of people who've helped me and this book get to the place it's at (in one way or another) is massive. I'd love to thank everyone who's been a part of my ML journey in one way or another and helped make this book what it is. Love y'all.

## CHAPTER 1

Working with Vectors, Matrices, and Arrays in NumPy

1.0 Introduction

NumPy is a foundational tool of the Python machine learning stack. NumPy allows for efficient operations on the data structures often used in machine learning: vectors, matrices, and tensors. While NumPy isn't the focus of this book, it will show up frequently in the following chapters. This chapter covers the most common NumPy operations we're likely to run into while working on machine learning workflows.

1.1 Creating a Vector

Problem

You need to create a vector.

Solution

Use NumPy to create a one-dimensional array:

```python
# Load library
import numpy as np

# Create a vector as a row
vector_row = np.array([1, 2, 3])

# Create a vector as a column
vector_column = np.array([[1],
                          [2],
                          [3]])
```

Discussion

NumPy's main data structure is the multidimensional array. A vector is just an array with a single dimension. To create a vector, we simply create a one-dimensional array. Just like vectors, these arrays can be represented horizontally (i.e., rows) or vertically (i.e., columns).

See Also

- Vectors, Math Is Fun (*https://oreil.ly/43I-b*)
- Euclidean vector, Wikipedia (*https://oreil.ly/er78t*)

1.2 Creating a Matrix

Problem

You need to create a matrix.

Solution

Use NumPy to create a two-dimensional array:

```
# Load library
import numpy as np

# Create a matrix
matrix = np.array([[1, 2],
                   [1, 2],
                   [1, 2]])
```

Discussion

To create a matrix we can use a NumPy two-dimensional array. In our solution, the matrix contains three rows and two columns (a column of 1s and a column of 2s).

NumPy actually has a dedicated matrix data structure:

```
matrix_object = np.mat([[1, 2],
                        [1, 2],
                        [1, 2]])

matrix([[1, 2],
        [1, 2],
        [1, 2]])
```

However, the matrix data structure is not recommended for two reasons. First, arrays are the de facto standard data structure of NumPy. Second, the vast majority of NumPy operations return arrays, not matrix objects.

See Also

- Matrix, Wikipedia (*https://oreil.ly/tnRJw*)
- Matrix, Wolfram MathWorld (*https://oreil.ly/76jUS*)

1.3 Creating a Sparse Matrix

Problem

Given data with very few nonzero values, you want to efficiently represent it.

Solution

Create a sparse matrix:

```
# Load libraries
import numpy as np
from scipy import sparse

# Create a matrix
matrix = np.array([[0, 0],
                   [0, 1],
                   [3, 0]])

# Create compressed sparse row (CSR) matrix
matrix_sparse = sparse.csr_matrix(matrix)
```

Discussion

A frequent situation in machine learning is having a huge amount of data; however, most of the elements in the data are zeros. For example, imagine a matrix where the columns are every movie on Netflix, the rows are every Netflix user, and the values are how many times a user has watched that particular movie. This matrix would have tens of thousands of columns and millions of rows! However, since most users do not watch most movies, the vast majority of elements would be zero.

A *sparse matrix* is a matrix in which most elements are 0. Sparse matrices store only nonzero elements and assume all other values will be zero, leading to significant computational savings. In our solution, we created a NumPy array with two nonzero values, then converted it into a sparse matrix. If we view the sparse matrix we can see that only the nonzero values are stored:

```
# View sparse matrix
print(matrix_sparse)

  (1, 1)    1
  (2, 0)    3
```

There are a number of types of sparse matrices. However, in *compressed sparse row* (CSR) matrices, `(1, 1)` and `(2, 0)` represent the (zero-indexed) indices of the nonzero values 1 and 3, respectively. For example, the element 1 is in the second row and second column. We can see the advantage of sparse matrices if we create a much larger matrix with many more zero elements and then compare this larger matrix with our original sparse matrix:

```
# Create larger matrix
matrix_large = np.array([[0, 0, 0, 0, 0, 0, 0, 0, 0, 0],
                         [0, 1, 0, 0, 0, 0, 0, 0, 0, 0],
                         [3, 0, 0, 0, 0, 0, 0, 0, 0, 0]])

# Create compressed sparse row (CSR) matrix
matrix_large_sparse = sparse.csr_matrix(matrix_large)

# View original sparse matrix
print(matrix_sparse)

  (1, 1)    1
  (2, 0)    3

# View larger sparse matrix
print(matrix_large_sparse)

  (1, 1)    1
  (2, 0)    3
```

As we can see, despite the fact that we added many more zero elements in the larger matrix, its sparse representation is exactly the same as our original sparse matrix. That is, the addition of zero elements did not change the size of the sparse matrix.

As mentioned, there are many different types of sparse matrices, such as compressed sparse column, list of lists, and dictionary of keys. While an explanation of the different types and their implications is outside the scope of this book, it is worth noting that while there is no "best" sparse matrix type, there are meaningful differences among them, and we should be conscious about why we are choosing one type over another.

See Also

- SciPy documentation: Sparse Matrices (*https://oreil.ly/zBBRB*)
- 101 Ways to Store a Sparse Matrix (*https://oreil.ly/sBQhN*)

1.4 Preallocating NumPy Arrays

Problem

You need to preallocate arrays of a given size with some value.

Solution

NumPy has functions for generating vectors and matrices of any size using 0s, 1s, or values of your choice:

```
# Load library
import numpy as np

# Generate a vector of shape (1,5) containing all zeros
vector = np.zeros(shape=5)

# View the matrix
print(vector)

array([0., 0., 0., 0., 0.])

# Generate a matrix of shape (3,3) containing all ones
matrix = np.full(shape=(3,3), fill_value=1)

# View the vector
print(matrix)

array([[1., 1., 1.],
       [1., 1., 1.],
       [1., 1., 1.]])
```

Discussion

Generating arrays prefilled with data is useful for a number of purposes, such as making code more performant or using synthetic data to test algorithms. In many programming languages, preallocating an array of default values (such as 0s) is considered common practice.

1.5 Selecting Elements

Problem

You need to select one or more elements in a vector or matrix.

Solution

NumPy arrays make it easy to select elements in vectors or matrices:

```
# Load library
import numpy as np

# Create row vector
vector = np.array([1, 2, 3, 4, 5, 6])

# Create matrix
matrix = np.array([[1, 2, 3],
```

```
       [4, 5, 6],
       [7, 8, 9]])

# Select third element of vector
vector[2]

3

# Select second row, second column
matrix[1,1]

5
```

Discussion

Like most things in Python, NumPy arrays are zero-indexed, meaning that the index of the first element is 0, not 1. With that caveat, NumPy offers a wide variety of methods for selecting (i.e., indexing and slicing) elements or groups of elements in arrays:

```
# Select all elements of a vector
vector[:]

array([1, 2, 3, 4, 5, 6])

# Select everything up to and including the third element
vector[:3]

array([1, 2, 3])

# Select everything after the third element
vector[3:]

array([4, 5, 6])

# Select the last element
vector[-1]

6

# Reverse the vector
vector[::-1]

array([6, 5, 4, 3, 2, 1])

# Select the first two rows and all columns of a matrix
matrix[:2,:]

array([[1, 2, 3],
       [4, 5, 6]])

# Select all rows and the second column
matrix[:,1:2]

array([[2],
       [5],
       [8]])
```

1.6 Describing a Matrix

Problem

You want to describe the shape, size, and dimensions of a matrix.

Solution

Use the shape, size, and ndim attributes of a NumPy object:

```
# Load library
import numpy as np

# Create matrix
matrix = np.array([[1, 2, 3, 4],
                   [5, 6, 7, 8],
                   [9, 10, 11, 12]])

# View number of rows and columns
matrix.shape

(3, 4)

# View number of elements (rows * columns)
matrix.size

12

# View number of dimensions
matrix.ndim

2
```

Discussion

This might seem basic (and it is); however, time and again it will be valuable to check the shape and size of an array both for further calculations and simply as a gut check after an operation.

1.7 Applying Functions over Each Element

Problem

You want to apply some function to all elements in an array.

Solution

Use the NumPy vectorize method:

```
# Load library
import numpy as np
```

```
# Create matrix
matrix = np.array([[1, 2, 3],
                   [4, 5, 6],
                   [7, 8, 9]])

# Create function that adds 100 to something
add_100 = lambda i: i + 100

# Create vectorized function
vectorized_add_100 = np.vectorize(add_100)

# Apply function to all elements in matrix
vectorized_add_100(matrix)

array([[101, 102, 103],
       [104, 105, 106],
       [107, 108, 109]])
```

Discussion

The NumPy `vectorize` method converts a function into a function that can apply to all elements in an array or slice of an array. It's worth noting that `vectorize` is essentially a `for` loop over the elements and does not increase performance. Furthermore, NumPy arrays allow us to perform operations between arrays even if their dimensions are not the same (a process called *broadcasting*). For example, we can create a much simpler version of our solution using broadcasting:

```
# Add 100 to all elements
matrix + 100

array([[101, 102, 103],
       [104, 105, 106],
       [107, 108, 109]])
```

Broadcasting does not work for all shapes and situations, but it is a common way of applying simple operations over all elements of a NumPy array.

1.8 Finding the Maximum and Minimum Values

Problem

You need to find the maximum or minimum value in an array.

Solution

Use NumPy's `max` and `min` methods:

```
# Load library
import numpy as np
```

```
# Create matrix
matrix = np.array([[1, 2, 3],
                   [4, 5, 6],
                   [7, 8, 9]])

# Return maximum element
np.max(matrix)

9

# Return minimum element
np.min(matrix)

1
```

Discussion

Often we want to know the maximum and minimum value in an array or subset of an array. This can be accomplished with the max and min methods. Using the axis parameter, we can also apply the operation along a certain axis:

```
# Find maximum element in each column
np.max(matrix, axis=0)

array([7, 8, 9])
```

```
# Find maximum element in each row
np.max(matrix, axis=1)

array([3, 6, 9])
```

1.9 Calculating the Average, Variance, and Standard Deviation

Problem

You want to calculate some descriptive statistics about an array.

Solution

Use NumPy's mean, var, and std:

```
# Load library
import numpy as np

# Create matrix
matrix = np.array([[1, 2, 3],
                   [4, 5, 6],
                   [7, 8, 9]])
```

```
# Return mean
np.mean(matrix)
```

```
5.0
```

```
# Return variance
np.var(matrix)
```

```
6.666666666666667
```

```
# Return standard deviation
np.std(matrix)
```

```
2.5819888974716112
```

Discussion

Just like with max and min, we can easily get descriptive statistics about the whole matrix or do calculations along a single axis:

```
# Find the mean value in each column
np.mean(matrix, axis=0)
```

```
array([ 4.,   5.,   6.])
```

1.10 Reshaping Arrays

Problem

You want to change the shape (number of rows and columns) of an array without changing the element values.

Solution

Use NumPy's reshape:

```
# Load library
import numpy as np
```

```
# Create 4x3 matrix
matrix = np.array([[1, 2, 3],
                   [4, 5, 6],
                   [7, 8, 9],
                   [10, 11, 12]])
```

```
# Reshape matrix into 2x6 matrix
matrix.reshape(2, 6)
```

```
array([[ 1,  2,  3,  4,  5,  6],
       [ 7,  8,  9, 10, 11, 12]])
```

Discussion

reshape allows us to restructure an array so that we maintain the same data but organize it as a different number of rows and columns. The only requirement is that the shape of the original and new matrix contain the same number of elements (i.e., are the same size). We can see the size of a matrix using size:

```
matrix.size
```
```
12
```

One useful argument in reshape is -1, which effectively means "as many as needed," so reshape(1, -1) means one row and as many columns as needed:

```
matrix.reshape(1, -1)
```
```
array([[ 1,  2,  3,  4,  5,  6,  7,  8,  9, 10, 11, 12]])
```

Finally, if we provide one integer, reshape will return a one-dimensional array of that length:

```
matrix.reshape(12)
```
```
array([ 1,  2,  3,  4,  5,  6,  7,  8,  9, 10, 11, 12])
```

1.11 Transposing a Vector or Matrix

Problem

You need to transpose a vector or matrix.

Solution

Use the T method:

```
# Load library
import numpy as np

# Create matrix
matrix = np.array([[1, 2, 3],
                   [4, 5, 6],
                   [7, 8, 9]])

# Transpose matrix
matrix.T

array([[1, 4, 7],
       [2, 5, 8],
       [3, 6, 9]])
```

Discussion

Transposing is a common operation in linear algebra where the column and row indices of each element are swapped. A nuanced point typically overlooked outside of a linear algebra class is that, technically, a vector can't be transposed because it's just a collection of values:

```
# Transpose vector
np.array([1, 2, 3, 4, 5, 6]).T

array([1, 2, 3, 4, 5, 6])
```

However, it is common to refer to transposing a vector as converting a row vector to a column vector (notice the second pair of brackets) or vice versa:

```
# Transpose row vector
np.array([[1, 2, 3, 4, 5, 6]]).T

array([[1],
       [2],
       [3],
       [4],
       [5],
       [6]])
```

1.12 Flattening a Matrix

Problem

You need to transform a matrix into a one-dimensional array.

Solution

Use the flatten method:

```
# Load library
import numpy as np

# Create matrix
matrix = np.array([[1, 2, 3],
                   [4, 5, 6],
                   [7, 8, 9]])

# Flatten matrix
matrix.flatten()

array([1, 2, 3, 4, 5, 6, 7, 8, 9])
```

Discussion

flatten is a simple method to transform a matrix into a one-dimensional array. Alternatively, we can use reshape to create a row vector:

```
matrix.reshape(1, -1)

array([[1, 2, 3, 4, 5, 6, 7, 8, 9]])
```

Another common way to flatten arrays is the ravel method. Unlike flatten, which returns a copy of the original array, ravel operates on the original object itself and is therefore slightly faster. It also lets us flatten lists of arrays, which we can't do with the flatten method. This operation is useful for flattening very large arrays and speeding up code:

```
# Create one matrix
matrix_a = np.array([[1, 2],
                     [3, 4]])

# Create a second matrix
matrix_b = np.array([[5, 6],
                     [7, 8]])

# Create a list of matrices
matrix_list = [matrix_a, matrix_b]

# Flatten the entire list of matrices
np.ravel(matrix_list)

array([1, 2, 3, 4, 5, 6, 7, 8])
```

1.13 Finding the Rank of a Matrix

Problem

You need to know the rank of a matrix.

Solution

Use NumPy's linear algebra method matrix_rank:

```
# Load library
import numpy as np

# Create matrix
matrix = np.array([[1, 1, 1],
                   [1, 1, 10],
                   [1, 1, 15]])

# Return matrix rank
np.linalg.matrix_rank(matrix)

2
```

Discussion

The *rank* of a matrix is the dimensions of the vector space spanned by its columns or rows. Finding the rank of a matrix is easy in NumPy thanks to `matrix_rank`.

See Also

- The Rank of a Matrix, CliffsNotes (*https://oreil.ly/Wg9ZG*)

1.14 Getting the Diagonal of a Matrix

Problem

You need to get the diagonal elements of a matrix.

Solution

Use NumPy's `diagonal`:

```
# Load library
import numpy as np

# Create matrix
matrix = np.array([[1, 2, 3],
                   [2, 4, 6],
                   [3, 8, 9]])

# Return diagonal elements
matrix.diagonal()

array([1, 4, 9])
```

Discussion

NumPy makes getting the diagonal elements of a matrix easy with `diagonal`. It is also possible to get a diagonal off the main diagonal by using the `offset` parameter:

```
# Return diagonal one above the main diagonal
matrix.diagonal(offset=1)

array([2, 6])

# Return diagonal one below the main diagonal
matrix.diagonal(offset=-1)

array([2, 8])
```

1.15 Calculating the Trace of a Matrix

Problem

You need to calculate the trace of a matrix.

Solution

Use trace:

```
# Load library
import numpy as np

# Create matrix
matrix = np.array([[1, 2, 3],
                   [2, 4, 6],
                   [3, 8, 9]])

# Return trace
matrix.trace()

14
```

Discussion

The *trace* of a matrix is the sum of the diagonal elements and is often used under the hood in machine learning methods. Given a NumPy multidimensional array, we can calculate the trace using trace. Alternatively, we can return the diagonal of a matrix and calculate its sum:

```
# Return diagonal and sum elements
sum(matrix.diagonal())

14
```

See Also

- The Trace of a Square Matrix (*https://oreil.ly/AhX1b*)

1.16 Calculating Dot Products

Problem

You need to calculate the dot product of two vectors.

Solution

Use NumPy's dot function:

```
# Load library
import numpy as np

# Create two vectors
vector_a = np.array([1,2,3])
vector_b = np.array([4,5,6])

# Calculate dot product
np.dot(vector_a, vector_b)

32
```

Discussion

The *dot product* of two vectors, a and b, is defined as:

$$\sum_{i=1}^{n} a_i b_i$$

where a_i is the ith element of vector a, and b_i is the ith element of vector b. We can use NumPy's dot function to calculate the dot product. Alternatively, in Python 3.5+ we can use the new @ operator:

```
# Calculate dot product
vector_a @ vector_b

32
```

See Also

- Vector Dot Product and Vector Length, Khan Academy (*https://oreil.ly/MpBt7*)
- Dot Product, Paul's Online Math Notes (*https://oreil.ly/EprM1*)

1.17 Adding and Subtracting Matrices

Problem

You want to add or subtract two matrices.

Solution

Use NumPy's add and subtract:

```
# Load library
import numpy as np

# Create matrix
matrix_a = np.array([[1, 1, 1],
```

```
                      [1, 1, 1],
                      [1, 1, 2]])

# Create matrix
matrix_b = np.array([[1, 3, 1],
                     [1, 3, 1],
                     [1, 3, 8]])

# Add two matrices
np.add(matrix_a, matrix_b)

array([[ 2,  4,  2],
       [ 2,  4,  2],
       [ 2,  4, 10]])

# Subtract two matrices
np.subtract(matrix_a, matrix_b)

array([[ 0, -2,  0],
       [ 0, -2,  0],
       [ 0, -2, -6]])
```

Discussion

Alternatively, we can simply use the + and − operators:

```
# Add two matrices
matrix_a + matrix_b

array([[ 2,  4,  2],
       [ 2,  4,  2],
       [ 2,  4, 10]])
```

1.18 Multiplying Matrices

Problem

You want to multiply two matrices.

Solution

Use NumPy's dot:

```
# Load library
import numpy as np

# Create matrix
matrix_a = np.array([[1, 1],
                     [1, 2]])

# Create matrix
matrix_b = np.array([[1, 3],
```

```
       [1, 2]])

# Multiply two matrices
np.dot(matrix_a, matrix_b)

array([[2, 5],
       [3, 7]])
```

Discussion

Alternatively, in Python 3.5+ we can use the @ operator:

```
# Multiply two matrices
matrix_a @ matrix_b

array([[2, 5],
       [3, 7]])
```

If we want to do element-wise multiplication, we can use the * operator:

```
# Multiply two matrices element-wise
matrix_a * matrix_b

array([[1, 3],
       [1, 4]])
```

See Also

- Array vs. Matrix Operations, MathWorks (*https://oreil.ly/_sFx5*)

1.19 Inverting a Matrix

Problem

You want to calculate the inverse of a square matrix.

Solution

Use NumPy's linear algebra inv method:

```
# Load library
import numpy as np

# Create matrix
matrix = np.array([[1, 4],
                   [2, 5]])

# Calculate inverse of matrix
np.linalg.inv(matrix)

array([[-1.66666667,  1.33333333],
       [ 0.66666667, -0.33333333]])
```

Discussion

The inverse of a square matrix, **A**, is a second matrix, $\mathbf{A}^{-1}$, such that:

$$\mathbf{A}\mathbf{A}^{-1} = \mathbf{I}$$

where **I** is the identity matrix. In NumPy we can use `linalg.inv` to calculate $\mathbf{A}^{-1}$ if it exists. To see this in action, we can multiply a matrix by its inverse, and the result is the identity matrix:

```
# Multiply matrix and its inverse
matrix @ np.linalg.inv(matrix)

array([[ 1.,  0.],
       [ 0.,  1.]])
```

See Also

- Inverse of a Matrix (*https://oreil.ly/SwRXC*)

1.20 Generating Random Values

Problem

You want to generate pseudorandom values.

Solution

Use NumPy's `random`:

```
# Load library
import numpy as np

# Set seed
np.random.seed(0)

# Generate three random floats between 0.0 and 1.0
np.random.random(3)

array([ 0.5488135 ,  0.71518937,  0.60276338])
```

Discussion

NumPy offers a wide variety of means to generate random numbers—many more than can be covered here. In our solution we generated floats; however, it is also common to generate integers:

```
# Generate three random integers between 0 and 10
np.random.randint(0, 11, 3)

array([3, 7, 9])
```

Alternatively, we can generate numbers by drawing them from a distribution (note this is not technically random):

```
# Draw three numbers from a normal distribution with mean 0.0
# and standard deviation of 1.0
np.random.normal(0.0, 1.0, 3)

array([-1.42232584,  1.52006949, -0.29139398])
```

```
# Draw three numbers from a logistic distribution with mean 0.0 and scale of 1.0
np.random.logistic(0.0, 1.0, 3)

array([-0.98118713, -0.08939902,  1.46416405])
```

```
# Draw three numbers greater than or equal to 1.0 and less than 2.0
np.random.uniform(1.0, 2.0, 3)

array([ 1.47997717,  1.3927848 ,  1.83607876])
```

Finally, sometimes it can be useful to return the same random numbers multiple times to get predictable, repeatable results. We can do this by setting the "seed" (an integer) of the pseudorandom generator. Random processes with the same seed will always produce the same output. We will use seeds throughout this book so that the code you see in the book and the code you run on your computer produces the same results.

## CHAPTER 2

Loading Data

2.0 Introduction

The first step in any machine learning endeavor is to get the raw data into our system. The raw data might be a logfile, dataset file, database, or cloud blob store such as Amazon S3. Furthermore, often we will want to retrieve data from multiple sources.

The recipes in this chapter look at methods of loading data from a variety of sources, including CSV files and SQL databases. We also cover methods of generating simulated data with desirable properties for experimentation. Finally, while there are many ways to load data in the Python ecosystem, we will focus on using the pandas library's extensive set of methods for loading external data, and using scikit-learn—an open source machine learning library in Python—for generating simulated data.

2.1 Loading a Sample Dataset

Problem

You want to load a preexisting sample dataset from the scikit-learn library.

Solution

scikit-learn comes with a number of popular datasets for you to use:

```
# Load scikit-learn's datasets
from sklearn import datasets

# Load digits dataset
digits = datasets.load_digits()

# Create features matrix
```

```
features = digits.data

# Create target vector
target = digits.target

# View first observation
features[0]

array([  0.,   0.,   5.,  13.,   9.,   1.,   0.,   0.,   0.,   0.,  13.,
        15.,  10.,  15.,   5.,   0.,   0.,   3.,  15.,   2.,   0.,  11.,
         8.,   0.,   0.,   4.,  12.,   0.,   0.,   8.,   8.,   0.,   0.,
         5.,   8.,   0.,   0.,   9.,   8.,   0.,   0.,   4.,  11.,   0.,
         1.,  12.,   7.,   0.,   0.,   2.,  14.,   5.,  10.,  12.,   0.,
         0.,   0.,   0.,   6.,  13.,  10.,   0.,   0.,   0.])
```

Discussion

Often we do not want to go through the work of loading, transforming, and cleaning a real-world dataset before we can explore some machine learning algorithm or method. Luckily, scikit-learn comes with some common datasets we can quickly load. These datasets are often called "toy" datasets because they are far smaller and cleaner than a dataset we would see in the real world. Some popular sample datasets in scikit-learn are:

load_iris

Contains 150 observations on the measurements of iris flowers. It is a good dataset for exploring classification algorithms.

load_digits

Contains 1,797 observations from images of handwritten digits. It is a good dataset for teaching image classification.

To see more details on any of these datasets, you can print the DESCR attribute:

```
# Load scikit-learn's datasets
from sklearn import datasets

# Load digits dataset
digits = datasets.load_digits()

# Print the attribute
print(digits.DESCR)

.. _digits_dataset:

Optical recognition of handwritten digits dataset
--------------------------------------------------

**Data Set Characteristics:**

    :Number of Instances: 1797
```

```
:Number of Attributes: 64
:Attribute Information: 8x8 image of integer pixels in the range 0..16.
:Missing Attribute Values: None
:Creator: E. Alpaydin (alpaydin '@' boun.edu.tr)
:Date: July; 1998
...
```

See Also

- scikit-learn toy datasets (*https://oreil.ly/WS1gc*)
- The Digit Dataset (*https://oreil.ly/0hukv*)

2.2 Creating a Simulated Dataset

Problem

You need to generate a dataset of simulated data.

Solution

scikit-learn offers many methods for creating simulated data. Of those, three methods are particularly useful: make_regression, make_classification, and make_blobs.

When we want a dataset designed to be used with linear regression, make_regression is a good choice:

```
# Load library
from sklearn.datasets import make_regression

# Generate features matrix, target vector, and the true coefficients
features, target, coefficients = make_regression(n_samples = 100,
                                                 n_features = 3,
                                                 n_informative = 3,
                                                 n_targets = 1,
                                                 noise = 0.0,
                                                 coef = True,
                                                 random_state = 1)

# View feature matrix and target vector
print('Feature Matrix\n', features[:3])
print('Target Vector\n', target[:3])

Feature Matrix
 [[ 1.29322588 -0.61736206 -0.11044703]
 [-2.793085    0.36633201  1.93752881]
 [ 0.80186103 -0.18656977  0.0465673 ]]
Target Vector
 [-10.37865986  25.5124503   19.67705609]
```

If we are interested in creating a simulated dataset for classification, we can use make_classification:

```
# Load library
from sklearn.datasets import make_classification

# Generate features matrix and target vector
features, target = make_classification(n_samples = 100,
                                        n_features = 3,
                                        n_informative = 3,
                                        n_redundant = 0,
                                        n_classes = 2,
                                        weights = [.25, .75],
                                        random_state = 1)

# View feature matrix and target vector
print('Feature Matrix\n', features[:3])
print('Target Vector\n', target[:3])

Feature Matrix
 [[ 1.06354768 -1.42632219  1.02163151]
 [ 0.23156977  1.49535261  0.33251578]
 [ 0.15972951  0.83533515 -0.40869554]]
Target Vector
 [1 0 0]
```

Finally, if we want a dataset designed to work well with clustering techniques, scikit-learn offers make_blobs:

```
# Load library
from sklearn.datasets import make_blobs

# Generate features matrix and target vector
features, target = make_blobs(n_samples = 100,
                              n_features = 2,
                              centers = 3,
                              cluster_std = 0.5,
                              shuffle = True,
                              random_state = 1)

# View feature matrix and target vector
print('Feature Matrix\n', features[:3])
print('Target Vector\n', target[:3])

Feature Matrix
 [[ -1.22685609   3.25572052]
 [ -9.57463218  -4.38310652]
 [-10.71976941  -4.20558148]]
Target Vector
 [0 1 1]
```

Discussion

As might be apparent from the solutions, make_regression returns a feature matrix of float values and a target vector of float values, while make_classification and make_blobs return a feature matrix of float values and a target vector of integers representing membership in a class.

scikit-learn's simulated datasets offer extensive options to control the type of data generated. scikit-learn's documentation contains a full description of all the parameters, but a few are worth noting.

In make_regression and make_classification, n_informative determines the number of features that are used to generate the target vector. If n_informative is less than the total number of features (n_features), the resulting dataset will have redundant features that can be identified through feature selection techniques.

In addition, make_classification contains a weights parameter that allows us to simulate datasets with imbalanced classes. For example, weights = [.25, .75] would return a dataset with 25% of observations belonging to one class and 75% of observations belonging to a second class.

For make_blobs, the centers parameter determines the number of clusters generated. Using the matplotlib visualization library, we can visualize the clusters generated by make_blobs:

```
# Load library
import matplotlib.pyplot as plt

# View scatterplot
plt.scatter(features[:,0], features[:,1], c=target)
plt.show()
```

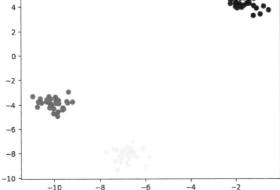

See Also

- `make_regression` documentation (*https://oreil.ly/VrtN3*)
- `make_classification` documentation (*https://oreil.ly/rehc-*)
- `make_blobs` documentation (*https://oreil.ly/1LZAI*)

2.3 Loading a CSV File

Problem

You need to import a comma-separated value (CSV) file.

Solution

Use the pandas library's `read_csv` to load a local or hosted CSV file into a pandas DataFrame:

```
# Load library
import pandas as pd

# Create URL
url = 'https://raw.githubusercontent.com/chrisalbon/sim_data/master/data.csv'

# Load dataset
dataframe = pd.read_csv(url)

# View first two rows
dataframe.head(2)
```

	integer	datetime	category
0	5	2015-01-01 00:00:00	0
1	5	2015-01-01 00:00:01	0

Discussion

There are two things to note about loading CSV files. First, it is often useful to take a quick look at the contents of the file before loading. It can be very helpful to see how a dataset is structured beforehand and what parameters we need to set to load in the file. Second, `read_csv` has over 30 parameters and therefore the documentation can be daunting. Fortunately, those parameters are mostly there to allow it to handle a wide variety of CSV formats.

CSV files get their names from the fact that the values are literally separated by commas (e.g., one row might be `2,"2015-01-01 00:00:00",0`); however, it is common for CSV files to use other separators, such as tabs (which are referred to as TSV files).

The pandas `sep` parameter allows us to define the delimiter used in the file. Although it is not always the case, a common formatting issue with CSV files is that the first line of the file is used to define column headers (e.g., `integer`, `datetime`, `category` in our solution). The `header` parameter allows us to specify if or where a header row exists. If a header row does not exist, we set `header=None`.

The `read_csv` function returns a pandas DataFrame: a common and useful object for working with tabular data that we'll cover in more depth throughout this book.

2.4 Loading an Excel File

Problem

You need to import an Excel spreadsheet.

Solution

Use the pandas library's `read_excel` to load an Excel spreadsheet:

```
# Load library
import pandas as pd

# Create URL
url = 'https://raw.githubusercontent.com/chrisalbon/sim_data/master/data.xlsx'

# Load data
dataframe = pd.read_excel(url, sheet_name=0, header=0)

# View the first two rows
dataframe.head(2)
```

	integer	datetime	category
	5	2015-01-01 00:00:00	0
0	5	2015-01-01 00:00:01	0
1	9	2015-01-01 00:00:02	0

Discussion

This solution is similar to our solution for reading CSV files. The main difference is the additional parameter, `sheet_name`, that specifies which sheet in the Excel file we wish to load. `sheet_name` can accept both strings, containing the name of the sheet, and integers, pointing to sheet positions (zero-indexed). If we need to load multiple sheets, we include them as a list. For example, `sheet_name=[0,1,2, "Monthly Sales"]` will return a dictionary of pandas DataFrames containing the first, second, and third sheets, and the sheet named `Monthly Sales`.

2.5 Loading a JSON File

Problem

You need to load a JSON file for data preprocessing.

Solution

The pandas library provides `read_json` to convert a JSON file into a pandas object:

```
# Load library
import pandas as pd

# Create URL
url = 'https://raw.githubusercontent.com/chrisalbon/sim_data/master/data.json'

# Load data
dataframe = pd.read_json(url, orient='columns')

# View the first two rows
dataframe.head(2)
```

	category	datetime	integer
0	0	2015-01-01 00:00:00	5
1	0	2015-01-01 00:00:01	5

Discussion

Importing JSON files into pandas is similar to the last few recipes we have seen. The key difference is the `orient` parameter, which indicates to pandas how the JSON file is structured. However, it might take some experimenting to figure out which argument (`split`, `records`, `index`, `columns`, or `values`) is the right one. Another helpful tool pandas offers is `json_normalize`, which can help convert semistructured JSON data into a pandas DataFrame.

See Also

- `json_normalize` documentation (*https://oreil.ly/nuvIB*)

2.6 Loading a Parquet File

Problem

You need to load a Parquet file.

Solution

The pandas `read_parquet` function allows us to read in Parquet files:

```
# Load library
import pandas as pd

# Create URL
url = 'https://machine-learning-python-cookbook.s3.amazonaws.com/data.parquet'

# Load data
dataframe = pd.read_parquet(url)

# View the first two rows
dataframe.head(2)
```

	category	datetime	integer
0	0	2015-01-01 00:00:00	5
1	0	2015-01-01 00:00:01	5

Discussion

Parquet is a popular data storage format in the large data space. It is often used with big data tools such as Hadoop and Spark. While PySpark is outside the focus of this book, it's highly likely companies operating on a large scale will use an efficient data storage format such as Parquet, and it's valuable to know how to read it into a dataframe and manipulate it.

See Also

- Apache Parquet documentation (*https://oreil.ly/M5bRq*)

2.7 Loading an Avro File

Problem

You need to load an Avro file into a pandas DataFrame.

Solution

The use the `pandavro` library's `read_avro` method:

```
# Load library
import requests
import pandavro as pdx

# Create URL
url = 'https://machine-learning-python-cookbook.s3.amazonaws.com/data.avro'
```

```
# Download file
r = requests.get(url)
open('data.avro', 'wb').write(r.content)

# Load data
dataframe = pdx.read_avro('data.avro')

# View the first two rows
dataframe.head(2)
```

	category	datetime	integer
0	0	2015-01-01 00:00:00	5
1	0	2015-01-01 00:00:01	5

Discussion

Apache Avro is an open source, binary data format that relies on schemas for the data structure. At the time of writing, it is not as common as Parquet. However, large binary data formats such as Avro, thrift, and Protocol Buffers are growing in popularity due to their efficient nature. If you work with large data systems, you're likely to run into one of these formats in the near future.

See Also

- Apache Avro documentation (*https://oreil.ly/Y1TJA*)

2.8 Querying a SQLite Database

Problem

You need to load data from a database using structured query language (SQL).

Solution

pandas' read_sql_query allows us to make an SQL query to a database and load it:

```
# Load libraries
import pandas as pd
from sqlalchemy import create_engine

# Create a connection to the database
database_connection = create_engine('sqlite:///sample.db')

# Load data
dataframe = pd.read_sql_query('SELECT * FROM data', database_connection)
```

```
# View first two rows
dataframe.head(2)
```

	first_name	last_name	age	preTestScore	postTestScore
0	Jason	Miller	42	4	25
1	Molly	Jacobson	52	24	94

Discussion

SQL is the lingua franca for pulling data from databases. In this recipe we first use `create_engine` to define a connection to an SQL database engine called SQLite. Next we use pandas' `read_sql_query` to query that database using SQL and put the results in a DataFrame.

SQL is a language in its own right and, while beyond the scope of this book, it is certainly worth knowing for anyone wanting to learn about machine learning. Our SQL query, `SELECT * FROM data`, asks the database to give us all columns (*) from the table called `data`.

Note that this is one of a few recipes in this book that will not run without extra code. Specifically, `create_engine('sqlite:///sample.db')` assumes that an SQLite database already exists.

See Also

- SQLite (*https://oreil.ly/8Y91T*)
- W3Schools SQL Tutorial (*https://oreil.ly/A7H1m*)

2.9 Querying a Remote SQL Database

Problem

You need to connect to, and read from, a remote SQL database.

Solution

Create a connection with `pymysql` and read it into a dataframe with pandas:

```
# Import libraries
import pymysql
import pandas as pd

# Create a DB connection
# Use the following example to start a DB instance
# https://github.com/kylegallatin/mysql-db-example
conn = pymysql.connect(
```

```
        host='localhost',
        user='root',
        password = "",
        db='db',
    )

    # Read the SQL query into a dataframe
    dataframe = pd.read_sql("select * from data", conn)

    # View the first two rows
    dataframe.head(2)
```

	integer	datetime	category
0	5	2015-01-01 00:00:00	0
1	5	2015-01-01 00:00:01	0

Discussion

Of all of the recipes presented in this chapter, this is probably the one we will use most in the real world. While connecting and reading from an example `sqlite` database is useful, it's likely not representative of tables you'll need to connect to in an enterprise environment. Most SQL instances that you'll connect to will require you to connect to the host and port of a remote machine, specifying a username and password for authentication. This example requires you to start a running SQL instance locally (*https://oreil.ly/Sxjqz*) that mimics a remote server on localhost so that you can get a sense of the workflow.

See Also

- PyMySQL documentation (*https://oreil.ly/8zSnj*)
- pandas Read SQL documentation (*https://oreil.ly/Yb7sH*)

2.10 Loading Data from a Google Sheet

Problem

You need to read in data directly from a Google Sheet.

Solution

Use pandas `read_CSV` and pass a URL that exports the Google Sheet as a CSV:

```
# Import libraries
import pandas as pd

# Google Sheet URL that downloads the sheet as a CSV
```

```
url = "https://docs.google.com/spreadsheets/d/"\
    "1ehC-9otcAuitqnmWksqt1mOrTRCL38dv0K9UjhwzTOA/export?format=csv"

# Read the CSV into a dataframe
dataframe = pd.read_csv(url)

# View the first two rows
dataframe.head(2)
```

	integer	datetime	category
0	5	2015-01-01 00:00:00	0
1	5	2015-01-01 00:00:01	0

Discussion

While Google Sheets can easily be downloaded, it's sometimes helpful to be able to read them directly into Python without any intermediate steps. The /export?format=csv query parameter at the end of the URL above creates an endpoint from which we can either download the file or read it into pandas.

See Also

- Google Sheets API (*https://oreil.ly/GRLzg*)

2.11 Loading Data from an S3 Bucket

Problem

You need to read a CSV file from an S3 bucket you have access to.

Solution

Add storage options to pandas giving it access to the S3 object:

```
# Import libraries
import pandas as pd

# S3 path to CSV
s3_uri = "s3://machine-learning-python-cookbook/data.csv"

# Set AWS credentials (replace with your own)
ACCESS_KEY_ID = "xxxxxxxxxxxxxx"
SECRET_ACCESS_KEY = "xxxxxxxxxxxxxxxx"

# Read the CSV into a dataframe
dataframe = pd.read_csv(s3_uri,storage_options={
        "key": ACCESS_KEY_ID,
        "secret": SECRET_ACCESS_KEY,
```

```
    }
)

# View first two rows
dataframe.head(2)
```

	integer	datetime	category
0	5	2015-01-01 00:00:00	0
1	5	2015-01-01 00:00:01	0

Discussion

Many enterprises now keep data in cloud provider blob stores such as Amazon S3 or Google Cloud Storage (GCS). It's common for machine learning practitioners to connect to these sources to retrieve data. Although the S3 URI (`s3://machine-learning-python-cookbook/data.csv`) is public, it still requires you to provide your own AWS access credentials to access it. It's worth noting that public objects also have HTTP URLs from which they can download files, such as this one for the CSV file (*https://oreil.ly/byelc*).

See Also

- Amazon S3 (*https://oreil.ly/E-CZX*)
- AWS Security Credentials (*https://oreil.ly/aHBBb*)

2.12 Loading Unstructured Data

Problem

You need to load unstructured data like text or images.

Solution

Use the base Python open function to load the information:

```
# Import libraries
import requests

# URL to download the txt file from
txt_url = "https://machine-learning-python-cookbook.s3.amazonaws.com/text.txt"

# Get the txt file
r = requests.get(txt_url)

# Write it to text.txt locally
with open('text.txt', 'wb') as f:
```

```
        f.write(r.content)

# Read in the file
with open('text.txt', 'r') as f:
    text = f.read()

# Print the content
print(text)

Hello there!
```

Discussion

While structured data can easily be read in from CSV, JSON, or various databases, unstructured data can be more challenging and may require custom processing down the line. Sometimes it's helpful to open and read in files using Python's basic open function. This allows us to open files and then read the content of that file.

See Also

- Python's open function (*https://oreil.ly/Xuuom*)
- Context managers in Python (*https://oreil.ly/UyZnL*)

## CHAPTER 3

Data Wrangling

3.0 Introduction

Data wrangling is a broad term used, often informally, to describe the process of transforming raw data into a clean, organized format ready for use. For us, data wrangling is only one step in preprocessing our data, but it is an important step.

The most common data structure used to "wrangle" data is the dataframe, which can be both intuitive and incredibly versatile. Dataframes are tabular, meaning that they are based on rows and columns like you would see in a spreadsheet. Here is a dataframe created from data about passengers on the *Titanic*:

```
# Load library
import pandas as pd

# Create URL
url = 'https://raw.githubusercontent.com/chrisalbon/sim_data/master/titanic.csv'

# Load data as a dataframe
dataframe = pd.read_csv(url)

# Show first five rows
dataframe.head(5)
```

	Name	PClass	Age	Sex	Survived	SexCode
0	Allen, Miss Elisabeth Walton	1st	29.00	female	1	1
1	Allison, Miss Helen Loraine	1st	2.00	female	0	1
2	Allison, Mr Hudson Joshua Creighton	1st	30.00	male	0	0
3	Allison, Mrs Hudson JC (Bessie Waldo Daniels)	1st	25.00	female	0	1
4	Allison, Master Hudson Trevor	1st	0.92	male	1	0

There are three important things to notice in this dataframe.

First, in a dataframe each row corresponds to one observation (e.g., a passenger) and each column corresponds to one feature (gender, age, etc.). For example, by looking at the first observation we can see that Miss Elisabeth Walton Allen stayed in first class, was 29 years old, was female, and survived the disaster.

Second, each column contains a name (e.g., Name, PClass, Age) and each row contains an index number (e.g., 0 for the lucky Miss Elisabeth Walton Allen). We will use these to select and manipulate observations and features.

Third, two columns, Sex and SexCode, contain the same information in different formats. In Sex, a woman is indicated by the string female, while in SexCode, a woman is indicated by using the integer 1. We will want all our features to be unique, and therefore we will need to remove one of these columns.

In this chapter, we will cover a wide variety of techniques to manipulate dataframes using the pandas library with the goal of creating a clean, well-structured set of observations for further preprocessing.

3.1 Creating a Dataframe

Problem

You want to create a new dataframe.

Solution

pandas has many methods for creating a new DataFrame object. One easy method is to instantiate a DataFrame using a Python dictionary. In the dictionary, each key is a column name and the value is a list, where each item corresponds to a row:

```
# Load library
import pandas as pd

# Create a dictionary
dictionary = {
  "Name": ['Jacky Jackson', 'Steven Stevenson'],
  "Age": [38, 25],
  "Driver": [True, False]
}

# Create DataFrame
dataframe = pd.DataFrame(dictionary)

# Show DataFrame
dataframe
```

	Name	Age	Driver
0	Jacky Jackson	38	True
1	Steven Stevenson	25	False

It's easy to add new columns to any dataframe using a list of values:

```
# Add a column for eye color
dataframe["Eyes"] = ["Brown", "Blue"]

# Show DataFrame
dataframe
```

	Name	Age	Driver	Eyes
0	Jacky Jackson	38	True	Brown
1	Steven Stevenson	25	False	Blue

Discussion

pandas offers what can feel like an infinite number of ways to create a DataFrame. In the real world, creating an empty DataFrame and then populating it will almost never happen. Instead, our DataFrames will be created from real data we have loaded from other sources (e.g., a CSV file or database).

3.2 Getting Information about the Data

Problem

You want to view some characteristics of a DataFrame.

Solution

One of the easiest things we can do after loading the data is view the first few rows using head:

```
# Load library
import pandas as pd

# Create URL
url = 'https://raw.githubusercontent.com/chrisalbon/sim_data/master/titanic.csv'

# Load data
dataframe = pd.read_csv(url)

# Show two rows
dataframe.head(2)
```

	Name	PClass	Age	Sex	Survived	SexCode
0	Allen, Miss Elisabeth Walton	1st	29.0	female	1	1
1	Allison, Miss Helen Loraine	1st	2.0	female	0	1

We can also take a look at the number of rows and columns:

```
# Show dimensions
dataframe.shape
```

```
(1313, 6)
```

We can get descriptive statistics for any numeric columns using `describe`:

```
# Show statistics
dataframe.describe()
```

	Age	Survived	SexCode
count	756.000000	1313.000000	1313.000000
mean	30.397989	0.342727	0.351866
std	14.259049	0.474802	0.477734
min	0.170000	0.000000	0.000000
25%	21.000000	0.000000	0.000000
50%	28.000000	0.000000	0.000000
75%	39.000000	1.000000	1.000000
max	71.000000	1.000000	1.000000

Additionally, the `info` method can show some helpful information:

```
# Show info
dataframe.info()
```

```
<class 'pandas.core.frame.DataFrame'>
RangeIndex: 1313 entries, 0 to 1312
Data columns (total 6 columns):
 #   Column    Non-Null Count  Dtype
---  ------    --------------  -----
 0   Name      1313 non-null   object
 1   PClass    1313 non-null   object
 2   Age       756 non-null    float64
 3   Sex       1313 non-null   object
 4   Survived  1313 non-null   int64
 5   SexCode   1313 non-null   int64
dtypes: float64(1), int64(2), object(3)
memory usage: 61.7+ KB
```

Discussion

After we load some data, it's a good idea to understand how it's structured and what kind of information it contains. Ideally, we would view the full data directly. But with most real-world cases, the data could have thousands to hundreds of thousands to millions of rows and columns. Instead, we have to rely on pulling samples to view small slices and calculating summary statistics of the data.

In our solution, we are using a toy dataset of the passengers of the *Titanic*. Using head, we can look at the first few rows (five by default) of the data. Alternatively, we can use tail to view the last few rows. With shape we can see how many rows and columns our DataFrame contains. With describe we can see some basic descriptive statistics for any numerical column. And, finally, info displays a number of helpful data points about the DataFrame, including index and column data types, non-null values, and memory usage.

It is worth noting that summary statistics do not always tell the full story. For example, pandas treats the columns Survived and SexCode as numeric columns because they contain 1s and 0s. However, in this case the numerical values represent categories. For example, if Survived equals 1, it indicates that the passenger survived the disaster. For this reason, some of the summary statistics provided don't make sense, such as the standard deviation of the SexCode column (an indicator of the passenger's gender).

3.3 Slicing DataFrames

Problem

You need to select a specific subset data or slices of a DataFrame.

Solution

Use loc or iloc to select one or more rows or values:

```
# Load library
import pandas as pd

# Create URL
url = 'https://raw.githubusercontent.com/chrisalbon/sim_data/master/titanic.csv'

# Load data
dataframe = pd.read_csv(url)

# Select first row
dataframe.iloc[0]

Name        Allen, Miss Elisabeth Walton
PClass                               1st
Age                                   29
Sex                               female
Survived                               1
```

```
SexCode                                    1
Name: 0, dtype: object
```

We can use : to define the slice of rows we want, such as selecting the second, third, and fourth rows:

```
# Select three rows
dataframe.iloc[1:4]
```

	Name	PClass	Age	Sex	Survived	SexCode
1	Allison, Miss Helen Loraine	1st	2.0	female	0	1
2	Allison, Mr Hudson Joshua Creighton	1st	30.0	male	0	0
3	Allison, Mrs Hudson JC (Bessie Waldo Daniels)	1st	25.0	female	0	1

We can even use it to get all rows up to a point, such as all rows up to and including the fourth row:

```
# Select four rows
dataframe.iloc[:4]
```

	Name	PClass	Age	Sex	Survived	SexCode
0	Allen, Miss Elisabeth Walton	1st	29.0	female	1	1
1	Allison, Miss Helen Loraine	1st	2.0	female	0	1
2	Allison, Mr Hudson Joshua Creighton	1st	30.0	male	0	0
3	Allison, Mrs Hudson JC (Bessie Waldo Daniels)	1st	25.0	female	0	1

DataFrames do not need to be numerically indexed. We can set the index of a DataFrame to any value where the value is unique to each row. For example, we can set the index to be passenger names and then select rows using a name:

```
# Set index
dataframe = dataframe.set_index(dataframe['Name'])

# Show row
dataframe.loc['Allen, Miss Elisabeth Walton']

Name           Allen, Miss Elisabeth Walton
PClass                                  1st
Age                                      29
Sex                                   female
Survived                                  1
SexCode                                   1
Name: Allen, Miss Elisabeth Walton, dtype: object
```

Discussion

All rows in a pandas DataFrame have a unique index value. By default, this index is an integer indicating the row position in the DataFrame; however, it does not have to be. DataFrame indexes can be set to be unique alphanumeric strings or customer numbers. To select individual rows and slices of rows, pandas provides two methods:

- loc is useful when the index of the DataFrame is a label (e.g., a string).
- iloc works by looking for the position in the DataFrame. For example, iloc[0] will return the first row regardless of whether the index is an integer or a label.

It is useful to be comfortable with both loc and iloc since they will come up a lot during data cleaning.

3.4 Selecting Rows Based on Conditionals

Problem

You want to select DataFrame rows based on some condition.

Solution

This can be done easily in pandas. For example, if we wanted to select all the women on the *Titanic*:

```
# Load library
import pandas as pd

# Create URL
url = 'https://raw.githubusercontent.com/chrisalbon/sim_data/master/titanic.csv'

# Load data
dataframe = pd.read_csv(url)

# Show top two rows where column 'sex' is 'female'
dataframe[dataframe['Sex'] == 'female'].head(2)
```

	Name	PClass	Age	Sex	Survived	SexCode
0	Allen, Miss Elisabeth Walton	1st	29.0	female	1	1
1	Allison, Miss Helen Loraine	1st	2.0	female	0	1

Take a moment to look at the format of this solution. Our conditional statement is dataframe['Sex'] == 'female'; by wrapping that in dataframe[] we are telling pandas to "select all the rows in the DataFrame where the value of dataframe['Sex'] is 'female'." These conditions result in a pandas series of booleans.

Multiple conditions are easy as well. For example, here we select all the rows where the passenger is a female 65 or older:

```
# Filter rows
dataframe[(dataframe['Sex'] == 'female') & (dataframe['Age'] >= 65)]
```

	Name	PClass	Age	Sex	Survived	SexCode
73	Crosby, Mrs Edward Gifford (Catherine Elizabet...	1st	69.0	female	1	1

Discussion

Conditionally selecting and filtering data is one of the most common tasks in data wrangling. You rarely want all the raw data from the source; instead, you are interested in only some subset of it. For example, you might only be interested in stores in certain states or the records of patients over a certain age.

3.5 Sorting Values

Problem

You need to sort a dataframe by the values in a column.

Solution

Use the pandas `sort_values` function:

```
# Load library
import pandas as pd

# Create URL
url = 'https://raw.githubusercontent.com/chrisalbon/sim_data/master/titanic.csv'

# Load data
dataframe = pd.read_csv(url)

# Sort the dataframe by age, show two rows
dataframe.sort_values(by=["Age"]).head(2)
```

	Name	PClass	Age	Sex	Survived	SexCode
763	Dean, Miss Elizabeth Gladys (Millvena)	3rd	0.17	female	1	1
751	Danbom, Master Gilbert Sigvard Emanuel	3rd	0.33	male	0	0

Discussion

During data analysis and exploration, it's often useful to sort a DataFrame by a particular column or set of columns. The by argument to `sort_values` takes a list of columns by which to sort the DataFrame and will sort based on the order of column names in the list.

By default, the `ascending` argument is set to `True`, so it will sort the values lowest to highest. If we wanted the oldest passengers instead of the youngest, we could set it to `False`.

3.6 Replacing Values

Problem

You need to replace values in a DataFrame.

Solution

The pandas `replace` method is an easy way to find and replace values. For example, we can replace any instance of `"female"` in the Sex column with `"Woman"`:

```
# Load library
import pandas as pd

# Create URL
url = 'https://raw.githubusercontent.com/chrisalbon/sim_data/master/titanic.csv'

# Load data
dataframe = pd.read_csv(url)

# Replace values, show two rows
dataframe['Sex'].replace("female", "Woman").head(2)

0    Woman
1    Woman
Name: Sex, dtype: object
```

We can also replace multiple values at the same time:

```
# Replace "female" and "male" with "Woman" and "Man"
dataframe['Sex'].replace(["female", "male"], ["Woman", "Man"]).head(5)

0    Woman
1    Woman
2      Man
3    Woman
4      Man
Name: Sex, dtype: object
```

We can also find and replace across the entire `DataFrame` object by specifying the whole dataframe instead of a single column:

```
# Replace values, show two rows
dataframe.replace(1, "One").head(2)
```

	Name	PClass	Age	Sex	Survived	SexCode
0	Allen, Miss Elisabeth Walton	1st	29	female	One	One
1	Allison, Miss Helen Loraine	1st	2	female	0	One

`replace` also accepts regular expressions:

```
# Replace values, show two rows
dataframe.replace(r"1st", "First", regex=True).head(2)
```

	Name	PClass	Age	Sex	Survived	SexCode
0	Allen, Miss Elisabeth Walton	First	29.0	female	1	1
1	Allison, Miss Helen Loraine	First	2.0	female	0	1

Discussion

`replace` is a tool we use to replace values. It is simple and yet has the powerful ability to accept regular expressions.

3.7 Renaming Columns

Problem

You want to rename a column in a pandas DataFrame.

Solution

Rename columns using the `rename` method:

```
# Load library
import pandas as pd

# Create URL
url = 'https://raw.githubusercontent.com/chrisalbon/sim_data/master/titanic.csv'

# Load data
dataframe = pd.read_csv(url)

# Rename column, show two rows
dataframe.rename(columns={'PClass': 'Passenger Class'}).head(2)
```

	Name	Passenger Class	Age	Sex	Survived	SexCode
0	Allen, Miss Elisabeth Walton	1st	29.0	female	1	1
1	Allison, Miss Helen Loraine	1st	2.0	female	0	1

Notice that the `rename` method can accept a dictionary as a parameter. We can use the dictionary to change multiple column names at once:

```
# Rename columns, show two rows
dataframe.rename(columns={'PClass': 'Passenger Class', 'Sex': 'Gender'}).head(2)
```

	Name	Passenger Class	Age	Gender	Survived	SexCode
0	Allen, Miss Elisabeth Walton	1st	29.0	female	1	1
1	Allison, Miss Helen Loraine	1st	2.0	female	0	1

Discussion

Using `rename` with a dictionary as an argument to the `columns` parameter is my preferred way to rename columns because it works with any number of columns. If we want to rename all columns at once, this helpful snippet of code creates a dictionary with the old column names as keys and empty strings as values:

```
# Load library
import collections

# Create dictionary
column_names = collections.defaultdict(str)

# Create keys
for name in dataframe.columns:
    column_names[name]

# Show dictionary
column_names

defaultdict(str,
            {'Age': '',
             'Name': '',
             'PClass': '',
             'Sex': '',
             'SexCode': '',
             'Survived': ''})
```

3.8 Finding the Minimum, Maximum, Sum, Average, and Count

Problem

You want to find the min, max, sum, average, or count of a numeric column.

Solution

pandas comes with some built-in methods for commonly used descriptive statistics such as `min`, `max`, `mean`, `sum`, and `count`:

```
# Load library
import pandas as pd

# Create URL
url = 'https://raw.githubusercontent.com/chrisalbon/sim_data/master/titanic.csv'

# Load data
dataframe = pd.read_csv(url)

# Calculate statistics
print('Maximum:', dataframe['Age'].max())
print('Minimum:', dataframe['Age'].min())
print('Mean:', dataframe['Age'].mean())
print('Sum:', dataframe['Age'].sum())
print('Count:', dataframe['Age'].count())

Maximum: 71.0
Minimum: 0.17
Mean: 30.397989417989415
Sum: 22980.879999999997
Count: 756
```

Discussion

In addition to the statistics used in the solution, pandas offers variance (var), standard deviation (std), kurtosis (kurt), skewness (skew), standard error of the mean (sem), mode (mode), median (median), value counts, and a number of others.

Furthermore, we can also apply these methods to the whole DataFrame:

```
# Show counts
dataframe.count()

Name        1313
PClass      1313
Age          756
Sex         1313
Survived    1313
SexCode     1313
dtype: int64
```

3.9 Finding Unique Values

Problem

You want to select all unique values in a column.

Solution

Use unique to view an array of all unique values in a column:

```
# Load library
import pandas as pd

# Create URL
url = 'https://raw.githubusercontent.com/chrisalbon/sim_data/master/titanic.csv'

# Load data
dataframe = pd.read_csv(url)

# Select unique values
dataframe['Sex'].unique()

array(['female', 'male'], dtype=object)
```

Alternatively, `value_counts` will display all unique values with the number of times each value appears:

```
# Show counts
dataframe['Sex'].value_counts()

male      851
female    462
Name: Sex, dtype: int64
```

Discussion

Both `unique` and `value_counts` are useful for manipulating and exploring categorical columns. Very often in categorical columns there will be classes that need to be handled in the data wrangling phase. For example, in the *Titanic* dataset, `PClass` is a column indicating the class of a passenger's ticket. There were three classes on the *Titanic*; however, if we use `value_counts` we can see a problem:

```
# Show counts
dataframe['PClass'].value_counts()

3rd    711
1st    322
2nd    279
*        1
Name: PClass, dtype: int64
```

While almost all passengers belong to one of three classes as expected, a single passenger has the class *. There are a number of strategies for handling this type of issue, which we will address in Chapter 5, but for now just realize that "extra" classes are common in categorical data and should not be ignored.

Finally, if we simply want to count the number of unique values, we can use `nunique`:

```
# Show number of unique values
dataframe['PClass'].nunique()

4
```

3.10 Handling Missing Values

Problem

You want to select missing values in a DataFrame.

Solution

isnull and notnull return booleans indicating whether a value is missing:

```
# Load library
import pandas as pd

# Create URL
url = 'https://raw.githubusercontent.com/chrisalbon/sim_data/master/titanic.csv'

# Load data
dataframe = pd.read_csv(url)

## Select missing values, show two rows
dataframe[dataframe['Age'].isnull()].head(2)
```

	Name	PClass	Age	Sex	Survived	SexCode
12	Aubert, Mrs Leontine Pauline	1st	NaN	female	1	1
13	Barkworth, Mr Algernon H	1st	NaN	male	1	0

Discussion

Missing values are a ubiquitous problem in data wrangling, yet many underestimate the difficulty of working with missing data. pandas uses NumPy's NaN (Not a Number) value to denote missing values, but it is important to note that NaN is not fully implemented natively in pandas. For example, if we wanted to replace all strings containing male with missing values, we get an error:

```
# Attempt to replace values with NaN
dataframe['Sex'] = dataframe['Sex'].replace('male', NaN)

-----------------------------------------------------------------

NameError                          Traceback (most recent call last)

<ipython-input-7-5682d714f87d> in <module>()
      1 # Attempt to replace values with NaN
----> 2 dataframe['Sex'] = dataframe['Sex'].replace('male', NaN)


NameError: name 'NaN' is not defined
-----------------------------------------------------------------
```

To have full functionality with NaN we need to import the NumPy library first:

```
# Load library
import numpy as np

# Replace values with NaN
dataframe['Sex'] = dataframe['Sex'].replace('male', np.nan)
```

Oftentimes a dataset uses a specific value to denote a missing observation, such as NONE, -999, or ... The pandas read_csv function includes a parameter allowing us to specify the values used to indicate missing values:

```
# Load data, set missing values
dataframe = pd.read_csv(url, na_values=[np.nan, 'NONE', -999])
```

We can also use the pandas fillna function to impute the missing values of a column. Here, we show the places where Age is null using the isna function and then fill those values with the mean age of passengers.

```
# Get a single null row
null_entry = dataframe[dataframe["Age"].isna()].head(1)

print(null_entry)
```

	Name	PClass	Age	Sex	Survived	SexCode
12	Aubert, Mrs Leontine Pauline	1st	NaN	female	1	1

```
# Fill all null values with the mean age of passengers
null_entry.fillna(dataframe["Age"].mean())
```

	Name	PClass	Age	Sex	Survived	SexCode
12	Aubert, Mrs Leontine Pauline	1st	30.397989	female	1	1

3.11 Deleting a Column

Problem

You want to delete a column from your DataFrame.

Solution

The best way to delete a column is to use drop with the parameter axis=1 (i.e., the column axis):

```
# Load library
import pandas as pd

# Create URL
url = 'https://raw.githubusercontent.com/chrisalbon/sim_data/master/titanic.csv'
```

```
# Load data
dataframe = pd.read_csv(url)

# Delete column
dataframe.drop('Age', axis=1).head(2)
```

	Name	PClass	Sex	Survived	SexCode
0	Allen, Miss Elisabeth Walton	1st	female	1	1
1	Allison, Miss Helen Loraine	1st	female	0	1

You can also use a list of column names as the main argument to drop multiple columns at once:

```
# Drop columns
dataframe.drop(['Age', 'Sex'], axis=1).head(2)
```

	Name	PClass	Survived	SexCode
0	Allen, Miss Elisabeth Walton	1st	1	1
1	Allison, Miss Helen Loraine	1st	0	1

If a column does not have a name (which can sometimes happen), you can drop it by its column index using `dataframe.columns`:

```
# Drop column
dataframe.drop(dataframe.columns[1], axis=1).head(2)
```

	Name	Age	Sex	Survived	SexCode
0	Allen, Miss Elisabeth Walton	29.0	female	1	1
1	Allison, Miss Helen Loraine	2.0	female	0	1

Discussion

`drop` is the idiomatic method of deleting a column. An alternative method is `del dataframe['Age']`, which works most of the time but is not recommended because of how it is called within pandas (the details of which are outside the scope of this book).

I recommend that you avoid using the pandas `inplace=True` argument. Many pandas methods include an `inplace` parameter that, when set to `True`, edits the DataFrame directly. This can lead to problems in more complex data processing pipelines because we are treating the DataFrames as mutable objects (which they technically are). I recommend treating DataFrames as immutable objects. For example:

```
# Create a new DataFrame
dataframe_name_dropped = dataframe.drop(dataframe.columns[0], axis=1)
```

In this example, we are not mutating the DataFrame `dataframe` but instead are making a new DataFrame that is an altered version of `dataframe` called `dataframe_name_dropped`. If you treat your DataFrames as immutable objects, you will save yourself a lot of headaches down the road.

3.12 Deleting a Row

Problem

You want to delete one or more rows from a DataFrame.

Solution

Use a boolean condition to create a new DataFrame excluding the rows you want to delete:

```
# Load library
import pandas as pd

# Create URL
url = 'https://raw.githubusercontent.com/chrisalbon/sim_data/master/titanic.csv'

# Load data
dataframe = pd.read_csv(url)

# Delete rows, show first three rows of output
dataframe[dataframe['Sex'] != 'male'].head(3)
```

	Name	PClass	Age	Sex	Survived	SexCode
0	Allen, Miss Elisabeth Walton	1st	29.0	female	1	1
1	Allison, Miss Helen Loraine	1st	2.0	female	0	1
3	Allison, Mrs Hudson JC (Bessie Waldo Daniels)	1st	25.00	female	0	1

Discussion

While technically you can use the `drop` method (for example, `dataframe.drop([0, 1], axis=0)` to drop the first two rows), a more practical method is simply to wrap a boolean condition inside `dataframe[]`. This enables us to use the power of conditionals to delete either a single row or (far more likely) many rows at once.

We can use boolean conditions to easily delete single rows by matching a unique value:

```
# Delete row, show first two rows of output
dataframe[dataframe['Name'] != 'Allison, Miss Helen Loraine'].head(2)
```

	Name	PClass	Age	Sex	Survived	SexCode
0	Allen, Miss Elisabeth Walton	1st	29.0	female	1	1
2	Allison, Mr Hudson Joshua Creighton	1st	30.0	male	0	0

We can even use it to delete a single row by specifying the row index:

```
# Delete row, show first two rows of output
dataframe[dataframe.index != 0].head(2)
```

	Name	PClass	Age	Sex	Survived	SexCode
1	Allison, Miss Helen Loraine	1st	2.0	female	0	1
2	Allison, Mr Hudson Joshua Creighton	1st	30.0	male	0	0

3.13 Dropping Duplicate Rows

Problem

You want to drop duplicate rows from your DataFrame.

Solution

Use drop_duplicates, but be mindful of the parameters:

```
# Load library
import pandas as pd

# Create URL
url = 'https://raw.githubusercontent.com/chrisalbon/sim_data/master/titanic.csv'

# Load data
dataframe = pd.read_csv(url)

# Drop duplicates, show first two rows of output
dataframe.drop_duplicates().head(2)
```

	Name	PClass	Age	Sex	Survived	SexCode
0	Allen, Miss Elisabeth Walton	1st	29.0	female	1	1
1	Allison, Miss Helen Loraine	1st	2.0	female	0	1

Discussion

A keen reader will notice that the solution didn't actually drop any rows:

```
# Show number of rows
print("Number Of Rows In The Original DataFrame:", len(dataframe))
print("Number Of Rows After Deduping:", len(dataframe.drop_duplicates()))
```

```
Number Of Rows In The Original DataFrame: 1313
Number Of Rows After Deduping: 1313
```

This is because `drop_duplicates` defaults to dropping only rows that match perfectly across all columns. Because every row in our DataFrame is unique, none will be dropped. However, often we want to consider only a subset of columns to check for duplicate rows. We can accomplish this using the `subset` parameter:

```
# Drop duplicates
dataframe.drop_duplicates(subset=['Sex'])
```

	Name	PClass	Age	Sex	Survived	SexCode
0	Allen, Miss Elisabeth Walton	1st	29.0	female	1	1
2	Allison, Mr Hudson Joshua Creighton	1st	30.0	male	0	0

Take a close look at the preceding output: we told `drop_duplicates` to only consider any two rows with the same value for `Sex` to be duplicates and to drop them. Now we are left with a DataFrame of only two rows: one woman and one man. You might be asking why `drop_duplicates` decided to keep these two rows instead of two different rows. The answer is that `drop_duplicates` defaults to keeping the first occurrence of a duplicated row and dropping the rest. We can control this behavior using the `keep` parameter:

```
# Drop duplicates
dataframe.drop_duplicates(subset=['Sex'], keep='last')
```

	Name	PClass	Age	Sex	Survived	SexCode
1307	Zabour, Miss Tamini	3rd	NaN	female	0	1
1312	Zimmerman, Leo	3rd	29.0	male	0	0

A related method is `duplicated`, which returns a boolean series denoting whether a row is a duplicate or not. This is a good option if you don't want to simply drop duplicates:

```
dataframe.duplicated()

0       False
1       False
2       False
3       False
4       False
        ...
1308    False
1309    False
1310    False
1311    False
1312    False
Length: 1313, dtype: bool
```

3.14 Grouping Rows by Values

Problem

You want to group individual rows according to some shared value.

Solution

groupby is one of the most powerful features in pandas:

```
# Load library
import pandas as pd

# Create URL
url = 'https://raw.githubusercontent.com/chrisalbon/sim_data/master/titanic.csv'

# Load data
dataframe = pd.read_csv(url)

# Group rows by the values of the column 'Sex', calculate mean # of each group
dataframe.groupby('Sex').mean(numeric_only=True)
```

Sex	Age	Survived	SexCode
female	29.396424	0.666667	1.0
male	31.014338	0.166863	0.0

Discussion

groupby is where data wrangling really starts to take shape. It is very common to have a DataFrame where each row is a person or an event and we want to group them according to some criterion and then calculate a statistic. For example, you can imagine a DataFrame where each row is an individual sale at a national restaurant chain and we want the total sales per restaurant. We can accomplish this by grouping rows by individual restaurants and then calculating the sum of each group.

Users new to groupby often write a line like this and are confused by what is returned:

```
# Group rows
dataframe.groupby('Sex')

<pandas.core.groupby.DataFrameGroupBy object at 0x10efacf28>
```

Why didn't it return something more useful? The reason is that groupby needs to be paired with some operation that we want to apply to each group, such as calculating an aggregate statistic (e.g., mean, median, sum). When talking about grouping we often use shorthand and say "group by gender," but that is incomplete. For grouping to be useful, we need to group by something and then apply a function to each of those groups:

```
# Group rows, count rows
dataframe.groupby('Survived')['Name'].count()

Survived
0    863
1    450
Name: Name, dtype: int64
```

Notice `Name` added after the groupby? That is because particular summary statistics are meaningful only to certain types of data. For example, while calculating the average age by gender makes sense, calculating the total age by gender does not. In this case, we group the data into survived or not, and then count the number of names (i.e., passengers) in each group.

We can also group by a first column, then group that grouping by a second column:

```
# Group rows, calculate mean
dataframe.groupby(['Sex','Survived'])['Age'].mean()

Sex     Survived
female  0          24.901408
        1          30.867143
male    0          32.320780
        1          25.951875
Name: Age, dtype: float64
```

3.15 Grouping Rows by Time

Problem

You need to group individual rows by time periods.

Solution

Use `resample` to group rows by chunks of time:

```
# Load libraries
import pandas as pd
import numpy as np

# Create date range
time_index = pd.date_range('06/06/2017', periods=100000, freq='30S')

# Create DataFrame
dataframe = pd.DataFrame(index=time_index)

# Create column of random values
dataframe['Sale_Amount'] = np.random.randint(1, 10, 100000)

# Group rows by week, calculate sum per week
dataframe.resample('W').sum()
```

	Sale_Amount
2017-06-11	86423
2017-06-18	101045
2017-06-25	100867
2017-07-02	100894
2017-07-09	100438
2017-07-16	10297

Discussion

Our standard *Titanic* dataset does not contain a datetime column, so for this recipe we have generated a simple DataFrame where each row is an individual sale. For each sale we know its date and time and its dollar amount (this data isn't realistic because the sales take place precisely 30 seconds apart and are exact dollar amounts, but for the sake of simplicity let's pretend).

The raw data looks like this:

```
# Show three rows
dataframe.head(3)
```

	Sale_Amount
2017-06-06 00:00:00	7
2017-06-06 00:00:30	2
2017-06-06 00:01:00	7

Notice that the date and time of each sale is the index of the DataFrame; this is because `resample` requires the index to be a datetime-like value.

Using `resample` we can group the rows by a wide array of time periods (offsets) and then we can calculate statistics on each time group:

```
# Group by two weeks, calculate mean
dataframe.resample('2W').mean()
```

	Sale_Amount
2017-06-11	5.001331
2017-06-25	5.007738
2017-07-09	4.993353
2017-07-23	4.950481

```
# Group by month, count rows
dataframe.resample('M').count()
```

	Sale_Amount
2017-06-30	72000
2017-07-31	28000

You might notice that in the two outputs the datetime index is a date even though we are grouping by weeks and months, respectively. The reason is that by default `resample` returns the label of the right "edge" (the last label) of the time group. We can control this behavior using the `label` parameter:

```
# Group by month, count rows
dataframe.resample('M', label='left').count()
```

	Sale_Amount
2017-05-31	72000
2017-06-30	28000

See Also

- List of pandas time offset aliases (*https://oreil.ly/BURbR*)

3.16 Aggregating Operations and Statistics

Problem

You need to aggregate an operation over each column (or a set of columns) in a dataframe.

Solution

Use the pandas `agg` method. Here, we can easily get the minimum value of every column:

```
# Load library
import pandas as pd

# Create URL
url = 'https://raw.githubusercontent.com/chrisalbon/sim_data/master/titanic.csv'

# Load data
dataframe = pd.read_csv(url)

# Get the minimum of every column
dataframe.agg("min")

Name          Abbing, Mr Anthony
PClass                         *
Age                         0.17
```

```
Sex                 female
Survived                 0
SexCode                  0
dtype: object
```

Sometimes, we want to apply specific functions to specific sets of columns:

```
# Mean Age, min and max SexCode
dataframe.agg({"Age":["mean"], "SexCode":["min", "max"]})
```

	Age	SexCode
mean	30.397989	NaN
min	NaN	0.0
max	NaN	1.0

We can also apply aggregate functions to groups to get more specific, descriptive statistics:

```
# Number of people who survived and didn't survive in each class
dataframe.groupby(
    ["PClass","Survived"]).agg({"Survived":["count"]}
).reset_index()
```

PClass	Survived		Count
0	*	0	1
1	1st	0	129
2	1st	1	193
3	2nd	0	160
4	2nd	1	119
5	3rd	0	573
6	3rd	1	138

Discussion

Aggregate functions are especially useful during exploratory data analysis to learn information about different subpopulations of data and the relationship between variables. By grouping the data and applying aggregate statistics, you can view patterns in the data that may prove useful during the machine learning or feature engineering process. While visual charts are also helpful, it's often useful to have such specific, descriptive statistics as a reference to better understand the data.

See Also

- pandas agg documentation (*https://oreil.ly/5xing*)

3.17 Looping over a Column

Problem

You want to iterate over every element in a column and apply some action.

Solution

You can treat a pandas column like any other sequence in Python and loop over it using the standard Python syntax:

```
# Load library
import pandas as pd

# Create URL
url = 'https://raw.githubusercontent.com/chrisalbon/sim_data/master/titanic.csv'

# Load data
dataframe = pd.read_csv(url)

# Print first two names uppercased
for name in dataframe['Name'][0:2]:
    print(name.upper())

ALLEN, MISS ELISABETH WALTON
ALLISON, MISS HELEN LORAINE
```

Discussion

In addition to loops (often called for loops), we can also use list comprehensions:

```
# Show first two names uppercased
[name.upper() for name in dataframe['Name'][0:2]]

['ALLEN, MISS ELISABETH WALTON', 'ALLISON, MISS HELEN LORAINE']
```

Despite the temptation to fall back on for loops, a more Pythonic solution would use the pandas apply method, described in Recipe 3.18.

3.18 Applying a Function over All Elements in a Column

Problem

You want to apply some function over all elements in a column.

Solution

Use apply to apply a built-in or custom function on every element in a column:

```
# Load library
import pandas as pd

# Create URL
url = 'https://raw.githubusercontent.com/chrisalbon/sim_data/master/titanic.csv'

# Load data
dataframe = pd.read_csv(url)

# Create function
def uppercase(x):
    return x.upper()

# Apply function, show two rows
dataframe['Name'].apply(uppercase)[0:2]

0    ALLEN, MISS ELISABETH WALTON
1    ALLISON, MISS HELEN LORAINE
Name: Name, dtype: object
```

Discussion

apply is a great way to do data cleaning and wrangling. It is common to write a function to perform some useful operation (separate first and last names, convert strings to floats, etc.) and then map that function to every element in a column.

3.19 Applying a Function to Groups

Problem

You have grouped rows using groupby and want to apply a function to each group.

Solution

Combine groupby and apply:

```
# Load library
import pandas as pd

# Create URL
url = 'https://raw.githubusercontent.com/chrisalbon/sim_data/master/titanic.csv'

# Load data
dataframe = pd.read_csv(url)

# Group rows, apply function to groups
dataframe.groupby('Sex').apply(lambda x: x.count())
```

Sex	Name	PClass	Age	Sex	Survived	SexCode
female	462	462	288	462	462	462
male	851	851	468	851	851	851

Discussion

In Recipe 3.18 I mentioned `apply`. `apply` is particularly useful when you want to apply a function to groups. By combining `groupby` and `apply` we can calculate custom statistics or apply any function to each group separately.

3.20 Concatenating DataFrames

Problem

You want to concatenate two DataFrames.

Solution

Use `concat` with `axis=0` to concatenate along the row axis:

```
# Load library
import pandas as pd

# Create DataFrame
data_a = {'id': ['1', '2', '3'],
          'first': ['Alex', 'Amy', 'Allen'],
          'last': ['Anderson', 'Ackerman', 'Ali']}
dataframe_a = pd.DataFrame(data_a, columns = ['id', 'first', 'last'])

# Create DataFrame
data_b = {'id': ['4', '5', '6'],
          'first': ['Billy', 'Brian', 'Bran'],
          'last': ['Bonder', 'Black', 'Balwner']}
dataframe_b = pd.DataFrame(data_b, columns = ['id', 'first', 'last'])

# Concatenate DataFrames by rows
pd.concat([dataframe_a, dataframe_b], axis=0)
```

	id	first	last
0	1	Alex	Anderson
1	2	Amy	Ackerman
2	3	Allen	Ali
0	4	Billy	Bonder
1	5	Brian	Black
2	6	Bran	Balwner

You can use `axis=1` to concatenate along the column axis:

```
# Concatenate DataFrames by columns
pd.concat([dataframe_a, dataframe_b], axis=1)
```

	id	first	last	id	first	last
0	1	Alex	Anderson	4	Billy	Bonder
1	2	Amy	Ackerman	5	Brian	Black
2	3	Allen	Ali	6	Bran	Balwner

Discussion

Concatenating is not a word you hear much outside of computer science and programming, so if you have not heard it before, do not worry. The informal definition of *concatenate* is to glue two objects together. In the solution we glued together two small DataFrames using the `axis` parameter to indicate whether we wanted to stack the two DataFrames on top of each other or place them side by side.

3.21 Merging DataFrames

Problem

You want to merge two DataFrames.

Solution

To inner join, use `merge` with the on parameter to specify the column to merge on:

```
# Load library
import pandas as pd

# Create DataFrame
employee_data = {'employee_id': ['1', '2', '3', '4'],
                 'name': ['Amy Jones', 'Allen Keys', 'Alice Bees',
                 'Tim Horton']}
dataframe_employees = pd.DataFrame(employee_data, columns = ['employee_id',
                                                             'name'])

# Create DataFrame
sales_data = {'employee_id': ['3', '4', '5', '6'],
              'total_sales': [23456, 2512, 2345, 1455]}
dataframe_sales = pd.DataFrame(sales_data, columns = ['employee_id',
                                                      'total_sales'])

# Merge DataFrames
pd.merge(dataframe_employees, dataframe_sales, on='employee_id')
```

	employee_id	name	total_sales
0	3	Alice Bees	23456
1	4	Tim Horton	2512

merge defaults to inner joins. If we want to do an outer join, we can specify that with the how parameter:

```
# Merge DataFrames
pd.merge(dataframe_employees, dataframe_sales, on='employee_id', how='outer')
```

	employee_id	name	total_sales
0	1	Amy Jones	NaN
1	2	Allen Keys	NaN
2	3	Alice Bees	23456.0
3	4	Tim Horton	2512.0
4	5	NaN	2345.0
5	6	NaN	1455.0

The same parameter can be used to specify left and right joins:

```
# Merge DataFrames
pd.merge(dataframe_employees, dataframe_sales, on='employee_id', how='left')
```

	employee_id	name	total_sales
0	1	Amy Jones	NaN
1	2	Allen Keys	NaN
2	3	Alice Bees	23456.0
3	4	Tim Horton	2512.0

We can also specify the column name in each DataFrame to merge on:

```
# Merge DataFrames
pd.merge(dataframe_employees,
         dataframe_sales,
         left_on='employee_id',
         right_on='employee_id')
```

	employee_id	name	total_sales
0	3	Alice Bees	23456
1	4	Tim Horton	2512

If, instead of merging on two columns, we want to merge on the indexes of each DataFrame, we can replace the left_on and right_on parameters with left_index=True and right_index=True.

Discussion

The data we need to use is often complex; it doesn't always come in one piece. Instead, in the real world, we're usually faced with disparate datasets from multiple database queries or files. To get all that data into one place, we can load each data query or data file into pandas as individual DataFrames and then merge them into a single DataFrame.

This process might be familiar to anyone who has used SQL, a popular language for doing merging operations (called *joins*). While the exact parameters used by pandas will be different, they follow the same general patterns used by other software languages and tools.

There are three aspects to specify with any `merge` operation. First, we have to specify the two DataFrames we want to merge. In the solution, we named them `dataframe_employees` and `dataframe_sales`. Second, we have to specify the name(s) of the columns to merge on—that is, the columns whose values are shared between the two DataFrames. For example, in our solution both DataFrames have a column named `employee_id`. To merge the two DataFrames we will match the values in each DataFrame's `employee_id` column. If these two columns use the same name, we can use the on parameter. However, if they have different names, we can use `left_on` and `right_on`.

What is the left and right DataFrame? The left DataFrame is the first one we specified in `merge`, and the right DataFrame is the second one. This language comes up again in the next sets of parameters we will need.

The last aspect, and most difficult for some people to grasp, is the type of merge operation we want to conduct. This is specified by the how parameter. `merge` supports the four main types of joins:

Inner
> Return only the rows that match in both DataFrames (e.g., return any row with an `employee_id` value appearing in both `dataframe_employees` and `dataframe_sales`).

Outer
> Return all rows in both DataFrames. If a row exists in one DataFrame but not in the other DataFrame, fill NaN values for the missing values (e.g., return all rows in both `dataframe_employee` and `dataframe_sales`).

Left

Return all rows from the left DataFrame but only rows from the right DataFrame that match with the left DataFrame. Fill `NaN` values for the missing values (e.g., return all rows from `dataframe_employees` but only rows from `dataframe_sales` that have a value for `employee_id` that appears in `dataframe_employees`).

Right

Return all rows from the right DataFrame but only rows from the left DataFrame that match with the right DataFrame. Fill `NaN` values for the missing values (e.g., return all rows from `dataframe_sales` but only rows from `dataframe_employees` that have a value for `employee_id` that appears in `dataframe_sales`).

If you did not understand all of that, I encourage you to play around with the `how` parameter in your code and see how it affects what `merge` returns.

See Also

- A Visual Explanation of SQL Joins (*https://oreil.ly/J1A4u*)
- pandas documentation: Merge, join, concatenate and compare (*https://oreil.ly/eNalU*)

## CHAPTER 4

Handling Numerical Data

4.0 Introduction

Quantitative data is the measurement of something—whether class size, monthly sales, or student scores. The natural way to represent these quantities is numerically (e.g., 29 students, $529,392 in sales). In this chapter, we will cover numerous strategies for transforming raw numerical data into features purpose-built for machine learning algorithms.

4.1 Rescaling a Feature

Problem

You need to rescale the values of a numerical feature to be between two values.

Solution

Use scikit-learn's `MinMaxScaler` to rescale a feature array:

```
# Load libraries
import numpy as np
from sklearn import preprocessing

# Create feature
feature = np.array([[-500.5],
                    [-100.1],
                    [0],
                    [100.1],
                    [900.9]])

# Create scaler
minmax_scale = preprocessing.MinMaxScaler(feature_range=(0, 1))
```

```
# Scale feature
scaled_feature = minmax_scale.fit_transform(feature)

# Show feature
scaled_feature

array([[ 0.        ],
       [ 0.28571429],
       [ 0.35714286],
       [ 0.42857143],
       [ 1.        ]])
```

Discussion

Rescaling is a common preprocessing task in machine learning. Many of the algorithms described later in this book will assume all features are on the same scale,
typically 0 to 1 or –1 to 1. There are a number of rescaling techniques, but one of
the simplest is called *min-max scaling*. Min-max scaling uses the minimum and maximum values of a feature to rescale values to within a range. Specifically, min-max
calculates:

$$x_i' = \frac{x_i - \min(x)}{\max(x) - \min(x)}$$

where x is the feature vector, x_i is an individual element of feature x, and x_i' is
the rescaled element. In our example, we can see from the outputted array that the
feature has been successfully rescaled to between 0 and 1:

```
array([[ 0.        ],
       [ 0.28571429],
       [ 0.35714286],
       [ 0.42857143],
       [ 1.        ]])
```

scikit-learn's `MinMaxScaler` offers two options to rescale a feature. One option is to
use `fit` to calculate the minimum and maximum values of the feature, and then
use `transform` to rescale the feature. The second option is to use `fit_transform` to
do both operations at once. There is no mathematical difference between the two
options, but there is sometimes a practical benefit to keeping the operations separate
because it allows us to apply the same transformation to different *sets* of the data.

See Also

- Feature scaling, Wikipedia (*https://oreil.ly/f2WiM*)

- About Feature Scaling and Normalization, Sebastian Raschka (*https://oreil.ly/
  Da0AH*)

4.2 Standardizing a Feature

Problem

You want to transform a feature to have a mean of 0 and a standard deviation of 1.

Solution

scikit-learn's StandardScaler performs both transformations:

```
# Load libraries
import numpy as np
from sklearn import preprocessing

# Create feature
x = np.array([[-1000.1],
              [-200.2],
              [500.5],
              [600.6],
              [9000.9]])

# Create scaler
scaler = preprocessing.StandardScaler()

# Transform the feature
standardized = scaler.fit_transform(x)

# Show feature
standardized

array([[-0.76058269],
       [-0.54177196],
       [-0.35009716],
       [-0.32271504],
       [ 1.97516685]])
```

Discussion

A common alternative to the min-max scaling discussed in Recipe 4.1 is rescaling of features to be approximately standard normally distributed. To achieve this, we use standardization to transform the data such that it has a mean, $\bar{x}$, of 0 and a standard deviation, σ, of 1. Specifically, each element in the feature is transformed so that:

$$x_i' = \frac{x_i - \bar{x}}{\sigma}$$

where x_i' is our standardized form of x_i. The transformed feature represents the number of standard deviations of the original value from the feature's mean value (also called a *z-score* in statistics).

Standardization is a common go-to scaling method for machine learning preprocessing and, in my experience, is used more often than min-max scaling. However, it depends on the learning algorithm. For example, principal component analysis often works better using standardization, while min-max scaling is often recommended for neural networks (both algorithms are discussed later in this book). As a general rule, I'd recommend defaulting to standardization unless you have a specific reason to use an alternative.

We can see the effect of standardization by looking at the mean and standard deviation of our solution's output:

```
# Print mean and standard deviation
print("Mean:", round(standardized.mean()))
print("Standard deviation:", standardized.std())

Mean: 0.0
Standard deviation: 1.0
```

If our data has significant outliers, it can negatively impact our standardization by affecting the feature's mean and variance. In this scenario, it is often helpful to instead rescale the feature using the median and quartile range. In scikit-learn, we do this using the RobustScaler method:

```
# Create scaler
robust_scaler = preprocessing.RobustScaler()

# Transform feature
robust_scaler.fit_transform(x)

array([[ -1.87387612],
       [ -0.875     ],
       [  0.        ],
       [  0.125     ],
       [ 10.61488511]])
```

4.3 Normalizing Observations

Problem

You want to rescale the feature values of observations to have unit norm (a total length of 1).

Solution

Use `Normalizer` with a norm argument:

```
# Load libraries
import numpy as np
from sklearn.preprocessing import Normalizer

# Create feature matrix
features = np.array([[0.5, 0.5],
                     [1.1, 3.4],
                     [1.5, 20.2],
                     [1.63, 34.4],
                     [10.9, 3.3]])

# Create normalizer
normalizer = Normalizer(norm="l2")

# Transform feature matrix
normalizer.transform(features)

array([[ 0.70710678,  0.70710678],
       [ 0.30782029,  0.95144452],
       [ 0.07405353,  0.99725427],
       [ 0.04733062,  0.99887928],
       [ 0.95709822,  0.28976368]])
```

Discussion

Many rescaling methods (e.g., min-max scaling and standardization) operate on features; however, we can also rescale across individual observations. `Normalizer` rescales the values on individual observations to have unit norm (the sum of their lengths is 1). This type of rescaling is often used when we have many equivalent features (e.g., text classification when every word or n-word group is a feature).

`Normalizer` provides three norm options with Euclidean norm (often called L2) being the default argument:

$$\| x \|_2 = \sqrt{x_1{}^2 + x_2{}^2 + \cdots + x_n{}^2}$$

where x is an individual observation and x_n is that observation's value for the nth feature.

```
# Transform feature matrix
features_l2_norm = Normalizer(norm="l2").transform(features)

# Show feature matrix
features_l2_norm
```

```
array([[ 0.70710678,  0.70710678],
       [ 0.30782029,  0.95144452],
       [ 0.07405353,  0.99725427],
       [ 0.04733062,  0.99887928],
       [ 0.95709822,  0.28976368]])
```

Alternatively, we can specify Manhattan norm (L1):

$$\| x \|_1 = \sum_{i=1}^{n} |x_i|.$$

```
# Transform feature matrix
features_l1_norm = Normalizer(norm="l1").transform(features)

# Show feature matrix
features_l1_norm
```

```
array([[ 0.5       ,  0.5       ],
       [ 0.24444444,  0.75555556],
       [ 0.06912442,  0.93087558],
       [ 0.04524008,  0.95475992],
       [ 0.76760563,  0.23239437]])
```

Intuitively, L2 norm can be thought of as the distance between two points in New York for a bird (i.e., a straight line), while L1 can be thought of as the distance for a human walking on the street (walk north one block, east one block, north one block, east one block, etc.), which is why it is called "Manhattan norm" or "Taxicab norm."

Practically, notice that norm="l1" rescales an observation's values so they sum to 1, which can sometimes be a desirable quality:

```
# Print sum
print("Sum of the first observation\'s values:",
    features_l1_norm[0, 0] + features_l1_norm[0, 1])
```

```
Sum of the first observation's values: 1.0
```

4.4 Generating Polynomial and Interaction Features

Problem

You want to create polynomial and interaction features.

Solution

Even though some choose to create polynomial and interaction features manually, scikit-learn offers a built-in method:

```
# Load libraries
import numpy as np
```

```
from sklearn.preprocessing import PolynomialFeatures

# Create feature matrix
features = np.array([[2, 3],
                     [2, 3],
                     [2, 3]])

# Create PolynomialFeatures object
polynomial_interaction = PolynomialFeatures(degree=2, include_bias=False)

# Create polynomial features
polynomial_interaction.fit_transform(features)

array([[ 2.,  3.,  4.,  6.,  9.],
       [ 2.,  3.,  4.,  6.,  9.],
       [ 2.,  3.,  4.,  6.,  9.]])
```

The degree parameter determines the maximum degree of the polynomial. For example, degree=2 will create new features raised to the second power:

$$x_1, \ x_2, \ x_1^2, \ x_1^2, \ x_2^2$$

while degree=3 will create new features raised to the second and third power:

$$x_1, \ x_2, \ x_1^2, \ x_2^2, \ x_1^3, \ x_2^3, \ x_1^2, \ x_1^3, \ x_2^3$$

Furthermore, by default PolynomialFeatures includes interaction features:

$$x_1 x_2$$

We can restrict the features created to only interaction features by setting interaction_only to True:

```
interaction = PolynomialFeatures(degree=2,
            interaction_only=True, include_bias=False)

interaction.fit_transform(features)

array([[ 2.,  3.,  6.],
       [ 2.,  3.,  6.],
       [ 2.,  3.,  6.]])
```

Discussion

Polynomial features are often created when we want to include the notion that there exists a nonlinear relationship between the features and the target. For example, we might suspect that the effect of age on the probability of having a major medical condition is not constant over time but increases as age increases. We can encode that nonconstant effect in a feature, x, by generating that feature's higher-order forms (x^2, x^3, etc.).

Additionally, often we run into situations where the effect of one feature is dependent on another feature. A simple example would be if we were trying to predict whether or not our coffee was sweet, and we had two features: (1) whether or not the coffee was stirred, and (2) whether or not we added sugar. Individually, each feature does not predict coffee sweetness, but the combination of their effects does. That is, a coffee would only be sweet if the coffee had sugar and was stirred. The effects of each feature on the target (sweetness) are dependent on each other. We can encode that relationship by including an interaction feature that is the product of the individual features.

4.5 Transforming Features

Problem

You want to make a custom transformation to one or more features.

Solution

In scikit-learn, use `FunctionTransformer` to apply a function to a set of features:

```
# Load libraries
import numpy as np
from sklearn.preprocessing import FunctionTransformer

# Create feature matrix
features = np.array([[2, 3],
                     [2, 3],
                     [2, 3]])

# Define a simple function
def add_ten(x: int) -> int:
    return x + 10

# Create transformer
ten_transformer = FunctionTransformer(add_ten)

# Transform feature matrix
ten_transformer.transform(features)

array([[12, 13],
       [12, 13],
       [12, 13]])
```

We can create the same transformation in pandas using `apply`:

```
# Load library
import pandas as pd

# Create DataFrame
df = pd.DataFrame(features, columns=["feature_1", "feature_2"])

# Apply function
df.apply(add_ten)
```

	feature_1	feature_2
0	12	13
1	12	13
2	12	13

Discussion

It is common to want to make some custom transformations to one or more features. For example, we might want to create a feature that is the natural log of the values of a different feature. We can do this by creating a function and then mapping it to features using either scikit-learn's `FunctionTransformer` or pandas' `apply`. In the solution we created a very simple function, `add_ten`, which added 10 to each input, but there is no reason we could not define a much more complex function.

4.6 Detecting Outliers

Problem

You want to identify extreme observations.

Solution

Detecting outliers is unfortunately more of an art than a science. However, a common method is to assume the data is normally distributed and, based on that assumption, "draw" an ellipse around the data, classifying any observation inside the ellipse as an inlier (labeled as 1) and any observation outside the ellipse as an outlier (labeled as -1):

```
# Load libraries
import numpy as np
from sklearn.covariance import EllipticEnvelope
from sklearn.datasets import make_blobs

# Create simulated data
features, _ = make_blobs(n_samples = 10,
                         n_features = 2,
                         centers = 1,
                         random_state = 1)
```

```
# Replace the first observation's values with extreme values
features[0,0] = 10000
features[0,1] = 10000

# Create detector
outlier_detector = EllipticEnvelope(contamination=.1)

# Fit detector
outlier_detector.fit(features)

# Predict outliers
outlier_detector.predict(features)
```

```
array([-1,  1,  1,  1,  1,  1,  1,  1,  1,  1])
```

In these arrays, values of -1 refer to outliers whereas values of 1 refer to inliers. A major limitation of this approach is the need to specify a contamination parameter, which is the proportion of observations that are outliers—a value that we don't know. Think of contamination as our estimate of the cleanliness of our data. If we expect our data to have few outliers, we can set contamination to something small. However, if we believe that the data is likely to have outliers, we can set it to a higher value.

Instead of looking at observations as a whole, we can instead look at individual features and identify extreme values in those features using interquartile range (IQR):

```
# Create one feature
feature = features[:,0]

# Create a function to return index of outliers
def indicies_of_outliers(x: int) -> np.array(int):
    q1, q3 = np.percentile(x, [25, 75])
    iqr = q3 - q1
    lower_bound = q1 - (iqr * 1.5)
    upper_bound = q3 + (iqr * 1.5)
    return np.where((x > upper_bound) | (x < lower_bound))

# Run function
indicies_of_outliers(feature)
```

```
(array([0]),)
```

IQR is the difference between the first and third quartile of a set of data. You can think of IQR as the spread of the bulk of the data, with outliers being observations far from the main concentration of data. Outliers are commonly defined as any value 1.5 IQRs less than the first quartile, or 1.5 IQRs greater than the third quartile.

Discussion

There is no single best technique for detecting outliers. Instead, we have a collection of techniques all with their own advantages and disadvantages. Our best strategy is often trying multiple techniques (e.g., both EllipticEnvelope and IQR-based detection) and looking at the results as a whole.

If at all possible, we should look at observations we detect as outliers and try to understand them. For example, if we have a dataset of houses and one feature is number of rooms, is an outlier with 100 rooms really a house or is it actually a hotel that has been misclassified?

See Also

- Three Ways to Detect Outliers (and the source of the IQR function used in this recipe) (*https://oreil.ly/wlwmH*)

4.7 Handling Outliers

Problem

You have outliers in your data that you want to identify and then reduce their impact on the data distribution.

Solution

Typically we can use three strategies to handle outliers. First, we can drop them:

```
# Load library
import pandas as pd

# Create DataFrame
houses = pd.DataFrame()
houses['Price'] = [534433, 392333, 293222, 4322032]
houses['Bathrooms'] = [2, 3.5, 2, 116]
houses['Square_Feet'] = [1500, 2500, 1500, 48000]

# Filter observations
houses[houses['Bathrooms'] < 20]
```

	Price	Bathrooms	Square_Feet
0	534433	2.0	1500
1	392333	3.5	2500
2	293222	2.0	1500

Second, we can mark them as outliers and include "Outlier" as a feature:

```
# Load library
import numpy as np

# Create feature based on boolean condition
houses["Outlier"] = np.where(houses["Bathrooms"] < 20, 0, 1)

# Show data
houses
```

	Price	Bathrooms	Square_Feet	Outlier
0	534433	2.0	1500	0
1	392333	3.5	2500	0
2	293222	2.0	1500	0
3	4322032	116.0	48000	1

Finally, we can transform the feature to dampen the effect of the outlier:

```
# Log feature
houses["Log_Of_Square_Feet"] = [np.log(x) for x in houses["Square_Feet"]]

# Show data
houses
```

	Price	Bathrooms	Square_Feet	Outlier	Log_Of_Square_Feet
0	534433	2.0	1500	0	7.313220
1	392333	3.5	2500	0	7.824046
2	293222	2.0	1500	0	7.313220
3	4322032	116.0	48000	1	10.778956

Discussion

Similar to detecting outliers, there is no hard-and-fast rule for handling them. How we handle them should be based on two aspects. First, we should consider what makes them outliers. If we believe they are errors in the data, such as from a broken sensor or a miscoded value, then we might drop the observation or replace outlier values with NaN since we can't trust those values. However, if we believe the outliers are genuine extreme values (e.g., a house [mansion] with 200 bathrooms), then marking them as outliers or transforming their values is more appropriate.

Second, how we handle outliers should be based on our goal for machine learning. For example, if we want to predict house prices based on features of the house, we might reasonably assume the price for mansions with over 100 bathrooms is driven by a different dynamic than regular family homes. Furthermore, if we are training a model to use as part of an online home loan web application, we might assume that our potential users will not include billionaires looking to buy a mansion.

So what should we do if we have outliers? Think about why they are outliers, have an end goal in mind for the data, and, most importantly, remember that not making a decision to address outliers is itself a decision with implications.

One additional point: if you do have outliers, standardization might not be appropriate because the mean and variance might be highly influenced by the outliers. In this case, use a rescaling method more robust against outliers, like RobustScaler.

See Also

- RobustScaler documentation (*https://oreil.ly/zgm-1*)

4.8 Discretizating Features

Problem

You have a numerical feature and want to break it up into discrete bins.

Solution

Depending on how we want to break up the data, there are two techniques we can use. First, we can binarize the feature according to some threshold:

```
# Load libraries
import numpy as np
from sklearn.preprocessing import Binarizer

# Create feature
age = np.array([[6],
                [12],
                [20],
                [36],
                [65]])

# Create binarizer
binarizer = Binarizer(threshold=18)

# Transform feature
binarizer.fit_transform(age)

array([[0],
       [0],
       [1],
       [1],
       [1]])
```

Second, we can break up numerical features according to multiple thresholds:

```
# Bin feature
np.digitize(age, bins=[20,30,64])

array([[0],
       [0],
       [1],
       [2],
       [3]])
```

Note that the arguments for the bins parameter denote the left edge of each bin. For example, the 20 argument does not include the element with the value of 20, only the two values smaller than 20. We can switch this behavior by setting the parameter right to True:

```
# Bin feature
np.digitize(age, bins=[20,30,64], right=True)

array([[0],
       [0],
       [0],
       [2],
       [3]])
```

Discussion

Discretization can be a fruitful strategy when we have reason to believe that a numerical feature should behave more like a categorical feature. For example, we might believe there is very little difference in the spending habits of 19- and 20-year-olds, but a significant difference between 20- and 21-year-olds (the age in the United States when young adults can consume alcohol). In that example, it could be useful to break up individuals in our data into those who can drink alcohol and those who cannot. Similarly, in other cases it might be useful to discretize our data into three or more bins.

In the solution, we saw two methods of discretization—scikit-learn's Binarizer for two bins and NumPy's digitize for three or more bins—however, we can also use digitize to binarize features like Binarizer by specifying only a single threshold:

```
# Bin feature
np.digitize(age, bins=[18])

array([[0],
       [0],
       [1],
       [1],
       [1]])
```

See Also

- digitize documentation (*https://oreil.ly/KipXX*)

4.9 Grouping Observations Using Clustering

Problem

You want to cluster observations so that similar observations are grouped together.

Solution

If you know that you have *k* groups, you can use k-means clustering to group similar observations and output a new feature containing each observation's group membership:

```
# Load libraries
import pandas as pd
from sklearn.datasets import make_blobs
from sklearn.cluster import KMeans

# Make simulated feature matrix
features, _ = make_blobs(n_samples = 50,
                         n_features = 2,
                         centers = 3,
                         random_state = 1)

# Create DataFrame
dataframe = pd.DataFrame(features, columns=["feature_1", "feature_2"])

# Make k-means clusterer
clusterer = KMeans(3, random_state=0)

# Fit clusterer
clusterer.fit(features)

# Predict values
dataframe["group"] = clusterer.predict(features)

# View first few observations
dataframe.head(5)
```

	feature_1	feature_2	group
0	−9.877554	−3.336145	0
1	−7.287210	−8.353986	2
2	−6.943061	−7.023744	2
3	−7.440167	−8.791959	2
4	−6.641388	−8.075888	2

Discussion

We are jumping ahead of ourselves a bit and will go into much more depth about clustering algorithms later in the book. However, I wanted to point out that we can use clustering as a preprocessing step. Specifically, we use unsupervised learning algorithms like k-means to cluster observations into groups. The result is a categorical feature with similar observations being members of the same group.

Don't worry if you did not understand all of that: just file away the idea that clustering can be used in preprocessing. And if you really can't wait, feel free to flip to Chapter 19 now.

4.10 Deleting Observations with Missing Values

Problem

You need to delete observations containing missing values.

Solution

Deleting observations with missing values is easy with a clever line of NumPy:

```
# Load library
import numpy as np

# Create feature matrix
features = np.array([[1.1, 11.1],
                     [2.2, 22.2],
                     [3.3, 33.3],
                     [4.4, 44.4],
                     [np.nan, 55]])

# Keep only observations that are not (denoted by ~) missing
features[~np.isnan(features).any(axis=1)]

array([[ 1.1,  11.1],
       [ 2.2,  22.2],
       [ 3.3,  33.3],
       [ 4.4,  44.4]])
```

Alternatively, we can drop missing observations using pandas:

```
# Load library
import pandas as pd

# Load data
dataframe = pd.DataFrame(features, columns=["feature_1", "feature_2"])

# Remove observations with missing values
dataframe.dropna()
```

	feature_1	feature_2
0	1.1	11.1
1	2.2	22.2
2	3.3	33.3
3	4.4	44.4

Discussion

Most machine learning algorithms cannot handle any missing values in the target and feature arrays. For this reason, we cannot ignore missing values in our data and must address the issue during preprocessing.

The simplest solution is to delete every observation that contains one or more missing values, a task quickly and easily accomplished using NumPy or pandas.

That said, we should be very reluctant to delete observations with missing values. Deleting them is the nuclear option, since our algorithm loses access to the information contained in the observation's nonmissing values.

Just as important, depending on the cause of the missing values, deleting observations can introduce bias into our data. There are three types of missing data:

Missing completely at random (MCAR)
> The probability that a value is missing is independent of everything. For example, a survey respondent rolls a die before answering a question: if she rolls a six, she skips that question.

Missing at random (MAR)
> The probability that a value is missing is not completely random but depends on the information captured in other features. For example, a survey asks about gender identity and annual salary, and women are more likely to skip the salary question; however, their nonresponse depends only on information we have captured in our gender identity feature.

Missing not at random (MNAR)
> The probability that a value is missing is not random and depends on information not captured in our features. For example, a survey asks about annual salary, and women are more likely to skip the salary question, and we do not have a gender identity feature in our data.

It is sometimes acceptable to delete observations if they are MCAR or MAR. However, if the value is MNAR, the fact that a value is missing is itself information. Deleting MNAR observations can inject bias into our data because we are removing observations produced by some unobserved systematic effect.

See Also

- Identifying the 3 Types of Missing Data (*https://oreil.ly/sz9Fx*)
- Missing-Data Imputation (*https://oreil.ly/swU2j*)

4.11 Imputing Missing Values

Problem

You have missing values in your data and want to impute them via a generic method or prediction.

Solution

You can impute missing values using k-nearest neighbors (KNN) or the scikit-learn SimpleImputer class. If you have a small amount of data, predict and impute the missing values using k-nearest neighbors:

```
# Load libraries
import numpy as np
from sklearn.impute import KNNImputer
from sklearn.preprocessing import StandardScaler
from sklearn.datasets import make_blobs

# Make a simulated feature matrix
features, _ = make_blobs(n_samples = 1000,
                         n_features = 2,
                         random_state = 1)

# Standardize the features
scaler = StandardScaler()
standardized_features = scaler.fit_transform(features)

# Replace the first feature's first value with a missing value
true_value = standardized_features[0,0]
standardized_features[0,0] = np.nan

# Predict the missing values in the feature matrix
knn_imputer = KNNImputer(n_neighbors=5)
features_knn_imputed = knn_imputer.fit_transform(standardized_features)

# Compare true and imputed values
print("True Value:", true_value)
print("Imputed Value:", features_knn_imputed[0,0])

True Value: 0.8730186114
Imputed Value: 1.09553327131
```

Alternatively, we can use scikit-learn's `SimpleImputer` class from the `imputer` module to fill in missing values with the feature's mean, median, or most frequent value. However, we will typically get worse results than with KNN:

```
# Load libraries
import numpy as np
from sklearn.impute import SimpleImputer
from sklearn.preprocessing import StandardScaler
from sklearn.datasets import make_blobs

# Make a simulated feature matrix
features, _ = make_blobs(n_samples = 1000,
                         n_features = 2,
                         random_state = 1)

# Standardize the features
scaler = StandardScaler()
standardized_features = scaler.fit_transform(features)

# Replace the first feature's first value with a missing value
true_value = standardized_features[0,0]
standardized_features[0,0] = np.nan

# Create imputer using the "mean" strategy
mean_imputer = SimpleImputer(strategy="mean")

# Impute values
features_mean_imputed = mean_imputer.fit_transform(features)

# Compare true and imputed values
print("True Value:", true_value)
print("Imputed Value:", features_mean_imputed[0,0])

True Value: 0.8730186114
Imputed Value: -3.05837272461
```

Discussion

There are two main strategies for replacing missing data with substitute values, each of which has strengths and weaknesses. First, we can use machine learning to predict the values of the missing data. To do this we treat the feature with missing values as a target vector and use the remaining subset of features to predict missing values. While we can use a wide range of machine learning algorithms to impute values, a popular choice is KNN. KNN is addressed in depth in Chapter 15, but the short explanation is that the algorithm uses the k nearest observations (according to some distance metric) to predict the missing value. In our solution we predicted the missing value using the five closest observations.

The downside to KNN is that in order to know which observations are the closest to the missing value, it needs to calculate the distance between the missing value and every single observation. This is reasonable in smaller datasets but quickly becomes problematic if a dataset has millions of observations. In such cases, approximate nearest neighbors (ANN) is a more feasible approach. We will discuss ANN in Recipe 15.5.

An alternative and more scalable strategy than KNN is to fill in the missing values of numerical data with the mean, median, or mode. For example, in our solution we used scikit-learn to fill in missing values with a feature's mean value. The imputed value is often not as close to the true value as when we used KNN, but we can scale mean-filling to data containing millions of observations more easily.

If we use imputation, it is a good idea to create a binary feature indicating whether the observation contains an imputed value.

See Also

- scikit-learn documentation: Imputation of Missing Values (*https://oreil.ly/1M4bn*)
- A Study of K-Nearest Neighbour as an Imputation Method (*https://oreil.ly/012--*)

## CHAPTER 5

Handling Categorical Data

5.0 Introduction

It is often useful to measure objects not in terms of their quantity but in terms of some quality. We frequently represent qualitative information in categories such as gender, colors, or brand of car. However, not all categorical data is the same. Sets of categories with no intrinsic ordering are called *nominal*. Examples of nominal categories include:

- Blue, Red, Green
- Man, Woman
- Banana, Strawberry, Apple

In contrast, when a set of categories has some natural ordering we refer to it as *ordinal*. For example:

- Low, Medium, High
- Young, Old
- Agree, Neutral, Disagree

Furthermore, categorical information is often represented in data as a vector or column of strings (e.g., `"Maine"`, `"Texas"`, `"Delaware"`). The problem is that most machine learning algorithms require inputs to be numerical values.

The k-nearest neighbors algorithm is an example of an algorithm that requires numerical data. One step in the algorithm is calculating the distances between observations—often using Euclidean distance:

$$\sqrt{\sum_{i=1}^{n} (x_i - y_i)^2}$$

where x and y are two observations and subscript i denotes the value for the observations' ith feature. However, the distance calculation obviously is impossible if the value of x_i is a string (e.g., "Texas"). Instead, we need to convert the string into some numerical format so that it can be input into the Euclidean distance equation. Our goal is to transform the data in a way that properly captures the information in the categories (ordinality, relative intervals between categories, etc.). In this chapter we will cover techniques for making this transformation as well as overcoming other challenges often encountered when handling categorical data.

5.1 Encoding Nominal Categorical Features

Problem

You have a feature with nominal classes that has no intrinsic ordering (e.g., apple, pear, banana), and you want to encode the feature into numerical values.

Solution

One-hot encode the feature using scikit-learn's `LabelBinarizer`:

```
# Import libraries
import numpy as np
from sklearn.preprocessing import LabelBinarizer, MultiLabelBinarizer

# Create feature
feature = np.array([["Texas"],
                    ["California"],
                    ["Texas"],
                    ["Delaware"],
                    ["Texas"]])

# Create one-hot encoder
one_hot = LabelBinarizer()

# One-hot encode feature
one_hot.fit_transform(feature)

array([[0, 0, 1],
       [1, 0, 0],
       [0, 0, 1],
       [0, 1, 0],
       [0, 0, 1]])
```

We can use the `classes_` attribute to output the classes:

```
# View feature classes
one_hot.classes_

array(['California', 'Delaware', 'Texas'],
      dtype='<U10')
```

If we want to reverse the one-hot encoding, we can use `inverse_transform`:

```
# Reverse one-hot encoding
one_hot.inverse_transform(one_hot.transform(feature))

array(['Texas', 'California', 'Texas', 'Delaware', 'Texas'],
      dtype='<U10')
```

We can even use pandas to one-hot encode the feature:

```
# Import library
import pandas as pd

# Create dummy variables from feature
pd.get_dummies(feature[:,0])
```

	California	Delaware	Texas
0	0	0	1
1	1	0	0
2	0	0	1
3	0	1	0
4	0	0	1

One helpful feature of scikit-learn is the ability to handle a situation where each observation lists multiple classes:

```
# Create multiclass feature
multiclass_feature = [("Texas", "Florida"),
                      ("California", "Alabama"),
                      ("Texas", "Florida"),
                      ("Delaware", "Florida"),
                      ("Texas", "Alabama")]

# Create multiclass one-hot encoder
one_hot_multiclass = MultiLabelBinarizer()

# One-hot encode multiclass feature
one_hot_multiclass.fit_transform(multiclass_feature)

array([[0, 0, 0, 1, 1],
       [1, 1, 0, 0, 0],
       [0, 0, 0, 1, 1],
       [0, 0, 1, 1, 0],
       [1, 0, 0, 0, 1]])
```

Once again, we can see the classes with the `classes_` method:

```
# View classes
one_hot_multiclass.classes_

array(['Alabama', 'California', 'Delaware', 'Florida', 'Texas'], dtype=object)
```

Discussion

We might think the proper strategy is to assign each class a numerical value (e.g., Texas = 1, California = 2). However, when our classes have no intrinsic ordering (e.g., Texas isn't "less" than California), our numerical values erroneously create an ordering that is not present.

The proper strategy is to create a binary feature for each class in the original feature. This is often called *one-hot encoding* (in machine learning literature) or *dummying* (in statistical and research literature). Our solution's feature was a vector containing three classes (i.e., Texas, California, and Delaware). In one-hot encoding, each class becomes its own feature with 1s when the class appears and 0s otherwise. Because our feature had three classes, one-hot encoding returned three binary features (one for each class). By using one-hot encoding we can capture the membership of an observation in a class while preserving the notion that the class lacks any sort of hierarchy.

Finally, it is often recommended that after one-hot encoding a feature, we drop one of the one-hot encoded features in the resulting matrix to avoid linear dependence.

See Also

- Dummy Variable Trap in Regression Models, Algosome (*https://oreil.ly/xjBhG*)
- Dropping one of the columns when using one-hot encoding, Cross Validated (*https://oreil.ly/CTdpG*)

5.2 Encoding Ordinal Categorical Features

Problem

You have an ordinal categorical feature (e.g., high, medium, low), and you want to transform it into numerical values.

Solution

Use the pandas DataFrame `replace` method to transform string labels to numerical equivalents:

```
# Load library
import pandas as pd
```

```
# Create features
dataframe = pd.DataFrame({"Score": ["Low", "Low", "Medium", "Medium", "High"]})

# Create mapper
scale_mapper = {"Low":1,
                "Medium":2,
                "High":3}

# Replace feature values with scale
dataframe["Score"].replace(scale_mapper)

0    1
1    1
2    2
3    2
4    3
Name: Score, dtype: int64
```

Discussion

Often we have a feature with classes that have some kind of natural ordering. A famous example is the Likert scale:

- Strongly Agree
- Agree
- Neutral
- Disagree
- Strongly Disagree

When encoding the feature for use in machine learning, we need to transform the ordinal classes into numerical values that maintain the notion of ordering. The most common approach is to create a dictionary that maps the string label of the class to a number and then apply that map to the feature.

It is important that our choice of numeric values is based on our prior information on the ordinal classes. In our solution, high is literally three times larger than low. This is fine in many instances but can break down if the assumed intervals between the classes are not equal:

```
dataframe = pd.DataFrame({"Score": ["Low",
                                    "Low",
                                    "Medium",
                                    "Medium",
                                    "High",
                                    "Barely More Than Medium"]})

scale_mapper = {"Low":1,
                "Medium":2,
```

```
                "Barely More Than Medium":3,
                "High":4}

dataframe["Score"].replace(scale_mapper)

0    1
1    1
2    2
3    2
4    4
5    3
Name: Score, dtype: int64
```

In this example, the distance between Low and Medium is the same as the distance between Medium and Barely More Than Medium, which is almost certainly not accurate. The best approach is to be conscious about the numerical values mapped to classes:

```
scale_mapper = {"Low":1,
                "Medium":2,
                "Barely More Than Medium":2.1,
                "High":3}

dataframe["Score"].replace(scale_mapper)

0    1.0
1    1.0
2    2.0
3    2.0
4    3.0
5    2.1
Name: Score, dtype: float64
```

5.3 Encoding Dictionaries of Features

Problem

You have a dictionary and want to convert it into a feature matrix.

Solution

Use DictVectorizer:

```
# Import library
from sklearn.feature_extraction import DictVectorizer

# Create dictionary
data_dict = [{"Red": 2, "Blue": 4},
             {"Red": 4, "Blue": 3},
             {"Red": 1, "Yellow": 2},
             {"Red": 2, "Yellow": 2}]
```

```
# Create dictionary vectorizer
dictvectorizer = DictVectorizer(sparse=False)

# Convert dictionary to feature matrix
features = dictvectorizer.fit_transform(data_dict)

# View feature matrix
features

array([[ 4.,  2.,  0.],
       [ 3.,  4.,  0.],
       [ 0.,  1.,  2.],
       [ 0.,  2.,  2.]])
```

By default `DictVectorizer` outputs a sparse matrix that only stores elements with a value other than 0. This can be very helpful when we have massive matrices (often encountered in natural language processing) and want to minimize the memory requirements. We can force `DictVectorizer` to output a dense matrix using `sparse=False`.

We can get the names of each generated feature using the `get_feature_names` method:

```
# Get feature names
feature_names = dictvectorizer.get_feature_names()

# View feature names
feature_names

['Blue', 'Red', 'Yellow']
```

While not necessary, for the sake of illustration we can create a pandas DataFrame to view the output better:

```
# Import library
import pandas as pd

# Create dataframe from features
pd.DataFrame(features, columns=feature_names)
```

	Blue	Red	Yellow
0	4.0	2.0	0.0
1	3.0	4.0	0.0
2	0.0	1.0	2.0
3	0.0	2.0	2.0

Discussion

A dictionary is a popular data structure used by many programming languages; however, machine learning algorithms expect the data to be in the form of a matrix. We can accomplish this using scikit-learn's `DictVectorizer`.

This is a common situation when working with natural language processing. For example, we might have a collection of documents and for each document we have a dictionary containing the number of times every word appears in the document. Using `DictVectorizer`, we can easily create a feature matrix where every feature is the number of times a word appears in each document:

```
# Create word count dictionaries for four documents
doc_1_word_count = {"Red": 2, "Blue": 4}
doc_2_word_count = {"Red": 4, "Blue": 3}
doc_3_word_count = {"Red": 1, "Yellow": 2}
doc_4_word_count = {"Red": 2, "Yellow": 2}

# Create list
doc_word_counts = [doc_1_word_count,
                   doc_2_word_count,
                   doc_3_word_count,
                   doc_4_word_count]

# Convert list of word count dictionaries into feature matrix
dictvectorizer.fit_transform(doc_word_counts)

array([[ 4.,  2.,  0.],
       [ 3.,  4.,  0.],
       [ 0.,  1.,  2.],
       [ 0.,  2.,  2.]])
```

In our toy example there are only three unique words (Red, Yellow, Blue) so there are only three features in our matrix; however, you can imagine that if each document was actually a book in a university library our feature matrix would be very large (and then we would want to set `sparse` to `True`).

See Also

- How to Create Dictionaries in Python (*https://oreil.ly/zu5hU*)
- SciPy Sparse Matrices (*https://oreil.ly/5nAsU*)

5.4 Imputing Missing Class Values

Problem

You have a categorical feature containing missing values that you want to replace with predicted values.

Solution

The ideal solution is to train a machine learning classifier algorithm to predict the missing values, commonly a k-nearest neighbors (KNN) classifier:

```
# Load libraries
import numpy as np
from sklearn.neighbors import KNeighborsClassifier

# Create feature matrix with categorical feature
X = np.array([[0, 2.10, 1.45],
              [1, 1.18, 1.33],
              [0, 1.22, 1.27],
              [1, -0.21, -1.19]])

# Create feature matrix with missing values in the categorical feature
X_with_nan = np.array([[np.nan, 0.87, 1.31],
                       [np.nan, -0.67, -0.22]])

# Train KNN learner
clf = KNeighborsClassifier(3, weights='distance')
trained_model = clf.fit(X[:,1:], X[:,0])

# Predict class of missing values
imputed_values = trained_model.predict(X_with_nan[:,1:])

# Join column of predicted class with their other features
X_with_imputed = np.hstack((imputed_values.reshape(-1,1), X_with_nan[:,1:]))

# Join two feature matrices
np.vstack((X_with_imputed, X))

array([[ 0.  ,  0.87,  1.31],
       [ 1.  , -0.67, -0.22],
       [ 0.  ,  2.1 ,  1.45],
       [ 1.  ,  1.18,  1.33],
       [ 0.  ,  1.22,  1.27],
       [ 1.  , -0.21, -1.19]])
```

An alternative solution is to fill in missing values with the feature's most frequent value:

```
from sklearn.impute import SimpleImputer

# Join the two feature matrices
X_complete = np.vstack((X_with_nan, X))

imputer = SimpleImputer(strategy='most_frequent')

imputer.fit_transform(X_complete)

array([[ 0.  ,  0.87,  1.31],
       [ 0.  , -0.67, -0.22],
```

```
[ 0.  ,  2.1 ,  1.45],
[ 1.  ,  1.18,  1.33],
[ 0.  ,  1.22,  1.27],
[ 1.  , -0.21, -1.19]])
```

Discussion

When we have missing values in a categorical feature, our best solution is to open our toolbox of machine learning algorithms to predict the values of the missing observations. We can accomplish this by treating the feature with the missing values as the target vector and the other features as the feature matrix. A commonly used algorithm is KNN (discussed in depth in Chapter 15), which assigns to the missing value the most frequent class of the k nearest observations.

Alternatively, we can fill in missing values with the most frequent class of the feature or even discard the observations with missing values. While less sophisticated than KNN, these options are much more scalable to larger data. In any case, it is advisable to include a binary feature indicating which observations contain imputed values.

See Also

- scikit-learn documentation: Imputation of Missing Values (*https://oreil.ly/joZ6J*)
- Overcoming Missing Values in a Random Forest Classifier (*https://oreil.ly/TcvOf*)
- A Study of K-Nearest Neighbour as an Imputation Method (*https://oreil.ly/ kDFEC*)

5.5 Handling Imbalanced Classes

Problem

You have a target vector with highly imbalanced classes, and you want to make adjustments so that you can handle the class imbalance.

Solution

Collect more data. If that isn't possible, change the metrics used to evaluate your model. If that doesn't work, consider using a model's built-in class weight parameters (if available), downsampling, or upsampling. We cover evaluation metrics in a later chapter, so for now let's focus on class weight parameters, downsampling, and upsampling.

To demonstrate our solutions, we need to create some data with imbalanced classes. Fisher's Iris dataset contains three balanced classes of 50 observations, each indicating the species of flower (*Iris setosa*, *Iris virginica*, and *Iris versicolor*). To unbalance the dataset, we remove 40 of the 50 *Iris setosa* observations and then merge the *Iris virginica* and *Iris versicolor* classes. The end result is a binary target vector indicating if an observation is an *Iris setosa* flower or not. The result is 10 observations of *Iris setosa* (class 0) and 100 observations of not *Iris setosa* (class 1):

```
# Load libraries
import numpy as np
from sklearn.ensemble import RandomForestClassifier
from sklearn.datasets import load_iris

# Load iris data
iris = load_iris()

# Create feature matrix
features = iris.data

# Create target vector
target = iris.target

# Remove first 40 observations
features = features[40:,:]
target = target[40:]

# Create binary target vector indicating if class 0
target = np.where((target == 0), 0, 1)

# Look at the imbalanced target vector
target
array([0, 0, 0, 0, 0, 0, 0, 0, 0, 0, 1, 1, 1, 1, 1, 1, 1, 1, 1, 1, 1, 1, 1,
       1, 1, 1, 1, 1, 1, 1, 1, 1, 1, 1, 1, 1, 1, 1, 1, 1, 1, 1, 1, 1, 1,
       1, 1, 1, 1, 1, 1, 1, 1, 1, 1, 1, 1, 1, 1, 1, 1, 1, 1, 1, 1, 1, 1,
       1, 1, 1, 1, 1, 1, 1, 1, 1, 1, 1, 1, 1, 1, 1, 1, 1, 1, 1, 1, 1, 1,
       1, 1, 1, 1, 1, 1, 1, 1, 1, 1, 1, 1, 1, 1, 1, 1, 1, 1])
```

Many algorithms in scikit-learn offer a parameter to weight classes during training to counteract the effect of their imbalance. While we have not covered it yet, Random ForestClassifier is a popular classification algorithm and includes a class_weight parameter; learn more about the RandomForestClassifier in Recipe 14.4. You can pass an argument explicitly specifying the desired class weights:

```
# Create weights
weights = {0: 0.9, 1: 0.1}

# Create random forest classifier with weights
RandomForestClassifier(class_weight=weights)

RandomForestClassifier(class_weight={0: 0.9, 1: 0.1})
```

Or you can pass balanced, which automatically creates weights inversely proportional to class frequencies:

```
# Train a random forest with balanced class weights
RandomForestClassifier(class_weight="balanced")

RandomForestClassifier(class_weight='balanced')
```

Alternatively, we can downsample the majority class or upsample the minority class. In *downsampling*, we randomly sample without replacement from the majority class (i.e., the class with more observations) to create a new subset of observations equal in size to the minority class. For example, if the minority class has 10 observations, we will randomly select 10 observations from the majority class and use those 20 observations as our data. Here we do exactly that using our unbalanced iris data:

```
# Indicies of each class's observations
i_class0 = np.where(target == 0)[0]
i_class1 = np.where(target == 1)[0]

# Number of observations in each class
n_class0 = len(i_class0)
n_class1 = len(i_class1)

# For every observation of class 0, randomly sample
# from class 1 without replacement
i_class1_downsampled = np.random.choice(i_class1, size=n_class0, replace=False)

# Join together class 0's target vector with the
# downsampled class 1's target vector
np.hstack((target[i_class0], target[i_class1_downsampled]))
```
```
array([0, 0, 0, 0, 0, 0, 0, 0, 0, 0, 1, 1, 1, 1, 1, 1, 1, 1, 1, 1])
```
```
# Join together class 0's feature matrix with the
# downsampled class 1's feature matrix
np.vstack((features[i_class0,:], features[i_class1_downsampled,:]))[0:5]
```
```
array([[ 5. ,  3.5,  1.3,  0.3],
       [ 4.5,  2.3,  1.3,  0.3],
       [ 4.4,  3.2,  1.3,  0.2],
       [ 5. ,  3.5,  1.6,  0.6],
       [ 5.1,  3.8,  1.9,  0.4]])
```

Our other option is to upsample the minority class. In *upsampling*, for every observation in the majority class, we randomly select an observation from the minority class with replacement. The result is the same number of observations from the minority and majority classes. Upsampling is implemented very similarly to downsampling, just in reverse:

```
# For every observation in class 1, randomly sample from class 0 with
# replacement
i_class0_upsampled = np.random.choice(i_class0, size=n_class1, replace=True)

# Join together class 0's upsampled target vector with class 1's target vector
np.concatenate((target[i_class0_upsampled], target[i_class1]))
```

```
array([0, 0, 0, 0, 0, 0, 0, 0, 0, 0, 0, 0, 0, 0, 0, 0, 0, 0, 0, 0, 0, 0, 0,
       0, 0, 0, 0, 0, 0, 0, 0, 0, 0, 0, 0, 0, 0, 0, 0, 0, 0, 0, 0, 0, 0, 0,
       0, 0, 0, 0, 0, 0, 0, 0, 0, 0, 0, 0, 0, 0, 0, 0, 0, 0, 0, 0, 0, 0, 0,
       0, 0, 0, 0, 0, 0, 0, 0, 0, 0, 0, 0, 0, 0, 0, 0, 0, 0, 0, 0, 0, 0, 0,
       0, 0, 0, 0, 0, 0, 0, 0, 1, 1, 1, 1, 1, 1, 1, 1, 1, 1, 1, 1, 1, 1, 1,
       1, 1, 1, 1, 1, 1, 1, 1, 1, 1, 1, 1, 1, 1, 1, 1, 1, 1, 1, 1, 1, 1, 1,
       1, 1, 1, 1, 1, 1, 1, 1, 1, 1, 1, 1, 1, 1, 1, 1, 1, 1, 1, 1, 1, 1, 1,
       1, 1, 1, 1, 1, 1, 1, 1, 1, 1, 1, 1, 1, 1, 1, 1, 1, 1, 1, 1, 1, 1, 1,
       1, 1, 1, 1, 1, 1, 1, 1, 1, 1, 1, 1, 1, 1, 1, 1])

# Join together class 0's upsampled feature matrix with class 1's feature matrix
np.vstack((features[i_class0_upsampled,:], features[i_class1,:]))[0:5]

array([[ 5. ,  3.5,  1.6,  0.6],
       [ 5. ,  3.5,  1.6,  0.6],
       [ 5. ,  3.3,  1.4,  0.2],
       [ 4.5,  2.3,  1.3,  0.3],
       [ 4.8,  3. ,  1.4,  0.3]])
```

Discussion

In the real world, imbalanced classes are everywhere—most visitors don't click the buy button, and many types of cancer are thankfully rare. For this reason, handling imbalanced classes is a common activity in machine learning.

Our best strategy is simply to collect more observations—especially observations from the minority class. However, often this is just not possible, so we have to resort to other options.

A second strategy is to use a model evaluation metric better suited to imbalanced classes. Accuracy is often used as a metric for evaluating the performance of a model, but when imbalanced classes are present, accuracy can be ill suited. For example, if only 0.5% of observations have some rare cancer, then even a naive model that predicts nobody has cancer will be 99.5% accurate. Clearly this is not ideal. Some better metrics we discuss in later chapters are confusion matrices, precision, recall, F_1 scores, and ROC curves.

A third strategy is to use the class weighing parameters included in implementations of some models. This allows the algorithm to adjust for imbalanced classes. Fortunately, many scikit-learn classifiers have a `class_weight` parameter, making it a good option.

The fourth and fifth strategies are related: downsampling and upsampling. In downsampling we create a random subset of the majority class of equal size to the minority class. In upsampling we repeatedly sample with replacement from the minority class to make it of equal size as the majority class. The decision between using downsampling and upsampling is context-specific, and in general we should try both to see which produces better results.

## CHAPTER 6

Handling Text

6.0 Introduction

Unstructured text data, like the contents of a book or a tweet, is both one of the most interesting sources of features and one of the most complex to handle. In this chapter, we will cover strategies for transforming text into information-rich features and use some out-of-the-box features (termed *embeddings*) that have become increasingly ubiquitous in tasks that involve natural language processing (NLP).

This is not to say that the recipes covered here are comprehensive. Entire academic disciplines focus on handling unstructured data such as text. In this chapter, we will cover some commonly used techniques; knowledge of these will add valuable tools to our preprocessing toolbox. In addition to many generic text processing recipes, we'll also demonstrate how you can import and leverage some pretrained machine learning models to generate richer text features.

6.1 Cleaning Text

Problem

You have some unstructured text data and want to complete some basic cleaning.

Solution

In the following example, we look at the text for three books and clean it by using Python's core string operations, in particular `strip`, `replace`, and `split`:

```
# Create text
text_data = ["   Interrobang. By Aishwarya Henriette     ",
             "Parking And Going. By Karl Gautier",
```

```
                 "    Today Is The night. By Jarek Prakash    "]

# Strip whitespaces
strip_whitespace = [string.strip() for string in text_data]

# Show text
strip_whitespace

['Interrobang. By Aishwarya Henriette',
 'Parking And Going. By Karl Gautier',
 'Today Is The night. By Jarek Prakash']

# Remove periods
remove_periods = [string.replace(".", "") for string in strip_whitespace]

# Show text
remove_periods

['Interrobang By Aishwarya Henriette',
 'Parking And Going By Karl Gautier',
 'Today Is The night By Jarek Prakash']
```

We also create and apply a custom transformation function:

```
# Create function
def capitalizer(string: str) -> str:
    return string.upper()

# Apply function
[capitalizer(string) for string in remove_periods]

['INTERROBANG BY AISHWARYA HENRIETTE',
 'PARKING AND GOING BY KARL GAUTIER',
 'TODAY IS THE NIGHT BY JAREK PRAKASH']
```

Finally, we can use regular expressions to make powerful string operations:

```
# Import library
import re

# Create function
def replace_letters_with_X(string: str) -> str:
    return re.sub(r"[a-zA-Z]", "X", string)

# Apply function
[replace_letters_with_X(string) for string in remove_periods]

['XXXXXXXXXXX XX XXXXXXXXX XXXXXXXXX',
 'XXXXXXX XXX XXXXX XX XXXX XXXXXXX',
 'XXXXX XX XXX XXXXX XX XXXXX XXXXXXX']
```

Discussion

Some text data will need to be cleaned before we can use it to build features, or
be preprocessed in some way prior to being fed into an algorithm. Most basic text

---

cleaning can be completed using Python's standard string operations. In the real world, we will most likely define a custom cleaning function (e.g., `capitalizer`) combining some cleaning tasks and apply that to the text data. Although cleaning strings can remove some information, it makes the data much easier to work with. Strings have many inherent methods that are useful for cleaning and processing; some additional examples can be found here:

```
# Define a string
s = "machine learning in python cookbook"

# Find the first index of the letter "n"
find_n = s.find("n")

# Whether or not the string starts with "m"
starts_with_m = s.startswith("m")

# Whether or not the string ends with "python"
ends_with_python = s.endswith("python")

# Is the string alphanumeric
is_alnum = s.isalnum()

# Is it composed of only alphabetical characters (not including spaces)
is_alpha = s.isalpha()

# Encode as utf-8
encode_as_utf8 = s.encode("utf-8")

# Decode the same utf-8
decode = encode_as_utf8.decode("utf-8")

print(
    find_n,
    starts_with_m,
    ends_with_python,
    is_alnum,
    is_alpha,
    encode_as_utf8,
    decode,
    sep = "|"
)
```

```
5|True|False|False|False|b'machine learning in python cookbook'|machine learning
in python cookbook
```

See Also

- Beginners Tutorial for Regular Expressions in Python (*https://oreil.ly/hSqsa*)

6.2 Parsing and Cleaning HTML

Problem

You have text data with HTML elements and want to extract just the text.

Solution

Use Beautiful Soup's extensive set of options to parse and extract from HTML:

```
# Load library
from bs4 import BeautifulSoup

# Create some HTML code
html = "<div class='full_name'>"\
       "<span style='font-weight:bold'>Masego"\
       "</span> Azra</div>"

# Parse html
soup = BeautifulSoup(html, "lxml")

# Find the div with the class "full_name", show text
soup.find("div", { "class" : "full_name" }).text

'Masego Azra'
```

Discussion

Despite the strange name, Beautiful Soup is a powerful Python library designed for scraping HTML. Typically Beautiful Soup is used to process HTML during live web scraping, but we can just as easily use it to extract text data embedded in static HTML. The full range of Beautiful Soup operations is beyond the scope of this book, but even the method we use in our solution shows how easy it can be to parse HTML and extract information from specific tags using find().

See Also

- Beautiful Soup (*https://oreil.ly/vh8h3*)

6.3 Removing Punctuation

Problem

You have a feature of text data and want to remove punctuation.

Solution

Define a function that uses `translate` with a dictionary of punctuation characters:

```
# Load libraries
import unicodedata
import sys

# Create text
text_data = ['Hi!!!! I. Love. This. Song....',
             '10000% Agree!!!! #LoveIT',
             'Right?!?!']

# Create a dictionary of punctuation characters
punctuation = dict.fromkeys(
    (i for i in range(sys.maxunicode)
    if unicodedata.category(chr(i)).startswith('P')
    ),
    None
)

# For each string, remove any punctuation characters
[string.translate(punctuation) for string in text_data]

['Hi I Love This Song', '10000 Agree LoveIT', 'Right']
```

Discussion

The Python `translate` method is popular due to its speed. In our solution, first we created a dictionary, `punctuation`, with all punctuation characters according to Unicode as its keys and `None` as its values. Next we translated all characters in the string that are in `punctuation` into `None`, effectively removing them. There are more readable ways to remove punctuation, but this somewhat hacky solution has the advantage of being far faster than alternatives.

It is important to be conscious of the fact that punctuation contains information (e.g., "Right?" versus "Right!"). Removing punctuation can be a necessary evil when we need to manually create features; however, if the punctuation is important we should make sure to take that into account. Depending on the downstream task we're trying to accomplish, punctuation might contain important information we want to keep (e.g., using a "?" to classify if some text contains a question).

6.4 Tokenizing Text

Problem

You have text and want to break it up into individual words.

Solution

Natural Language Toolkit for Python (NLTK) has a powerful set of text manipulation operations, including word tokenizing:

```
# Load library
from nltk.tokenize import word_tokenize

# Create text
string = "The science of today is the technology of tomorrow"

# Tokenize words
word_tokenize(string)

['The', 'science', 'of', 'today', 'is', 'the', 'technology', 'of', 'tomorrow']
```

We can also tokenize into sentences:

```
# Load library
from nltk.tokenize import sent_tokenize

# Create text
string = "The science of today is the technology of tomorrow. Tomorrow is today."

# Tokenize sentences
sent_tokenize(string)

['The science of today is the technology of tomorrow.', 'Tomorrow is today.']
```

Discussion

Tokenization, especially word tokenization, is a common task after cleaning text data because it is the first step in the process of turning the text into data we will use to construct useful features. Some pretrained NLP models (such as Google's BERT) utilize model-specific tokenization techniques; however, word-level tokenization is still a fairly common tokenization approach before getting features from individual words.

6.5 Removing Stop Words

Problem

Given tokenized text data, you want to remove extremely common words (e.g., *a, is, of, on*) that contain little informational value.

Solution

Use NLTK's `stopwords`:

```
# Load library
from nltk.corpus import stopwords

# You will have to download the set of stop words the first time
# import nltk
# nltk.download('stopwords')

# Create word tokens
tokenized_words = ['i',
                   'am',
                   'going',
                   'to',
                   'go',
                   'to',
                   'the',
                   'store',
                   'and',
                   'park']

# Load stop words
stop_words = stopwords.words('english')

# Remove stop words
[word for word in tokenized_words if word not in stop_words]

['going', 'go', 'store', 'park']
```

Discussion

While "stop words" can refer to any set of words we want to remove before process-ing, frequently the term refers to extremely common words that themselves contain little information value. Whether or not you choose to remove stop words will depend on your individual use case. NLTK has a list of common stop words that we can use to find and remove stop words in our tokenized words:

```
# Show stop words
stop_words[:5]

['i', 'me', 'my', 'myself', 'we']
```

Note that NLTK's stopwords assumes the tokenized words are all lowercased.

6.6 Stemming Words

Problem

You have tokenized words and want to convert them into their root forms.

Solution

Use NLTK's `PorterStemmer`:

```
# Load library
from nltk.stem.porter import PorterStemmer

# Create word tokens
tokenized_words = ['i', 'am', 'humbled', 'by', 'this', 'traditional', 'meeting']

# Create stemmer
porter = PorterStemmer()

# Apply stemmer
[porter.stem(word) for word in tokenized_words]

['i', 'am', 'humbl', 'by', 'thi', 'tradit', 'meet']
```

Discussion

Stemming reduces a word to its stem by identifying and removing affixes (e.g., gerunds) while keeping the root meaning of the word. For example, both "tradition" and "traditional" have "tradit" as their stem, indicating that while they are different words, they represent the same general concept. By stemming our text data, we transform it to something less readable but closer to its base meaning and thus more suitable for comparison across observations. NLTK's `PorterStemmer` implements the widely used Porter stemming algorithm to remove or replace common suffixes to produce the word stem.

See Also

- The Porter Stemming Algorithm (*https://oreil.ly/Z4NTp*)

6.7 Tagging Parts of Speech

Problem

You have text data and want to tag each word or character with its part of speech.

Solution

Use NLTK's pretrained parts-of-speech tagger:

```
# Load libraries
from nltk import pos_tag
from nltk import word_tokenize

# Create text
```

```
text_data = "Chris loved outdoor running"

# Use pretrained part of speech tagger
text_tagged = pos_tag(word_tokenize(text_data))

# Show parts of speech
text_tagged

[('Chris', 'NNP'), ('loved', 'VBD'), ('outdoor', 'RP'), ('running', 'VBG')]
```

The output is a list of tuples with the word and the tag of the part of speech. NLTK uses the Penn Treebank parts for speech tags. Some examples of the Penn Treebank tags are:

Tag	Part of speech
NNP	Proper noun, singular
NN	Noun, singular or mass
RB	Adverb
VBD	Verb, past tense
VBG	Verb, gerund or present participle
JJ	Adjective
PRP	Personal pronoun

Once the text has been tagged, we can use the tags to find certain parts of speech. For example, here are all nouns:

```
# Filter words
[word for word, tag in text_tagged if tag in ['NN','NNS','NNP','NNPS'] ]

['Chris']
```

A more realistic situation would be to have data where every observation contains a tweet, and we want to convert those sentences into features for individual parts of speech (e.g., a feature with 1 if a proper noun is present, and 0 otherwise):

```
# Import libraries
from sklearn.preprocessing import MultiLabelBinarizer

# Create text
tweets = ["I am eating a burrito for breakfast",
          "Political science is an amazing field",
          "San Francisco is an awesome city"]

# Create list
tagged_tweets = []

# Tag each word and each tweet
for tweet in tweets:
    tweet_tag = nltk.pos_tag(word_tokenize(tweet))
    tagged_tweets.append([tag for word, tag in tweet_tag])
```

```
# Use one-hot encoding to convert the tags into features
one_hot_multi = MultiLabelBinarizer()
one_hot_multi.fit_transform(tagged_tweets)

array([[1, 1, 0, 1, 0, 1, 1, 1, 0],
       [1, 0, 1, 1, 0, 0, 0, 0, 1],
       [1, 0, 1, 1, 1, 0, 0, 0, 1]])
```

Using `classes_` we can see that each feature is a part-of-speech tag:

```
# Show feature names
one_hot_multi.classes_

array(['DT', 'IN', 'JJ', 'NN', 'NNP', 'PRP', 'VBG', 'VBP', 'VBZ'], dtype=object)
```

Discussion

If our text is English and not on a specialized topic (e.g., medicine) the simplest solution is to use NLTK's pretrained parts-of-speech tagger. However, if `pos_tag` is not very accurate, NLTK also gives us the ability to train our own tagger. The major downside of training a tagger is that we need a large corpus of text where the tag of each word is known. Constructing this tagged corpus is obviously labor intensive and is probably going to be a last resort.

See Also

- Alphabetical list of part-of-speech tags used in the Penn Treebank Project (*https://oreil.ly/31xKf*)

6.8 Performing Named-Entity Recognition

Problem

You want to perform named-entity recognition in freeform text (such as "Person," "State," etc.).

Solution

Use spaCy's default named-entity recognition pipeline and models to extract entites from text:

```
# Import libraries
import spacy

# Load the spaCy package and use it to parse the text
# make sure you have run "python -m spacy download en"
nlp = spacy.load("en_core_web_sm")
doc = nlp("Elon Musk offered to buy Twitter using $21B of his own money.")
```

```
# Print each entity
print(doc.ents)

# For each entity print the text and the entity label
for entity in doc.ents:
    print(entity.text, entity.label_, sep=",")

(Elon Musk, Twitter, 21B)
Elon Musk, PERSON
Twitter, ORG
21B, MONEY
```

Discussion

Named-entity recognition is the process of recognizing specific entities from text. Tools like spaCy offer preconfigured pipelines, and even pretrained or fine-tuned machine learning models that can easily identify these entities. In this case, we use spaCy to identify a person ("Elon Musk"), organization ("Twitter"), and money value ("21B") from the raw text. Using this information, we can extract structured information from the unstructured textual data. This information can then be used in downstream machine learning models or data analysis.

Training a custom named-entity recognition model is outside the scope of this example; however, it is often done using deep learning and other NLP techniques.

See Also

- spaCy Named Entity Recognition documentation (*https://oreil.ly/cN8KM*)
- Named-entity recognition, Wikipedia (*https://oreil.ly/G8WDF*)

6.9 Encoding Text as a Bag of Words

Problem

You have text data and want to create a set of features indicating the number of times an observation's text contains a particular word.

Solution

Use scikit-learn's CountVectorizer:

```
# Load library
import numpy as np
from sklearn.feature_extraction.text import CountVectorizer

# Create text
text_data = np.array(['I love Brazil. Brazil!',
```

```
                  'Sweden is best',
                  'Germany beats both'])

# Create the bag of words feature matrix
count = CountVectorizer()
bag_of_words = count.fit_transform(text_data)

# Show feature matrix
bag_of_words

<3x8 sparse matrix of type '<class 'numpy.int64'>'
    with 8 stored elements in Compressed Sparse Row format>
```

This output is a sparse array, which is often necessary when we have a large amount of text. However, in our toy example we can use `toarray` to view a matrix of word counts for each observation:

```
bag_of_words.toarray()

array([[0, 0, 0, 2, 0, 0, 1, 0],
       [0, 1, 0, 0, 0, 1, 0, 1],
       [1, 0, 1, 0, 1, 0, 0, 0]], dtype=int64)
```

We can use the `get_feature_names` method to view the word associated with each feature:

```
# Show feature names
count.get_feature_names_out()

array(['beats', 'best', 'both', 'brazil', 'germany', 'is', 'love',
       'sweden'], dtype=object)
```

Note that the I from `I love Brazil` is not considered a token because the default `token_pattern` only considers tokens of two or more alphanumeric characters.

Still, this might be confusing so, for the sake of clarity, here is what the feature matrix looks like with the words as column names (each row is one observation):

beats	best	both	brazil	germany	is	love	sweden
0	0	0	2	0	0	1	0
0	1	0	0	0	1	0	1
1	0	1	0	1	0	0	0

Discussion

One of the most common methods of transforming text into features is using a bag-of-words model. Bag-of-words models output a feature for every unique word in text data, with each feature containing a count of occurrences in observations. For example, in our solution, the sentence "I love Brazil. Brazil!" has a value of 2 in the "brazil" feature because the word *brazil* appears two times.

The text data in our solution was purposely small. In the real world, a single observation of text data could be the contents of an entire book! Since our bag-of-words model creates a feature for every unique word in the data, the resulting matrix can contain thousands of features. This means the size of the matrix can sometimes become very large in memory. Luckily, we can exploit a common characteristic of bag-of-words feature matrices to reduce the amount of data we need to store.

Most words likely do not occur in most observations, and therefore bag-of-words feature matrices will contain mostly 0s as values. We call these types of matrices *sparse*. Instead of storing all values of the matrix, we can store only nonzero values and then assume all other values are 0. This will save memory when we have large feature matrices. One of the nice features of `CountVectorizer` is that the output is a sparse matrix by default.

`CountVectorizer` comes with a number of useful parameters to make it easy to create bag-of-words feature matrices. First, while by default every feature is a word, that does not have to be the case. Instead we can set every feature to be the combination of two words (called a 2-gram) or even three words (3-gram). `ngram_range` sets the minimum and maximum size of our *n*-grams. For example, `(2,3)` will return all 2-grams and 3-grams. Second, we can easily remove low-information filler words by using `stop_words`, either with a built-in list or a custom list. Finally, we can restrict the words or phrases we want to consider to a certain list of words using `vocabulary`. For example, we could create a bag-of-words feature matrix only for occurrences of country names:

```
# Create feature matrix with arguments
count_2gram = CountVectorizer(ngram_range=(1,2),
                              stop_words="english",
                              vocabulary=['brazil'])
bag = count_2gram.fit_transform(text_data)

# View feature matrix
bag.toarray()

array([[2],
       [0],
       [0]])

# View the 1-grams and 2-grams
count_2gram.vocabulary_

{'brazil': 0}
```

See Also

- *n*-gram, Wikipedia (*https://oreil.ly/XWIrM*)
- Bag of Words Meets Bags of Popcorn (*https://oreil.ly/IiyRV*)

6.10 Weighting Word Importance

Problem

You want a bag of words with words weighted by their importance to an observation.

Solution

Compare the frequency of the word in a document (a tweet, movie review, speech transcript, etc.) with the frequency of the word in all other documents using term frequency-inverse document frequency (*tf-idf*). scikit-learn makes this easy with TfidfVectorizer:

```
# Load libraries
import numpy as np
from sklearn.feature_extraction.text import TfidfVectorizer

# Create text
text_data = np.array(['I love Brazil. Brazil!',
                      'Sweden is best',
                      'Germany beats both'])

# Create the tf-idf feature matrix
tfidf = TfidfVectorizer()
feature_matrix = tfidf.fit_transform(text_data)

# Show tf-idf feature matrix
feature_matrix

<3x8 sparse matrix of type '<class 'numpy.float64'>'
    with 8 stored elements in Compressed Sparse Row format>
```

Just as in Recipe 6.9, the output is a sparse matrix. However, if we want to view the output as a dense matrix, we can use toarray:

```
# Show tf-idf feature matrix as dense matrix
feature_matrix.toarray()

array([[ 0.        , 0.        , 0.        , 0.89442719, 0.        ,
         0.        , 0.4472136 , 0.        ],
       [ 0.        , 0.57735027, 0.        , 0.        , 0.        ,
         0.57735027, 0.        , 0.57735027],
       [ 0.57735027, 0.        , 0.57735027, 0.        , 0.57735027,
         0.        , 0.        , 0.        ]])
```

vocabulary_ shows us the word of each feature:

```
# Show feature names
tfidf.vocabulary_

{'love': 6,
 'brazil': 3,
```

```
'sweden': 7,
'is': 5,
'best': 1,
'germany': 4,
'beats': 0,
'both': 2}
```

Discussion

The more a word appears in a document, the more likely it is that the word is important to that document. For example, if the word *economy* appears frequently, it is evidence that the document might be about economics. We call this *term frequency* (*tf*).

In contrast, if a word appears in many documents, it is likely less important to any individual document. For example, if every document in some text data contains the word *after* then it is probably an unimportant word. We call this *document frequency* (*df*).

By combining these two statistics, we can assign a score to every word representing how important that word is in a document. Specifically, we multiply *tf* to the inverse of document frequency (*idf*):

$$tf\text{-}idf(t, d) = tf(t, d) \times idf(t)$$

where t is a word (term) and d is a document. There are a number of variations in how *tf* and *idf* are calculated. In scikit-learn, *tf* is simply the number of times a word appears in the document, and *idf* is calculated as:

$$idf(t) = log\frac{1 + n_d}{1 + df(d, t)} + 1$$

where n_d is the number of documents, and $df(d, t)$ is term t's document frequency (i.e., the number of documents where the term appears).

By default, scikit-learn then normalizes the *tf-idf* vectors using the Euclidean norm (L2 norm). The higher the resulting value, the more important the word is to a document.

See Also

- scikit-learn documentation: *tf–idf* term weighting (*https://oreil.ly/40WeT*)

6.11 Using Text Vectors to Calculate Text Similarity in a Search Query

Problem

You want to use *tf-idf* vectors to implement a text search function in Python.

Solution

Calculate the cosine similarity between *tf-idf* vectors using scikit-learn:

```
# Load libraries
import numpy as np
from sklearn.feature_extraction.text import TfidfVectorizer
from sklearn.metrics.pairwise import linear_kernel

# Create searchable text data
text_data = np.array(['I love Brazil. Brazil!',
                      'Sweden is best',
                      'Germany beats both'])

# Create the tf-idf feature matrix
tfidf = TfidfVectorizer()
feature_matrix = tfidf.fit_transform(text_data)

# Create a search query and transform it into a tf-idf vector
text = "Brazil is the best"
vector = tfidf.transform([text])

# Calculate the cosine similarities between the input vector and all other
  vectors
cosine_similarities = linear_kernel(vector, feature_matrix).flatten()

# Get the index of the most relevent items in order
related_doc_indicies = cosine_similarities.argsort()[:-10:-1]

# Print the most similar texts to the search query along with the cosine
  similarity
print([(text_data[i], cosine_similarities[i]) for i in related_doc_indicies])

[
  (
    'Sweden is best', 0.6666666666666666),
    ('I love Brazil. Brazil!', 0.5163977794943222),
    ('Germany beats both', 0.0
    )
]
```

Discussion

Text vectors are incredibly useful for NLP use cases such as search engines. After calculating the *tf-idf* vectors of a set of sentences or documents, we can use the same `tfidf` object to vectorize future sets of text. Then, we can compute cosine similarity between our input vector and the matrix of other vectors and sort by the most relevant documents.

Cosine similarities take on the range of [0, 1.0], with 0 being least similar and 1 being most similar. Since we're using *tf-idf* vectors to compute the similarity between vectors, the frequency of a word's occurrence is also taken into account. However, with a small corpus (set of documents) even "frequent" words may not appear frequently. In this example, "Sweden is best" is the most relevant text to our search query "Brazil is the best". Since the query mentions Brazil, we might expect "I love Brazil. Brazil!" to be the most relevant; however, "Sweden is best" is the most similar due to the words "is" and "best". As the number of documents we add to our corpus increases, less important words will be weighted less and have less effect on our cosine similarity calculation.

See Also

- Cosine Similarity, Geeks for Geeks (*https://oreil.ly/-5Odv*)
- Nvidia Gave Me a $15K Data Science Workstation—Here's What I Did with It (building a Pubmed search engine in Python) (*https://oreil.ly/pAxbR*)

6.12 Using a Sentiment Analysis Classifier

Problem

You want to classify the sentiment of some text to use as a feature or in downstream data analysis.

Solution

Use the `transformers` library's sentiment classifier.

```
# Import libraries
from transformers import pipeline

# Create an NLP pipeline that runs sentiment analysis
classifier = pipeline("sentiment-analysis")

# Classify some text
# (this may download some data and models the first time you run it)
sentiment_1 = classifier("I hate machine learning! It's the absolute worst.")
sentiment_2 = classifier(
    "Machine learning is the absolute"
```

```
        "bees knees I love it so much!"
    )

    # Print sentiment output
    print(sentiment_1, sentiment_2)

    [
      {
        'label': 'NEGATIVE',
        'score': 0.9998020529747009
      }
    ]
    [
      {
        'label': 'POSITIVE',
        'score': 0.9990628957748413
      }
    ]
```

Discussion

The `transformers` library is an extremely popular library for NLP tasks and contains
a number of easy-to-use APIs for training models or using pretrained ones. We'll
talk more about NLP and this library in Chapter 22, but this example serves as a
high-level introduction to the power of using pretrained classifiers in your machine
learning pipelines to generate features, classify text, or analyze unstructured data.

See Also

- Hugging Face Transformers Quick Tour (*https://oreil.ly/7hT6W*)

## CHAPTER 7

Handling Dates and Times

7.0 Introduction

Dates and times (datetimes), such as the time of a particular sale or the date of a public health statistic, are frequently encountered during preprocessing for machine learning. *Longitudinal data* (or *time series data*) is data that's collected repeatedly for the same variables over points in time. In this chapter, we will build a toolbox of strategies for handling time series data, including tackling time zones and creating lagged time features. Specifically, we will focus on the time series tools in the pandas library, which centralizes the functionality of many other general libraries such as `datetime`.

7.1 Converting Strings to Dates

Problem

Given a vector of strings representing dates and times, you want to transform them into time series data.

Solution

Use pandas' `to_datetime` with the format of the date and/or time specified in the `format` parameter:

```
# Load libraries
import numpy as np
import pandas as pd

# Create strings
date_strings = np.array(['03-04-2005 11:35 PM',
```

```
                    '23-05-2010 12:01 AM',
                    '04-09-2009 09:09 PM'])
```

```
# Convert to datetimes
[pd.to_datetime(date, format='%d-%m-%Y %I:%M %p') for date in date_strings]
```

```
[Timestamp('2005-04-03 23:35:00'),
 Timestamp('2010-05-23 00:01:00'),
 Timestamp('2009-09-04 21:09:00')]
```

We might also want to add an argument to the errors parameter to handle problems:

```
# Convert to datetimes
[pd.to_datetime(date, format="%d-%m-%Y %I:%M %p", errors="coerce")
 for date in date_strings]
```

```
[Timestamp('2005-04-03 23:35:00'),
 Timestamp('2010-05-23 00:01:00'),
 Timestamp('2009-09-04 21:09:00')]
```

If errors="coerce", then any problem that occurs will not raise an error (the default behavior) but instead will set the value causing the error to NaT (a missing value). This allows you to deal with outliers by filling them with null values, as opposed to troubleshooting errors for individual records in the data.

Discussion

When dates and times come as strings, we need to convert them into a data type Python can understand. While there are a number of Python tools for converting strings to datetimes, following our use of pandas in other recipes we can use to_datetime to conduct the transformation. One obstacle to using strings to represent dates and times is that the format of the strings can vary significantly between data sources. For example, one vector of dates might represent March 23, 2015 as "03-23-15" while another might use "3|23|2015". We can use the format parameter to specify the exact format of the string. Here are some common date and time formatting codes:

Code	Description	Example
%Y	Full year	2001
%m	Month w/ zero padding	04
%d	Day of the month w/ zero padding	09
%I	Hour (12hr clock) w/ zero padding	02
%p	AM or PM	AM
%M	Minute w/ zero padding	05
%S	Second w/ zero padding	09

See Also

- Python strftime Cheatsheet (complete list of Python string time codes) (*https://oreil.ly/4-tN6*)

7.2 Handling Time Zones

Problem

You have time series data and want to add or change time zone information.

Solution

Unless specified, pandas objects have no time zone. We can add a time zone using `tz` during creation:

```
# Load library
import pandas as pd

# Create datetime
pd.Timestamp('2017-05-01 06:00:00', tz='Europe/London')

Timestamp('2017-05-01 06:00:00+0100', tz='Europe/London')
```

We can add a time zone to a previously created datetime using `tz_localize`:

```
# Create datetime
date = pd.Timestamp('2017-05-01 06:00:00')

# Set time zone
date_in_london = date.tz_localize('Europe/London')

# Show datetime
date_in_london

Timestamp('2017-05-01 06:00:00+0100', tz='Europe/London')
```

We also can convert to a different time zone:

```
# Change time zone
date_in_london.tz_convert('Africa/Abidjan')

Timestamp('2017-05-01 05:00:00+0000', tz='Africa/Abidjan')
```

Finally, the pandas `Series` objects can apply `tz_localize` and `tz_convert` to every element:

```
# Create three dates
dates = pd.Series(pd.date_range('2/2/2002', periods=3, freq='M'))

# Set time zone
dates.dt.tz_localize('Africa/Abidjan')
```

```
0    2002-02-28 00:00:00+00:00
1    2002-03-31 00:00:00+00:00
2    2002-04-30 00:00:00+00:00
dtype: datetime64[ns, Africa/Abidjan]
```

Discussion

pandas supports two sets of strings representing timezones; however, I suggest using the pytz library strings. We can see all the strings used to represent time zones by importing all_timezones:

```
# Load library
from pytz import all_timezones

# Show two time zones
all_timezones[0:2]

['Africa/Abidjan', 'Africa/Accra']
```

7.3 Selecting Dates and Times

Problem

You have a vector of dates and you want to select one or more.

Solution

Use two boolean conditions as the start and end dates:

```
# Load library
import pandas as pd

# Create data frame
dataframe = pd.DataFrame()

# Create datetimes
dataframe['date'] = pd.date_range('1/1/2001', periods=100000, freq='H')

# Select observations between two datetimes
dataframe[(dataframe['date'] > '2002-1-1 01:00:00') &
          (dataframe['date'] <= '2002-1-1 04:00:00')]
```

	date
8762	2002-01-01 02:00:00
8763	2002-01-01 03:00:00
8764	2002-01-01 04:00:00

Alternatively, we can set the date column as the DataFrame's index and then slice using loc:

```
# Set index
dataframe = dataframe.set_index(dataframe['date'])

# Select observations between two datetimes
dataframe.loc['2002-1-1 01:00:00':'2002-1-1 04:00:00']
```

date	date
2002-01-01 01:00:00	2002-01-01 01:00:00
2002-01-01 02:00:00	2002-01-01 02:00:00
2002-01-01 03:00:00	2002-01-01 03:00:00
2002-01-01 04:00:00	2002-01-01 04:00:00

Discussion

Whether we use boolean conditions or index slicing is situation dependent. If we wanted to do some complex time series manipulation, it might be worth the overhead of setting the date column as the index of the DataFrame, but if we wanted to do some simple data wrangling, the boolean conditions might be easier.

7.4 Breaking Up Date Data into Multiple Features

Problem

You have a column of dates and times and you want to create features for year, month, day, hour, and minute.

Solution

Use the time properties in pandas `Series.dt`:

```
# Load library
import pandas as pd

# Create data frame
dataframe = pd.DataFrame()

# Create five dates
dataframe['date'] = pd.date_range('1/1/2001', periods=150, freq='W')

# Create features for year, month, day, hour, and minute
dataframe['year'] = dataframe['date'].dt.year
dataframe['month'] = dataframe['date'].dt.month
dataframe['day'] = dataframe['date'].dt.day
dataframe['hour'] = dataframe['date'].dt.hour
dataframe['minute'] = dataframe['date'].dt.minute

# Show three rows
dataframe.head(3)
```

	date	year	month	day	hour	minute
0	2001-01-07	2001	1	7	0	0
1	2001-01-14	2001	1	14	0	0
2	2001-01-21	2001	1	21	0	0

Discussion

Sometimes it can be useful to break up a column of dates into components. For example, we might want a feature that includes just the year of the observation or we might want to consider only the month of some observations so we can compare them regardless of year.

7.5 Calculating the Difference Between Dates

Problem

You have two datetime features and want to calculate the time between them for each observation.

Solution

Subtract the two date features using pandas:

```
# Load library
import pandas as pd

# Create data frame
dataframe = pd.DataFrame()

# Create two datetime features
dataframe['Arrived'] = [pd.Timestamp('01-01-2017'), pd.Timestamp('01-04-2017')]
dataframe['Left'] = [pd.Timestamp('01-01-2017'), pd.Timestamp('01-06-2017')]

# Calculate duration between features
dataframe['Left'] - dataframe['Arrived']

0   0 days
1   2 days
dtype: timedelta64[ns]
```

Often we will want to remove the **days** output and keep only the numerical value:

```
# Calculate duration between features
pd.Series(delta.days for delta in (dataframe['Left'] - dataframe['Arrived']))

0   0
1   2
dtype: int64
```

Discussion

There are times when the feature we want is the change (delta) between two points in time. For example, we might have the dates a customer checks in and checks out of a hotel, but the feature we want is the duration of the customer's stay. pandas makes this calculation easy using the TimeDelta data type.

See Also

- pandas documentation: Time Deltas (*https://oreil.ly/fbgp-*)

7.6 Encoding Days of the Week

Problem

You have a vector of dates and want to know the day of the week for each date.

Solution

Use the pandas Series.dt method day_name():

```
# Load library
import pandas as pd

# Create dates
dates = pd.Series(pd.date_range("2/2/2002", periods=3, freq="M"))

# Show days of the week
dates.dt.day_name()
0     Thursday
1       Sunday
2      Tuesday
dtype: object
```

If we want the output to be a numerical value and therefore more usable as a machine learning feature, we can use weekday where the days of the week are represented as integers (Monday is 0):

```
# Show days of the week
dates.dt.weekday

0    3
1    6
2    1
dtype: int64
```

Discussion

Knowing the weekday can be helpful if, for instance, we wanted to compare total sales on Sundays for the past three years. pandas makes creating a feature vector containing weekday information easy.

See Also

- pandas Series datetimelike properties (*https://oreil.ly/3Au86*)

7.7 Creating a Lagged Feature

Problem

You want to create a feature that is lagged *n* time periods.

Solution

Use the pandas `shift` method:

```python
# Load library
import pandas as pd

# Create data frame
dataframe = pd.DataFrame()

# Create data
dataframe["dates"] = pd.date_range("1/1/2001", periods=5, freq="D")
dataframe["stock_price"] = [1.1,2.2,3.3,4.4,5.5]

# Lagged values by one row
dataframe["previous_days_stock_price"] = dataframe["stock_price"].shift(1)

# Show data frame
dataframe
```

	dates	stock_price	previous_days_stock_price
0	2001-01-01	1.1	NaN
1	2001-01-02	2.2	1.1
2	2001-01-03	3.3	2.2
3	2001-01-04	4.4	3.3
4	2001-01-05	5.5	4.4

Discussion

Very often data is based on regularly spaced time periods (e.g., every day, every hour, every three hours) and we are interested in using values in the past to make predictions (often called *lagging* a feature). For example, we might want to predict a stock's price using the price it was the day before. With pandas we can use `shift` to lag values by one row, creating a new feature containing past values.

In our solution, the first row for `previous_days_stock_price` is a missing value because there is no previous `stock_price` value.

7.8 Using Rolling Time Windows

Problem

Given time series data, you want to calculate a statistic for a rolling time.

Solution

Use the pandas DataFrame `rolling` method:

```
# Load library
import pandas as pd

# Create datetimes
time_index = pd.date_range("01/01/2010", periods=5, freq="M")

# Create data frame, set index
dataframe = pd.DataFrame(index=time_index)

# Create feature
dataframe["Stock_Price"] = [1,2,3,4,5]

# Calculate rolling mean
dataframe.rolling(window=2).mean()
```

	Stock_Price
2010-01-31	NaN
2010-02-28	1.5
2010-03-31	2.5
2010-04-30	3.5
2010-05-31	4.5

Discussion

Rolling (also called *moving*) *time windows* are conceptually simple but can be difficult to understand at first. Imagine we have monthly observations for a stock's price. It is often useful to have a time window of a certain number of months and then move over the observations calculating a statistic for all observations in the time window.

For example, if we have a time window of three months and we want a rolling mean, we would calculate:

1. mean(January, February, March)
2. mean(February, March, April)
3. mean(March, April, May)
4. etc.

Another way to put it: our three-month time window "walks" over the observations, calculating the window's mean at each step.

The pandas rolling method allows us to specify the size of the window by using window and then quickly calculate some common statistics, including the max value (max()), mean value (mean()), count of values (count()), and rolling correlation (corr()).

Rolling means are often used to smooth time series data because using the mean of the entire time window dampens the effect of short-term fluctuations.

See Also

- pandas documentation: Rolling Windows (*https://oreil.ly/a5gZQ*)
- What Are Moving Average or Smoothing Techniques? (*https://oreil.ly/aoOSe*)

7.9 Handling Missing Data in Time Series

Problem

You have missing values in time series data.

Solution

In addition to the missing data strategies previously discussed, when we have time series data we can use interpolation to fill gaps caused by missing values:

```
# Load libraries
import pandas as pd
import numpy as np

# Create date
time_index = pd.date_range("01/01/2010", periods=5, freq="M")

# Create data frame, set index
dataframe = pd.DataFrame(index=time_index)
```

```
# Create feature with a gap of missing values
dataframe["Sales"] = [1.0,2.0,np.nan,np.nan,5.0]

# Interpolate missing values
dataframe.interpolate()
```

	Sales
2010-01-31	1.0
2010-02-28	2.0
2010-03-31	3.0
2010-04-30	4.0
2010-05-31	5.0

Alternatively, we can replace missing values with the last known value (i.e., forward filling):

```
# Forward fill
dataframe.ffill()
```

	Sales
2010-01-31	1.0
2010-02-28	2.0
2010-03-31	2.0
2010-04-30	2.0
2010-05-31	5.0

We can also replace missing values with the latest known value (i.e., backfilling):

```
# Backfill
dataframe.bfill()
```

	Sales
2010-01-31	1.0
2010-02-28	2.0
2010-03-31	5.0
2010-04-30	5.0
2010-05-31	5.0

Discussion

Interpolation is a technique for filling gaps caused by missing values by, in effect, drawing a line or curve between the known values bordering the gap and using that line or curve to predict reasonable values. Interpolation can be particularly useful when the time intervals are constant, the data is not prone to noisy fluctuations, and the gaps caused by missing values are small. For example, in our solution, a gap of two missing values was bordered by 2.0 and 5.0. By fitting a line starting at 2.0 and ending at 5.0, we can make reasonable guesses for the two missing values between 3.0 and 4.0.

If we believe the line between the two known points is nonlinear, we can use interpolate's method parameter to specify the interpolation method:

```
# Interpolate missing values
dataframe.interpolate(method="quadratic")
```

	Sales
2010-01-31	1.000000
2010-02-28	2.000000
2010-03-31	3.059808
2010-04-30	4.038069
2010-05-31	5.000000

Finally, we may have large gaps of missing values but do not want to interpolate values across the entire gap. In these cases we can use limit to restrict the number of interpolated values and limit_direction to set whether to interpolate values forward from the last known value before the gap or vice versa:

```
# Interpolate missing values
dataframe.interpolate(limit=1, limit_direction="forward")
```

	Sales
2010-01-31	1.0
2010-02-28	2.0
2010-03-31	3.0
2010-04-30	NaN
2010-05-31	5.0

Backfilling and forward filling are forms of naive interpolation, where we draw a flat line from a known value and use it to fill in missing values. One (minor) advantage back filling and forward filling have over interpolation is that they don't require known values on *both* sides of missing values.

## CHAPTER 8

Handling Images

8.0 Introduction

Image classification is one of the most exciting areas of machine learning. The ability of computers to recognize patterns and objects from images is an incredibly powerful tool in our toolkit. However, before we can apply machine learning to images, we often first need to transform the raw images to features usable by our learning algorithms. As with textual data, there are also many pretrained classifiers available for images that we can use to extract features or objects of interest to use as inputs to our own models.

To work with images, we will primarily use the Open Source Computer Vision Library (OpenCV). While there are a number of good libraries out there, OpenCV is the most popular and well-documented library for handling images. It can occasionally be challenging to install, but if you run into issues, there are many guides online. This book in particular was written with `opencv-python-headless==4.7.0.68`. You can also run these chapters with the ML in Python Cookbook Runner (*https://oreil.ly/ MLwPython*) to ensure all commands are reproducible.

Throughout this chapter, we will use as examples a set of images, which is available to download from GitHub (*https://oreil.ly/gV5Zc*).

8.1 Loading Images

Problem

You want to load an image for preprocessing.

Solution

Use OpenCV's `imread`:

```
# Load libraries
import cv2
import numpy as np
from matplotlib import pyplot as plt

# Load image as grayscale
image = cv2.imread("images/plane.jpg", cv2.IMREAD_GRAYSCALE)
```

If we want to view the image, we can use the Python plotting library Matplotlib:

```
# Show image
plt.imshow(image, cmap="gray"), plt.axis("off")
plt.show()
```

Discussion

Fundamentally, images are data, and when we use `imread`, we convert that data into a data type we are very familiar with—a NumPy array:

```
# Show data type
type(image)
```

```
numpy.ndarray
```

We have transformed the image into a matrix whose elements correspond to individual pixels. We can even take a look at the actual values of the matrix:

```
# Show image data
image
```

```
array([[140, 136, 146, ..., 132, 139, 134],
       [144, 136, 149, ..., 142, 124, 126],
       [152, 139, 144, ..., 121, 127, 134],
       ...,
       [156, 146, 144, ..., 157, 154, 151],
       [146, 150, 147, ..., 156, 158, 157],
       [143, 138, 147, ..., 156, 157, 157]], dtype=uint8)
```

The resolution of our image is 3600 × 2270, the exact dimensions of our matrix:

```
# Show dimensions
image.shape
```

```
(2270, 3600)
```

What does each element in the matrix actually represent? In grayscale images, the value of an individual element is the pixel intensity. Intensity values range from black (0) to white (255). For example, the intensity of the top leftmost pixel in our image has a value of 140:

```
# Show first pixel
image[0,0]
```

```
140
```

In a matrix representing a color image, each element actually contains three values corresponding to blue, green, and red values, respectively (BGR):

```
# Load image in color
image_bgr = cv2.imread("images/plane.jpg", cv2.IMREAD_COLOR)
```

```
# Show pixel
image_bgr[0,0]
```

```
array([195, 144, 111], dtype=uint8)
```

One small caveat: by default OpenCV uses BGR, but many image applications—including Matplotlib—use red, green, blue (RGB), meaning the red and the blue values are swapped. To properly display OpenCV color images in Matplotlib, we first need to convert the color to RGB (apologies to hardcopy readers for whom there are no color images):

```
# Convert to RGB
image_rgb = cv2.cvtColor(image_bgr, cv2.COLOR_BGR2RGB)
```

```
# Show image
plt.imshow(image_rgb), plt.axis("off")
plt.show()
```

See Also

- Difference Between RGB and BGR (*https://oreil.ly/N1Ub6*)
- RGB color model, Wikipedia (*https://oreil.ly/OEesQ*)

8.2 Saving Images

Problem

You want to save an image for preprocessing.

Solution

Use OpenCV's `imwrite`:

```
# Load libraries
import cv2
import numpy as np
from matplotlib import pyplot as plt

# Load image as grayscale
image = cv2.imread("images/plane.jpg", cv2.IMREAD_GRAYSCALE)

# Save image
cv2.imwrite("images/plane_new.jpg", image)

True
```

Discussion

OpenCV's `imwrite` saves images to the filepath specified. The format of the image is defined by the filename's extension (*.jpg*, *.png*, etc.). One behavior to be careful about: `imwrite` will overwrite existing files without outputting an error or asking for confirmation.

8.3 Resizing Images

Problem

You want to resize an image for further preprocessing.

Solution

Use `resize` to change the size of an image:

```
# Load libraries
import cv2
```

```
import numpy as np
from matplotlib import pyplot as plt

# Load image as grayscale
image = cv2.imread("images/plane_256x256.jpg", cv2.IMREAD_GRAYSCALE)

# Resize image to 50 pixels by 50 pixels
image_50x50 = cv2.resize(image, (50, 50))

# View image
plt.imshow(image_50x50, cmap="gray"), plt.axis("off")
plt.show()
```

Discussion

Resizing images is a common task in image preprocessing for two reasons. First, images come in all shapes and sizes, and to be usable as features, images must have the same dimensions. Standardizing (resizing) images does come at the cost of losing some information present in the larger image, as can be seen in the picture of the airplane. Images are matrices of information, and when we reduce the size of the image, we are reducing the size of that matrix and the information it contains. Second, machine learning can require thousands or hundreds of thousands of images. When those images are very large they can take up a lot of memory, and by resizing them we can dramatically reduce memory usage. Some common image sizes for machine learning are 32 × 32, 64 × 64, 96 × 96, and 256 × 256. In essence, the method we choose for image resizing will often be a tradeoff between the statistical performance of our model and computational cost to train it. The Pillow library offers many options for resizing images (*https://oreil.ly/NiJn_*) for this reason.

8.4 Cropping Images

Problem

You want to remove the outer portion of the image to change its dimensions.

Solution

The image is encoded as a two-dimensional NumPy array, so we can crop the image easily by slicing the array:

```
# Load libraries
import cv2
import numpy as np
from matplotlib import pyplot as plt

# Load image in grayscale
image = cv2.imread("images/plane_256x256.jpg", cv2.IMREAD_GRAYSCALE)

# Select first half of the columns and all rows
image_cropped = image[:,:128]

# Show image
plt.imshow(image_cropped, cmap="gray"), plt.axis("off")
plt.show()
```

Discussion

Since OpenCV represents images as a matrix of elements, by selecting the rows and columns we want to keep we can easily crop the image. Cropping can be particularly useful if we know that we want to keep only a certain part of every image. For example, if our images come from a stationary security camera we can crop all the images so they contain only the area of interest.

See Also

- Slicing NumPy Arrays (*https://oreil.ly/8JN5p*)

8.5 Blurring Images

Problem

You want to smooth out an image.

Solution

To blur an image, each pixel is transformed to be the average value of its neighbors. This neighbor and the operation performed are mathematically represented as a kernel (don't worry if you don't know what a kernel is). The size of this kernel determines the amount of blurring, with larger kernels producing smoother images. Here we blur an image by averaging the values of a 5 × 5 kernel around each pixel:

```
# Load libraries
import cv2
import numpy as np
from matplotlib import pyplot as plt

# Load image as grayscale
image = cv2.imread("images/plane_256x256.jpg", cv2.IMREAD_GRAYSCALE)

# Blur image
image_blurry = cv2.blur(image, (5,5))

# Show image
plt.imshow(image_blurry, cmap="gray"), plt.axis("off")
plt.show()
```

To highlight the effect of kernel size, here is the same blurring with a 100 × 100 kernel:

```
# Blur image
image_very_blurry = cv2.blur(image, (100,100))

# Show image
plt.imshow(image_very_blurry, cmap="gray"), plt.xticks([]), plt.yticks([])
plt.show()
```

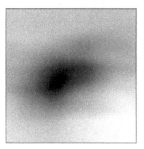

Discussion

Kernels are widely used in image processing to do everything from sharpening to edge detection and will come up repeatedly in this chapter. The blurring kernel we used looks like this:

```
# Create kernel
kernel = np.ones((5,5)) / 25.0

# Show kernel
kernel

array([[ 0.04,  0.04,  0.04,  0.04,  0.04],
       [ 0.04,  0.04,  0.04,  0.04,  0.04],
       [ 0.04,  0.04,  0.04,  0.04,  0.04],
       [ 0.04,  0.04,  0.04,  0.04,  0.04],
       [ 0.04,  0.04,  0.04,  0.04,  0.04]])
```

The center element in the kernel is the pixel being examined, while the remaining elements are its neighbors. Since all elements have the same value (normalized to add up to 1), each has an equal say in the resulting value of the pixel of interest. We can manually apply a kernel to an image using `filter2D` to produce a similar blurring effect:

```
# Apply kernel
image_kernel = cv2.filter2D(image, -1, kernel)

# Show image
plt.imshow(image_kernel, cmap="gray"), plt.xticks([]), plt.yticks([])
plt.show()
```

See Also

- Image Kernels Explained Visually (*https://oreil.ly/9yvdg*)
- Kernel (image processing), Wikipedia (*https://oreil.ly/ByREC*)

8.6 Sharpening Images

Problem

You want to sharpen an image.

Solution

Create a kernel that highlights the target pixel. Then apply it to the image using
`filter2D`:

```
# Load libraries
import cv2
import numpy as np
from matplotlib import pyplot as plt

# Load image as grayscale
image = cv2.imread("images/plane_256x256.jpg", cv2.IMREAD_GRAYSCALE)

# Create kernel
kernel = np.array([[0, -1, 0],
                   [-1, 5,-1],
                   [0, -1, 0]])

# Sharpen image
image_sharp = cv2.filter2D(image, -1, kernel)

# Show image
plt.imshow(image_sharp, cmap="gray"), plt.axis("off")
plt.show()
```

Discussion

Sharpening works similarly to blurring, except instead of using a kernel to average the neighboring values, we constructed a kernel to highlight the pixel itself. The resulting effect makes contrasts in edges stand out more.

8.7 Enhancing Contrast

Problem

We want to increase the contrast between pixels in an image.

Solution

Histogram equalization is a tool for image processing that can make objects and shapes stand out. When we have a grayscale image, we can apply OpenCV's equalizeHist directly on the image:

```
# Load libraries
import cv2
import numpy as np
from matplotlib import pyplot as plt

# Load image
image = cv2.imread("images/plane_256x256.jpg", cv2.IMREAD_GRAYSCALE)

# Enhance image
image_enhanced = cv2.equalizeHist(image)

# Show image
plt.imshow(image_enhanced, cmap="gray"), plt.axis("off")
plt.show()
```

However, when we have a color image, we first need to convert the image to the YUV color format. The Y is the luma, or brightness, and U and V denote the color. After the conversion, we can apply equalizeHist to the image and then convert it back to BGR or RGB (apologies to hardcopy readers for whom there are no color images):

```
# Load image
image_bgr = cv2.imread("images/plane.jpg")

# Convert to YUV
image_yuv = cv2.cvtColor(image_bgr, cv2.COLOR_BGR2YUV)

# Apply histogram equalization
image_yuv[:, :, 0] = cv2.equalizeHist(image_yuv[:, :, 0])

# Convert to RGB
image_rgb = cv2.cvtColor(image_yuv, cv2.COLOR_YUV2RGB)

# Show image
plt.imshow(image_rgb), plt.axis("off")
plt.show()
```

Discussion

While a detailed explanation of how histogram equalization works is beyond the scope of this book, the short explanation is that it transforms the image so that it uses a wider range of pixel intensities.

While the resulting image often does not look "realistic," we need to remember that the image is just a visual representation of the underlying data. If histogram equalization is able to make objects of interest more distinguishable from other objects or backgrounds (which is not always the case), then it can be a valuable addition to our image preprocessing pipeline.

8.8 Isolating Colors

Problem

You want to isolate a color in an image.

Solution

Define a range of colors and then apply a mask to the image (apologies to hardcopy readers for whom there are no color images):

```
# Load libraries
import cv2
import numpy as np
from matplotlib import pyplot as plt

# Load image
image_bgr = cv2.imread('images/plane_256x256.jpg')

# Convert BGR to HSV
image_hsv = cv2.cvtColor(image_bgr, cv2.COLOR_BGR2HSV)

# Define range of blue values in HSV
lower_blue = np.array([50,100,50])
upper_blue = np.array([130,255,255])

# Create mask
mask = cv2.inRange(image_hsv, lower_blue, upper_blue)

# Mask image
image_bgr_masked = cv2.bitwise_and(image_bgr, image_bgr, mask=mask)

# Convert BGR to RGB
image_rgb = cv2.cvtColor(image_bgr_masked, cv2.COLOR_BGR2RGB)

# Show image
plt.imshow(image_rgb), plt.axis("off")
plt.show()
```

Discussion

Isolating colors in OpenCV is straightforward. First we convert an image into HSV (hue, saturation, and value). Second, we define a range of values we want to isolate, which is probably the most difficult and time-consuming part. Third, we create a mask for the image. Image masking is a common technique meant to extract regions of interest. In this case, our mask keeps only the white areas:

```
# Show image
plt.imshow(mask, cmap='gray'), plt.axis("off")
plt.show()
```

Finally, we apply the mask to the image using bitwise_and and convert to our desired output format.

8.9 Binarizing Images

Problem

Given an image, you want to output a simplified version.

Solution

Thresholding is the process of setting pixels with intensity greater than some value to be white and less than the value to be black. A more advanced technique is *adaptive thresholding*, where the threshold value for a pixel is determined by the pixel intensities of its neighbors. This can be helpful when lighting conditions change over different regions in an image:

```
# Load libraries
import cv2
import numpy as np
from matplotlib import pyplot as plt

# Load image as grayscale
image_grey = cv2.imread("images/plane_256x256.jpg", cv2.IMREAD_GRAYSCALE)

# Apply adaptive thresholding
max_output_value = 255
neighborhood_size = 99
subtract_from_mean = 10
image_binarized = cv2.adaptiveThreshold(image_grey,
                                        max_output_value,
```

```
                                   cv2.ADAPTIVE_THRESH_GAUSSIAN_C,
                                   cv2.THRESH_BINARY,
                                   neighborhood_size,
                                   subtract_from_mean)

# Show image
plt.imshow(image_binarized, cmap="gray"), plt.axis("off")
plt.show()
```

Discussion

The process of binarizing an image involves converting a greyscale image to its black
and white form. Our solution has four important arguments in adaptiveThreshold.
max_output_value simply determines the maximum intensity of the output pixel
intensities. cv2.ADAPTIVE_THRESH_GAUSSIAN_C sets a pixel's threshold to be a weighted sum of the neighboring pixel intensities. The weights are determined by a Gaussian window. Alternatively, we could set the threshold to simply the mean of the
neighboring pixels with cv2.ADAPTIVE_THRESH_MEAN_C:

```
# Apply cv2.ADAPTIVE_THRESH_MEAN_C
image_mean_threshold = cv2.adaptiveThreshold(image_grey,
                                   max_output_value,
                                   cv2.ADAPTIVE_THRESH_MEAN_C,
                                   cv2.THRESH_BINARY,
                                   neighborhood_size,
                                   subtract_from_mean)

# Show image
plt.imshow(image_mean_threshold, cmap="gray"), plt.axis("off")
plt.show()
```

The last two parameters are the block size (the size of the neighborhood used to determine a pixel's threshold) and a constant subtracted from the calculated threshold (used to manually fine-tune the threshold).

A major benefit of thresholding is *denoising* an image—keeping only the most important elements. For example, thresholding is often applied to photos of printed text to isolate the letters from the page.

8.10 Removing Backgrounds

Problem

You want to isolate the foreground of an image.

Solution

Mark a rectangle around the desired foreground, then run the GrabCut algorithm:

```
# Load library
import cv2
import numpy as np
from matplotlib import pyplot as plt

# Load image and convert to RGB
image_bgr = cv2.imread('images/plane_256x256.jpg')
image_rgb = cv2.cvtColor(image_bgr, cv2.COLOR_BGR2RGB)

# Rectangle values: start x, start y, width, height
rectangle = (0, 56, 256, 150)

# Create initial mask
mask = np.zeros(image_rgb.shape[:2], np.uint8)

# Create temporary arrays used by grabCut
bgdModel = np.zeros((1, 65), np.float64)
fgdModel = np.zeros((1, 65), np.float64)

# Run grabCut
cv2.grabCut(image_rgb, # Our image
            mask, # The Mask
            rectangle, # Our rectangle
            bgdModel, # Temporary array for background
            fgdModel, # Temporary array for background
            5, # Number of iterations
            cv2.GC_INIT_WITH_RECT) # Initiative using our rectangle

# Create mask where sure and likely backgrounds set to 0, otherwise 1
mask_2 = np.where((mask==2) | (mask==0), 0, 1).astype('uint8')

# Multiply image with new mask to subtract background
```

```
image_rgb_nobg = image_rgb * mask_2[:, :, np.newaxis]

# Show image
plt.imshow(image_rgb_nobg), plt.axis("off")
plt.show()
```

Discussion

The first thing we notice is that even though GrabCut did a pretty good job, there
are still areas of background left in the image. We could go back and manually mark
those areas as background, but in the real world we have thousands of images and
manually fixing them individually is not feasible. Therefore, we would do well by
simply accepting that the image data will still contain some background noise.

In our solution, we start by marking a rectangle around the area that contains the
foreground. GrabCut assumes everything outside this rectangle to be background
and uses that information to figure out what is likely background inside the square.
(To learn how the algorithm does this, see this explanation from Itay Blumenthal
(*https://oreil.ly/DTGwb*).) Then a mask is created that denotes the different defi-
nitely/likely background/foreground regions:

```
# Show mask
plt.imshow(mask, cmap='gray'), plt.axis("off")
plt.show()
```

The black region is the area outside our rectangle that is assumed to be definitely background. The gray area is what GrabCut considered likely background, while the white area is likely foreground.

This mask is then used to create a second mask that merges the black and gray regions:

```
# Show mask
plt.imshow(mask_2, cmap='gray'), plt.axis("off")
plt.show()
```

The second mask is then applied to the image so that only the foreground remains.

8.11 Detecting Edges

Problem

You want to find the edges in an image.

Solution

Use an edge detection technique like the Canny edge detector:

```
# Load libraries
import cv2
import numpy as np
from matplotlib import pyplot as plt

# Load image as grayscale
image_gray = cv2.imread("images/plane_256x256.jpg", cv2.IMREAD_GRAYSCALE)

# Calculate median intensity
median_intensity = np.median(image_gray)

# Set thresholds to be one standard deviation above and below median intensity
lower_threshold = int(max(0, (1.0 - 0.33) * median_intensity))
upper_threshold = int(min(255, (1.0 + 0.33) * median_intensity))

# Apply Canny edge detector
```

```
image_canny = cv2.Canny(image_gray, lower_threshold, upper_threshold)

# Show image
plt.imshow(image_canny, cmap="gray"), plt.axis("off")
plt.show()
```

Discussion

Edge detection is a major topic of interest in computer vision. Edges are important
because they are areas of high information. For example, in our image one patch of
sky looks very much like another and is unlikely to contain unique or interesting
information. However, patches where the background sky meets the airplane contain
a lot of information (e.g., an object's shape). Edge detection allows us to remove low-
information areas and isolate the areas of images containing the most information.

There are many edge detection techniques (Sobel filters, Laplacian edge detector,
etc.). However, our solution uses the commonly used Canny edge detector. How the
Canny detector works is too detailed for this book, but there is one point that we
need to address. The Canny detector requires two parameters denoting low and high
gradient threshold values. Potential edge pixels between the low and high thresholds
are considered weak edge pixels, while those above the high threshold are considered
strong edge pixels. OpenCV's Canny method includes the low and high thresholds as
required parameters. In our solution, we set the lower and upper thresholds to be one
standard deviation below and above the image's median pixel intensity. However, we
often get better results if we determine a good pair of low and high threshold values
through manual trial and error on a few images before running Canny on our entire
collection of images.

See Also

- Canny Edge Detector, Wikipedia (*https://oreil.ly/gG9xo*)
- Canny Edge Detection Auto Thresholding (*https://oreil.ly/YvjM5*)

8.12 Detecting Corners

Problem

You want to detect the corners in an image.

Solution

Use OpenCV's implementation of the Harris corner detector, cornerHarris:

```python
# Load libraries
import cv2
import numpy as np
from matplotlib import pyplot as plt

# Load image
image_bgr = cv2.imread("images/plane_256x256.jpg")
image_gray = cv2.cvtColor(image_bgr, cv2.COLOR_BGR2GRAY)
image_gray = np.float32(image_gray)

# Set corner detector parameters
block_size = 2
aperture = 29
free_parameter = 0.04

# Detect corners
detector_responses = cv2.cornerHarris(image_gray,
                                      block_size,
                                      aperture,
                                      free_parameter)

# Large corner markers
detector_responses = cv2.dilate(detector_responses, None)

# Only keep detector responses greater than threshold, mark as white
threshold = 0.02
image_bgr[detector_responses >
          threshold *
          detector_responses.max()] = [255,255,255]

# Convert to grayscale
image_gray = cv2.cvtColor(image_bgr, cv2.COLOR_BGR2GRAY)

# Show image
plt.imshow(image_gray, cmap="gray"), plt.axis("off")
plt.show()
```

Discussion

The *Harris corner detector* is a commonly used method of detecting the intersection of two edges. Our interest in detecting corners is motivated by the same reason as for detecting edges: corners are points of high information. A complete explanation of the Harris corner detector is available in the external resources at the end of this recipe, but a simplified explanation is that it looks for windows (also called *neighborhoods* or *patches*) where small movements of the window (imagine shaking the window) create big changes in the contents of the pixels inside the window. cornerHarris contains three important parameters that we can use to control the edges detected. First, block_size is the size of the neighbor around each pixel used for corner detection. Second, aperture is the size of the Sobel kernel used (don't worry if you don't know what that is), and finally there is a free parameter where larger values correspond to identifying softer corners.

The output is a grayscale image depicting potential corners:

```
# Show potential corners
plt.imshow(detector_responses, cmap='gray'), plt.axis("off")
plt.show()
```

We then apply thresholding to keep only the most likely corners. Alternatively, we can use a similar detector, the Shi-Tomasi corner detector, which works in a similar way to the Harris detector (goodFeaturesToTrack) to identify a fixed number of strong corners. goodFeaturesToTrack takes three major parameters—the number of corners to detect, the minimum quality of the corner (0 to 1), and the minimum Euclidean distance between corners:

```
# Load images
image_bgr = cv2.imread('images/plane_256x256.jpg')
image_gray = cv2.cvtColor(image_bgr, cv2.COLOR_BGR2GRAY)

# Number of corners to detect
corners_to_detect = 10
minimum_quality_score = 0.05
minimum_distance = 25

# Detect corners
corners = cv2.goodFeaturesToTrack(image_gray,
                                  corners_to_detect,
                                  minimum_quality_score,
                                  minimum_distance)
corners = np.int16(corners)

# Draw white circle at each corner
for corner in corners:
    x, y = corner[0]
    cv2.circle(image_bgr, (x,y), 10, (255,255,255), -1)

# Convert to grayscale
image_rgb = cv2.cvtColor(image_bgr, cv2.COLOR_BGR2GRAY)

# Show image
plt.imshow(image_rgb, cmap='gray'), plt.axis("off")
plt.show()
```

See Also

- OpenCV's cornerHarris (*https://oreil.ly/vLMBj*)
- OpenCV's goodFeaturesToTrack (*https://oreil.ly/Ra-x6*)

8.13 Creating Features for Machine Learning

Problem

You want to convert an image into an observation for machine learning.

Solution

Use NumPy's `flatten` to convert the multidimensional array containing image data into a vector containing the observation's values:

```
# Load libraries
import cv2
import numpy as np
from matplotlib import pyplot as plt

# Load image as grayscale
image = cv2.imread("images/plane_256x256.jpg", cv2.IMREAD_GRAYSCALE)

# Resize image to 10 pixels by 10 pixels
image_10x10 = cv2.resize(image, (10, 10))

# Convert image data to one-dimensional vector
image_10x10.flatten()
```

```
array([133, 130, 130, 129, 130, 129, 129, 128, 128, 127, 135, 131, 131,
       131, 130, 130, 129, 128, 128, 128, 134, 132, 131, 131, 130, 129,
       129, 128, 130, 133, 132, 158, 130, 133, 130,  46,  97,  26, 132,
       143, 141,  36,  54,  91,   9,   9,  49, 144, 179,  41, 142,  95,
        32,  36,  29,  43, 113, 141, 179, 187, 141, 124,  26,  25, 132,
       135, 151, 175, 174, 184, 143, 151,  38, 133, 134, 139, 174, 177,
       169, 174, 155, 141, 135, 137, 137, 152, 169, 168, 168, 179, 152,
       139, 136, 135, 137, 143, 159, 166, 171, 175], dtype=uint8)
```

Discussion

Images are presented as a grid of pixels. If an image is in grayscale, each pixel is presented by one value (i.e., pixel intensity is 1 if white, 0 if black). For example, imagine we have a 10 × 10–pixel image:

```
plt.imshow(image_10x10, cmap="gray"), plt.axis("off")
plt.show()
```

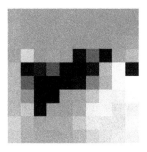

In this case, the dimensions of the image's data will be 10 × 10:

```
image_10x10.shape
```

```
(10, 10)
```

And if we flatten the array, we get a vector of length 100 (10 multiplied by 10):

```
image_10x10.flatten().shape
```

```
(100,)
```

This is the feature data for our image that can be joined with the vectors from other images to create the data we will feed to our machine learning algorithms.

If the image is in color, instead of each pixel being represented by one value, it is represented by multiple values (most often three) representing the channels (red, green, blue, etc.) that blend to make the final color of that pixel. For this reason, if our 10 × 10 image is in color, we will have 300 feature values for each observation:

```
# Load image in color
image_color = cv2.imread("images/plane_256x256.jpg", cv2.IMREAD_COLOR)

# Resize image to 10 pixels by 10 pixels
image_color_10x10 = cv2.resize(image_color, (10, 10))

# Convert image data to one-dimensional vector, show dimensions
image_color_10x10.flatten().shape
```

```
(300,)
```

One of the major challenges of image processing and computer vision is that since every pixel location in a collection of images is a feature, as the images get larger, the number of features explodes:

```
# Load image in grayscale
image_256x256_gray = cv2.imread("images/plane_256x256.jpg", cv2.IMREAD_GRAYSCALE)

# Convert image data to one-dimensional vector, show dimensions
image_256x256_gray.flatten().shape

(65536,)
```

And the number of features grows even larger when the image is in color:

```
# Load image in color
image_256x256_color = cv2.imread("images/plane_256x256.jpg", cv2.IMREAD_COLOR)

# Convert image data to one-dimensional vector, show dimensions
image_256x256_color.flatten().shape

(196608,)
```

As the output shows, even a small color image has almost 200,000 features, which can cause problems when we are training our models because the number of features might far exceed the number of observations.

This problem will motivate dimensionality strategies discussed in a later chapter, which attempt to reduce the number of features while not losing an excessive amount of information contained in the data.

8.14 Encoding Color Histograms as Features

Problem

You want to create a set of features representing the colors appearing in an image.

Solution

Compute the histograms for each color channel:

```
# Load libraries
import cv2
import numpy as np
from matplotlib import pyplot as plt

np.random.seed(0)

# Load image
image_bgr = cv2.imread("images/plane_256x256.jpg", cv2.IMREAD_COLOR)

# Convert to RGB
image_rgb = cv2.cvtColor(image_bgr, cv2.COLOR_BGR2RGB)

# Create a list for feature values
features = []
```

```
# Calculate the histogram for each color channel
colors = ("r","g","b")

# For each channel: calculate histogram and add to feature value list
for i, channel in enumerate(colors):
    histogram = cv2.calcHist([image_rgb], # Image
                    [i], # Index of channel
                    None, # No mask
                    [256], # Histogram size
                    [0,256]) # Range
    features.extend(histogram)

# Create a vector for an observation's feature values
observation = np.array(features).flatten()

# Show the observation's value for the first five features
observation[0:5]

array([ 1008.,   217.,   184.,   165.,   116.], dtype=float32)
```

Discussion

In the RGB color model, each color is the combination of three color channels (i.e., red, green, blue). In turn, each channel can take on one of 256 values (represented by an integer between 0 and 255). For example, the top leftmost pixel in our image has the following channel values:

```
# Show RGB channel values
image_rgb[0,0]

array([107, 163, 212], dtype=uint8)
```

A histogram is a representation of the distribution of values in data. Here's a simple example:

```
# Import pandas
import pandas as pd

# Create some data
data = pd.Series([1, 1, 2, 2, 3, 3, 3, 4, 5])

# Show the histogram
data.hist(grid=False)
plt.show()
```

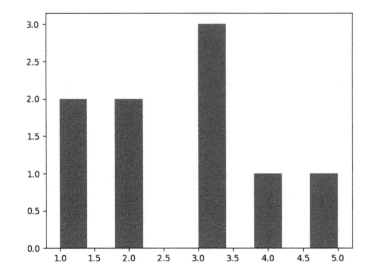

In this example, we have some data with two 1s, two 2s, three 3s, one 4, and one 5. In the histogram, each bar represents the number of times each value (1, 2, etc.) appears in our data.

We can apply this same technique to each of the color channels, but instead of five possible values, we have 256 (the number of possible values for a channel value). The x-axis represents the 256 possible channel values, and the y-axis represents the number of times a particular channel value appears across all pixels in an image (apologies to hardcopy readers for whom there are no color images):

```
# Calculate the histogram for each color channel
colors = ("r","g","b")

# For each channel: calculate histogram, make plot
for i, channel in enumerate(colors):
    histogram = cv2.calcHist([image_rgb], # Image
                    [i], # Index of channel
                    None, # No mask
                    [256], # Histogram size
                    [0,256]) # Range
    plt.plot(histogram, color = channel)
    plt.xlim([0,256])

# Show plot
plt.show()
```

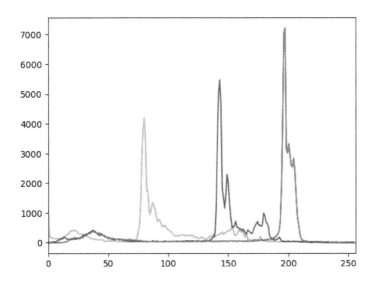

As we can see in the histogram, barely any pixels contain the blue channel values between 0 and ~180, while many pixels contain blue channel values between ~190 and ~210. This distribution of channel values is shown for all three channels. The histogram, however, is not simply a visualization; it has 256 features for each color channel, making for 768 total features representing the distribution of colors in an image.

See Also

- Histogram, Wikipedia (*https://oreil.ly/nPbJT*)
- pandas documentation: Histogram (*https://oreil.ly/h60M5*)
- OpenCV tutorial: Histogram (*https://oreil.ly/BuX1C*)

8.15 Using Pretrained Embeddings as Features

Problem

You want to load pretrained embeddings from an existing model in PyTorch and use them as input to one of your own models.

Solution

Use `torchvision.models` to select a model and then retrieve an embedding from it for a given image:

```
# Load libraries
import cv2
import numpy as np
import torch
from torchvision import transforms
import torchvision.models as models

# Load image
image_bgr = cv2.imread("images/plane.jpg", cv2.IMREAD_COLOR)

# Convert to pytorch data type
convert_tensor = transforms.ToTensor()
pytorch_image = convert_tensor(np.array(image_rgb))

# Load the pretrained model
model = models.resnet18(pretrained=True)

# Select the specific layer of the model we want output from
layer = model._modules.get('avgpool')

# Set model to evaluation mode
model.eval()

# Infer the embedding with the no_grad option
with torch.no_grad():
    embedding = model(pytorch_image.unsqueeze(0))

print(embedding.shape)

torch.Size([1, 1000])
```

Discussion

In the ML space, *transfer learning* is often defined as taking information learned from one task and using it as input to another task. Instead of starting from zero, we can use representations already learned from large pretrained image models (such as ResNet) to get a head start on our own machine learning models. More intuitively, you can understand how we could use the weights of a model trained to recognize cats as a good start for a model we want to train to recognize dogs. By sharing information form one model to another, we can leverage the information learned from other datasets and model architectures without the overhead of training a model from scratch.

The entire application of transfer learning in computer vision is outside the scope of this book; however, there are many different ways we can extract embeddings-based representations of images outside of PyTorch. In TensorFlow, another common library for deep learning, we can use `tensorflow_hub`:

```
# Load libraries
import cv2
```

```
import tensorflow as tf
import tensorflow_hub as hub

# Load image
image_bgr = cv2.imread("images/plane.jpg", cv2.IMREAD_COLOR)
image_rgb = cv2.cvtColor(image_bgr, cv2.COLOR_BGR2RGB)

# Convert to tensorflow data type
tf_image = tf.image.convert_image_dtype([image_rgb], tf.float32)

# Create the model and get embeddings using the inception V1 model
embedding_model = hub.KerasLayer(
    "https://tfhub.dev/google/imagenet/inception_v1/feature_vector/5"
)
embeddings = embedding_model(tf_image)

# Print the shape of the embedding
print(embeddings.shape)

(1, 1024)
```

See Also

- PyTorch tutorial: Transfer Learning for Computer Vision (*https://oreil.ly/R8RTk*)
- TensorFlow Hub (*https://oreil.ly/iwHI6*)

8.16 Detecting Objects with OpenCV

Problem

You want to detect objects in images using pretrained cascade classifiers with OpenCV.

Solution

Download and run one of OpenCV's Haar cascade classifiers (*https://oreil.ly/XlXbm*). In this case, we use a pretrained face detection model to detect and draw a rectangle around a face in an image:

```
# Import libraries
import cv2
from matplotlib import pyplot as plt

# first run:
# mkdir models && cd models
# wget https://tinyurl.com/mrc6jwhp
face_cascade = cv2.CascadeClassifier()
face_cascade.load(
    cv2.samples.findFile(
```

```
            "models/haarcascade_frontalface_default.xml"
    )
)

# Load image
image_bgr = cv2.imread("images/kyle_pic.jpg", cv2.IMREAD_COLOR)
image_rgb = cv2.cvtColor(image_bgr, cv2.COLOR_BGR2RGB)

# Detect faces and draw a rectangle
faces = face_cascade.detectMultiScale(image_rgb)
for (x,y,w,h) in faces:
    cv2.rectangle(image_rgb, (x, y),
                            (x + h, y + w),
                            (0, 255, 0), 5)

# Show the image
plt.subplot(1, 1, 1)
plt.imshow(image_rgb)
plt.show()
```

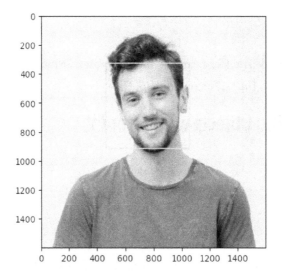

Discussion

Haar cascade classifiers are machine learning models used to learn a set of image features (specifically Haar features) that can be used to detect objects in images. The features themselves are simple rectangular features that are determined by calculating the difference in sums between rectangular regions. Subsequently, a gradient boosting algorithm is applied to learn the most important features and, finally, create a relatively strong model using cascading classifiers.

While the details of this process are outside the scope of this book, it's noteworthy that these pretrained models can be easily downloaded from places such as the

OpenCV GitHub (*https://oreil.ly/273DA*) as XML files and applied to images without training a model yourself. This is useful in cases where you want to add simple binary image features such as `contains_face` (or any other object) to your data.

See Also

- OpenCV tutorial: Cascade Classifier (*https://oreil.ly/dFhu6*)

8.17 Classifying Images with Pytorch

Problem

You want to classify images using pretrained deep learning models in Pytorch.

Solution

Use `torchvision.models` to select a pretrained image classification model and feed the image through it:

```
# Load libraries
import cv2
import json
import numpy as np
import torch
from torchvision import transforms
from torchvision.models import resnet18
import urllib.request

# Get imagenet classes
with urllib.request.urlopen(
    "https://raw.githubusercontent.com/raghakot/keras-vis/master/resources/"
    ):
    imagenet_class_index = json.load(url)

# Instantiate pretrained model
model = resnet18(pretrained=True)

# Load image
image_bgr = cv2.imread("images/plane.jpg", cv2.IMREAD_COLOR)
image_rgb = cv2.cvtColor(image_bgr, cv2.COLOR_BGR2RGB)

# Convert to pytorch data type
convert_tensor = transforms.ToTensor()
pytorch_image = convert_tensor(np.array(image_rgb))

# Set model to evaluation mode
model.eval()

# Make a prediction
```

```
prediction = model(pytorch_image.unsqueeze(0))

# Get the index of the highest predicted probability
_, index = torch.max(prediction, 1)

# Convert that to a percentage value
percentage = torch.nn.functional.softmax(prediction, dim=1)[0] * 100

# Print the name of the item at the index along with the percent confidence
print(imagenet_class_index[str(index.tolist()[0])][1],
    percentage[index.tolist()[0]].item())

airship 6.0569939613342285
```

Discussion

Many pretrained deep learning models for image classification are easily available via both PyTorch and TensorFlow. In this example, we used ResNet18, a deep neural network architecture that was trained on the ImageNet dataset that is 18 layers deep. Deeper ResNet models, such as ResNet101 and ResNet152, are also available in Pytorch—and beyond that there are many other image models to choose from. Models trained on the ImageNet dataset are able to output predicted probabilities for all classes defined in the `imagenet_class_index` variable in the previous code snippet, which we downloaded from GitHub.

Like the facial recognition example in OpenCV (see Recipe 8.16), we can use the predicted image classes as downstream features for future ML models or handy metadata tags that add more information to our images.

See Also

- PyTorch documentation: Models and Pre-trained Weights (*https://oreil.ly/MhlxR*)

## CHAPTER 9

Dimensionality Reduction Using Feature Extraction

9.0 Introduction

It is common to have access to thousands and even hundreds of thousands of features. For example, in Chapter 8 we transformed a 256×256–pixel color image into 196,608 features. Furthermore, because each of these pixels can take one of 256 possible values, our observation can take 256^{196608} different configurations. Many machine learning algorithms have trouble learning from such data, because it will never be practical to collect enough observations for the algorithms to operate correctly. Even in more tabular, structured datasets we can easily end up with thousands of features after the feature engineering process.

Fortunately, not all features are created equal, and the goal of *feature extraction* for dimensionality reduction is to transform our set of features, $p_{original}$, such that we end up with a new set, p_{new}, where $p_{original} > p_{new}$, while still keeping much of the underlying information. Put another way, we reduce the number of features with only a small loss in our data's ability to generate high-quality predictions. In this chapter, we will cover a number of feature extraction techniques to do just this.

One downside of the feature extraction techniques we discuss is that the new features we generate will not be interpretable by humans. They will contain as much or nearly as much ability to train our models but will appear to the human eye as a collection of random numbers. If we wanted to maintain our ability to interpret our models, dimensionality reduction through *feature selection* is a better option (and will be discussed in Chapter 10). During feature selection we remove features we deem unimportant but keep other features as they currently are. Although this may not let us keep information from all features as feature extraction does, it leaves the features we don't drop intact—and therefore fully interpretable by humans during analysis.

9.1 Reducing Features Using Principal Components

Problem

Given a set of features, you want to reduce the number of features while retaining the variance (important information) in the data.

Solution

Use principal component analysis with scikit's PCA:

```
# Load libraries
from sklearn.preprocessing import StandardScaler
from sklearn.decomposition import PCA
from sklearn import datasets

# Load the data
digits = datasets.load_digits()

# Standardize the feature matrix
features = StandardScaler().fit_transform(digits.data)

# Create a PCA that will retain 99% of variance
pca = PCA(n_components=0.99, whiten=True)

# Conduct PCA
features_pca = pca.fit_transform(features)

# Show results
print("Original number of features:", features.shape[1])
print("Reduced number of features:", features_pca.shape[1])

Original number of features: 64
Reduced number of features: 54
```

Discussion

Principal component analysis (PCA) is a popular linear dimensionality reduction technique. PCA projects observations onto the (hopefully fewer) principal components of the feature matrix that retain the most *variance* in the data, which, practically, means we retain information. PCA is an unsupervised technique, meaning that it does not use the information from the target vector and instead only considers the feature matrix.

For a mathematical description of how PCA works, see the external resources listed at the end of this recipe. However, we can understand the intuition behind PCA using a simple example. In Figure 9-1, our data contains two features, x_1 and x_2. Looking at the visualization, it should be clear that observations are spread out like a cigar, with a lot of length and very little height. More specifically, we can say that the variance of the "length" is significantly greater than the "height." Instead of length and height, we refer to the "direction" with the most variance as the first principal component and the "direction" with the second-most variance as the second principal component (and so on).

If we wanted to reduce our features, one strategy would be to project all observations in our two-dimensional space onto the one-dimensional principal component. We would lose the information captured in the second principal component, but in some situations that would be an acceptable trade-off. This is PCA.

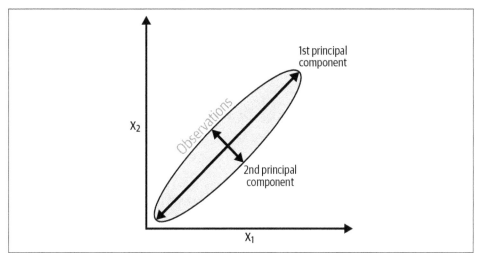

Figure 9-1. The first and second principal components of PCA

PCA is implemented in scikit-learn using the PCA class. n_components has two operations, depending on the argument provided. If the argument is greater than 1, pca will return that many features. This leads to the question of how to select the optimal number of features. Fortunately, if the argument to n_components is between 0 and 1, pca returns the minimum number of features that retain that much variance. It's common to use values of 0.95 and 0.99, meaning 95% and 99% of the variance of the original features has been retained, respectively. whiten=True transforms the values of each principal component so that they have zero mean and unit variance. Another parameter and argument is svd_solver="randomized", which implements a stochastic algorithm to find the first principal components in often significantly less time.

The output of our solution shows that PCA enables us to reduce our dimensionality by 10 features while still retaining 99% of the information (variance) in the feature matrix.

See Also

- scikit-learn documentation: PCA (*https://oreil.ly/OT_gN*)
- Principal Component Analysis with Linear Algebra, Jeff Jauregui (*https://oreil.ly/Uns61*)

9.2 Reducing Features When Data Is Linearly Inseparable

Problem

You suspect you have linearly inseparable data and want to reduce the dimensions.

Solution

Use an extension of principal component analysis that uses kernels to allow for nonlinear dimensionality reduction:

```
# Load libraries
from sklearn.decomposition import PCA, KernelPCA
from sklearn.datasets import make_circles

# Create linearly inseparable data
features, _ = make_circles(n_samples=1000, random_state=1, noise=0.1, factor=0.1)

# Apply kernel PCA with radius basis function (RBF) kernel
kpca = KernelPCA(kernel="rbf", gamma=15, n_components=1)
features_kpca = kpca.fit_transform(features)

print("Original number of features:", features.shape[1])
print("Reduced number of features:", features_kpca.shape[1])

Original number of features: 2
Reduced number of features: 1
```

Discussion

PCA is able to reduce the dimensionality of our feature matrix (i.e., the number of features). Standard PCA uses linear projection to reduce the features. If the data is *linearly separable* (i.e., you can draw a straight line or hyperplane between different classes) then PCA works well. However, if your data is not linearly separable (i.e., you can only separate classes using a curved decision boundary), the linear transformation will not work as well. In our solution we used scikit-learn's `make_circles` to generate a simulated dataset with a target vector of two classes and two features. `make_circles` makes linearly inseparable data; specifically, one class is surrounded on all sides by the other class, as shown in Figure 9-2.

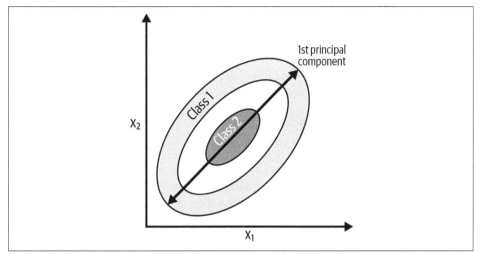

Figure 9-2. The first principal component projected on linearly inseparable data

If we used linear PCA to reduce the dimensions of our data, the two classes would be linearly projected onto the first principal component such that they would become intertwined, as shown in Figure 9-3.

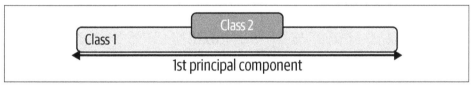

Figure 9-3. The first principal component of linearly inseparable data without kernel PCA

Ideally, we would want a transformation that would reduce the dimensions and make the data linearly separable. Kernel PCA can do both, as shown in Figure 9-4.

Figure 9-4. The first principal component of linearly inseparable data with kernel PCA

Kernels allow us to project the linearly inseparable data into a higher dimension where it is linearly separable; this is called the "kernel trick." Don't worry if you don't understand the details of the kernel trick; just think of kernels as different ways of projecting the data. There are a number of kernels we can use in scikit-learn's kernelPCA class, specified using the kernel parameter. A common kernel to use is the Gaussian radial basis function kernel rbf, but other options are the polynomial kernel (poly) and sigmoid kernel (sigmoid). We can even specify a linear projection (linear), which will produce the same results as standard PCA.

One downside of kernel PCA is that we need to specify a number of parameters. For example, in Recipe 9.1 we set n_components to 0.99 to make PCA select the number of components to retain 99% of the variance. We don't have this option in kernel PCA. Instead we have to define the number of components (e.g., n_components=1). Furthermore, kernels come with their own hyperparameters that we will have to set; for example, the radial basis function requires a gamma value.

So how do we know which values to use? Through trial and error. Specifically, we can train our machine learning model multiple times, each time with a different kernel or different value of the parameter. Once we find the combination of values that produces the highest quality predicted values, we are done. This is a common theme in machine learning, and we will learn about this strategy in depth in Chapter 12.

See Also

- scikit-learn documentation on Kernel PCA (*https://oreil.ly/SCAX-*)
- Kernel Tricks and Nonlinear Dimensionality Reduction via RBF Kernel PCA (*https://oreil.ly/ktm5Z*)

9.3 Reducing Features by Maximizing Class Separability

Problem

You want to reduce the number of features to be used by a classifier by maximizing the separation between the classes.

Solution

Try *linear discriminant analysis* (LDA) to project the features onto component axes that maximize the separation of classes:

```
# Load libraries
from sklearn import datasets
from sklearn.discriminant_analysis import LinearDiscriminantAnalysis

# Load Iris flower dataset:
iris = datasets.load_iris()
features = iris.data
target = iris.target

# Create and run an LDA, then use it to transform the features
lda = LinearDiscriminantAnalysis(n_components=1)
features_lda = lda.fit(features, target).transform(features)
```

```
# Print the number of features
print("Original number of features:", features.shape[1])
print("Reduced number of features:", features_lda.shape[1])

Original number of features: 4
Reduced number of features: 1
```

We can use `explained_variance_ratio_` to view the amount of variance explained by each component. In our solution the single component explained over 99% of the variance:

```
lda.explained_variance_ratio_

array([0.9912126])
```

Discussion

LDA is a classification that is also a popular technique for dimensionality reduction. LDA works similarly to PCA in that it projects our feature space onto a lower-dimensional space. However, in PCA we were interested only in the component axes that maximize the variance in the data, while in LDA we have the additional goal of maximizing the differences between classes. In Figure 9-5, we have data comprising two target classes and two features. If we project the data onto the y-axis, the two classes are not easily separable (i.e., they overlap), while if we project the data onto the x-axis, we are left with a feature vector (i.e., we reduced our dimensionality by one) that still preserves class separability. In the real world, of course, the relationship between the classes will be more complex and the dimensionality will be higher, but the concept remains the same.

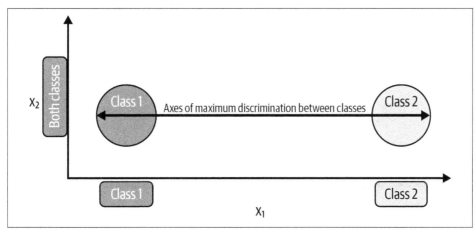

Figure 9-5. LDA attempts to maximize the difference between our classes

In scikit-learn, LDA is implemented using `LinearDiscriminantAnalysis`, which includes a parameter, n_components, indicating the number of features we want returned. To figure out what argument value to use with n_components (e.g., how many parameters to keep), we can take advantage of the fact that explained_variance_ratio_ tells us the variance explained by each outputted feature and is a sorted array. For example:

```
lda.explained_variance_ratio_

array([0.9912126])
```

Specifically, we can run `LinearDiscriminantAnalysis` with n_components set to None to return the ratio of variance explained by every component feature, then calculate how many components are required to get above some threshold of variance explained (often 0.95 or 0.99):

```
# Create and run LDA
lda = LinearDiscriminantAnalysis(n_components=None)
features_lda = lda.fit(features, target)

# Create array of explained variance ratios
lda_var_ratios = lda.explained_variance_ratio_

# Create function
def select_n_components(var_ratio, goal_var: float) -> int:
    # Set initial variance explained so far
    total_variance = 0.0

    # Set initial number of features
    n_components = 0

    # For the explained variance of each feature:
    for explained_variance in var_ratio:

        # Add the explained variance to the total
        total_variance += explained_variance

        # Add one to the number of components
        n_components += 1

        # If we reach our goal level of explained variance
        if total_variance >= goal_var:
            # End the loop
            break

    # Return the number of components
    return n_components

# Run function
select_n_components(lda_var_ratios, 0.95)
```

```
1
```

See Also

- Comparison of LDA and PCA 2D Projection of Iris Dataset (*https://oreil.ly/evGsx*)

- Linear Discriminant Analysis (*https://oreil.ly/uOB81*)

9.4 Reducing Features Using Matrix Factorization

Problem

You have a feature matrix of nonnegative values and want to reduce the dimensionality.

Solution

Use *nonnegative matrix factorization* (NMF) to reduce the dimensionality of the feature matrix:

```
# Load libraries
from sklearn.decomposition import NMF
from sklearn import datasets

# Load the data
digits = datasets.load_digits()

# Load feature matrix
features = digits.data

# Create, fit, and apply NMF
nmf = NMF(n_components=10, random_state=4)
features_nmf = nmf.fit_transform(features)

# Show results
print("Original number of features:", features.shape[1])
print("Reduced number of features:", features_nmf.shape[1])

Original number of features: 64
Reduced number of features: 10
```

Discussion

NMF is an unsupervised technique for linear dimensionality reduction that *factorizes* (i.e., breaks up into multiple matrices whose product approximates the original matrix) the feature matrix into matrices representing the latent relationship between observations and their features. Intuitively, NMF can reduce dimensionality because in matrix multiplication, the two factors (matrices being multiplied) can have significantly fewer dimensions than the product matrix. Formally, given a desired number of returned features, r, NMF factorizes our feature matrix such that:

$$V \approx WH$$

where **V** is our $n \times d$ feature matrix (i.e., d features, n observations), **W** is an $n \times r$ matrix, and **H** is an $r \times d$ matrix. By adjusting the value of r we can set the amount of dimensionality reduction desired.

One major requirement of NMF is that, as the name implies, the feature matrix cannot contain negative values. Additionally, unlike PCA and other techniques we have examined, NMF does not provide the explained variance of the outputted features. Thus, the best way for us to find the optimum value of n_components is by trying a range of values to find the one that produces the best result in our end model (see Chapter 12).

See Also

- Non-negative matrix factorization, Wikipedia (*https://oreil.ly/HJ_Qe*)

9.5 Reducing Features on Sparse Data

Problem

You have a sparse feature matrix and want to reduce the dimensionality.

Solution

Use *Truncated Singular Value Decomposition* (TSVD):

```
# Load libraries
from sklearn.preprocessing import StandardScaler
from sklearn.decomposition import TruncatedSVD
from scipy.sparse import csr_matrix
from sklearn import datasets
import numpy as np

# Load the data
digits = datasets.load_digits()

# Standardize feature matrix
features = StandardScaler().fit_transform(digits.data)

# Make sparse matrix
features_sparse = csr_matrix(features)

# Create a TSVD
tsvd = TruncatedSVD(n_components=10)

# Conduct TSVD on sparse matrix
features_sparse_tsvd = tsvd.fit(features_sparse).transform(features_sparse)
```

```
# Show results
print("Original number of features:", features_sparse.shape[1])
print("Reduced number of features:", features_sparse_tsvd.shape[1])

Original number of features: 64
Reduced number of features: 10
```

Discussion

TSVD is similar to PCA and, in fact, PCA often uses nontruncated *Singular Value Decomposition* (SVD) in one of its steps. Given d features, SVD will create factor matrices that are $d \times d$, whereas TSVD will return factors that are $n \times n$, where n is previously specified by a parameter. The practical advantage of TSVD is that, unlike PCA, it works on sparse feature matrices.

One issue with TSVD: because of how it uses a random number generator, the signs of the output can flip between fittings. An easy workaround is to use `fit` only once per preprocessing pipeline, then use `transform` multiple times.

As with linear discriminant analysis, we have to specify the number of features (components) we want to output. This is done with the `n_components` parameter. A natural question is: what is the optimum number of components? One strategy is to include `n_components` as a hyperparameter to optimize during model selection (i.e., choose the value for `n_components` that produces the best-trained model). Alternatively, because TSVD provides the ratio of the original feature matrix's variance explained by each component, we can select the number of components that explain a desired amount of variance (95% and 99% are common values). For example, in our solution, the first three outputted components explain approximately 30% of the original data's variance:

```
# Sum of first three components' explained variance ratios
tsvd.explained_variance_ratio_[0:3].sum()

0.3003938537287226
```

We can automate the process by creating a function that runs TSVD with `n_components` set to one less than the number of original features and then calculate the number of components that explain a desired amount of the original data's variance:

```
# Create and run a TSVD with one less than number of features
tsvd = TruncatedSVD(n_components=features_sparse.shape[1]-1)
features_tsvd = tsvd.fit(features)

# List of explained variances
tsvd_var_ratios = tsvd.explained_variance_ratio_

# Create a function
```

```
def select_n_components(var_ratio, goal_var):
    # Set initial variance explained so far
    total_variance = 0.0

    # Set initial number of features
    n_components = 0

    # For the explained variance of each feature:
    for explained_variance in var_ratio:

        # Add the explained variance to the total
        total_variance += explained_variance

        # Add one to the number of components
        n_components += 1

        # If we reach our goal level of explained variance
        if total_variance >= goal_var:
            # End the loop
            break

    # Return the number of components
    return n_components

# Run function
select_n_components(tsvd_var_ratios, 0.95)

40
```

See Also

- scikit-learn documentation: TruncatedSVD (*https://oreil.ly/nD1pF*)

## CHAPTER 10

Dimensionality Reduction Using Feature Selection

10.0 Introduction

In Chapter 9, we discussed how to reduce the dimensionality of our feature matrix by creating new features with (ideally) similar abilities to train quality models but with significantly fewer dimensions. This is called *feature extraction*. In this chapter we will cover an alternative approach: selecting high-quality, informative features and dropping less useful features. This is called *feature selection*.

There are three types of feature selection methods: filter, wrapper, and embedded. *Filter methods* select the best features by examining their statistical properties. Methods where we explicitly set a threshold for a statistic or manually select the number of features we want to keep are examples of feature selection by filtering. Wrapper methods use trial and error to find the subset of features that produces models with the highest quality predictions. *Wrapper methods* are often the most effective, as they find the best result through actual experimentation as opposed to naive assumptions. Finally, *embedded methods* select the best feature subset as part of, as an extension of, a learning algorithm's training process.

Ideally, we'd describe all three methods in this chapter. However, since embedded methods are closely intertwined with specific learning algorithms, they are difficult to explain prior to a deeper dive into the algorithms themselves. Therefore, in this chapter we cover only filter and wrapper feature selection methods, leaving the discussion of particular embedded methods until the chapters where those learning algorithms are discussed in depth.

10.1 Thresholding Numerical Feature Variance

Problem

You have a set of numerical features and want to filter out those with low variance (i.e., likely containing little information).

Solution

Select a subset of features with variances above a given threshold:

```
# Load libraries
from sklearn import datasets
from sklearn.feature_selection import VarianceThreshold

# Import some data to play with
iris = datasets.load_iris()

# Create features and target
features = iris.data
target = iris.target

# Create thresholder
thresholder = VarianceThreshold(threshold=.5)

# Create high variance feature matrix
features_high_variance = thresholder.fit_transform(features)

# View high variance feature matrix
features_high_variance[0:3]
array([[ 5.1,  1.4,  0.2],
       [ 4.9,  1.4,  0.2],
       [ 4.7,  1.3,  0.2]])
```

Discussion

Variance thresholding (VT) is an example of feature selection by filtering, and one of the most basic approaches to feature selection. It is motivated by the idea that features with low variance are likely less interesting (and less useful) than features with high variance. VT first calculates the variance of each feature:

$$Var(x) = \frac{1}{n}\sum_{i=1}^{n}(x_i - \mu)^2$$

where x is the feature vector, x_i is an individual feature value, and μ is that feature's mean value. Next, it drops all features whose variance does not meet that threshold.

Keep two things in mind when employing VT. First, the variance is not centered; that is, it is in the squared unit of the feature itself. Therefore, VT will not work when feature sets contain different units (e.g., one feature is in years while another is in dollars). Second, the variance threshold is selected manually, so we have to use our own judgment for a good value to select (or use a model selection technique described in Chapter 12). We can see the variance for each feature using `variances_`:

```
# View variances
thresholder.fit(features).variances_

array([0.68112222, 0.18871289, 3.09550267, 0.57713289])
```

Finally, if the features have been standardized (to mean zero and unit variance), then for obvious reasons VT will not work correctly:

```
# Load library
from sklearn.preprocessing import StandardScaler

# Standardize feature matrix
scaler = StandardScaler()
features_std = scaler.fit_transform(features)

# Caculate variance of each feature
selector = VarianceThreshold()
selector.fit(features_std).variances_

array([1., 1., 1., 1.])
```

10.2 Thresholding Binary Feature Variance

Problem

You have a set of binary categorical features and want to filter out those with low variance (i.e., likely containing little information).

Solution

Select a subset of features with a Bernoulli random variable variance above a given threshold:

```
# Load library
from sklearn.feature_selection import VarianceThreshold

# Create feature matrix with:
# Feature 0: 80% class 0
# Feature 1: 80% class 1
# Feature 2: 60% class 0, 40% class 1
features = [[0, 1, 0],
            [0, 1, 1],
            [0, 1, 0],
```

```
           [0, 1, 1],
           [1, 0, 0]]

# Run threshold by variance
thresholder = VarianceThreshold(threshold=(.75 * (1 - .75)))
thresholder.fit_transform(features)

array([[0],
       [1],
       [0],
       [1],
       [0]])
```

Discussion

As with numerical features, one strategy for selecting highly informative categorical features and filtering out less informative ones is to examine their variances. In binary features (i.e., Bernoulli random variables), variance is calculated as:

$$\text{Var}\,(x) = p(1 - p)$$

where p is the proportion of observations of class 1. Therefore, by setting p, we can remove features where the vast majority of observations are one class.

10.3 Handling Highly Correlated Features

Problem

You have a feature matrix and suspect some features are highly correlated.

Solution

Use a correlation matrix to check for highly correlated features. If highly correlated features exist, consider dropping one of the correlated features:

```
# Load libraries
import pandas as pd
import numpy as np

# Create feature matrix with two highly correlated features
features = np.array([[1, 1, 1],
                     [2, 2, 0],
                     [3, 3, 1],
                     [4, 4, 0],
                     [5, 5, 1],
                     [6, 6, 0],
                     [7, 7, 1],
                     [8, 7, 0],
                     [9, 7, 1]])
```

```
# Convert feature matrix into DataFrame
dataframe = pd.DataFrame(features)

# Create correlation matrix
corr_matrix = dataframe.corr().abs()

# Select upper triangle of correlation matrix
upper = corr_matrix.where(np.triu(np.ones(corr_matrix.shape),
                                  k=1).astype(bool))

# Find index of feature columns with correlation greater than 0.95
to_drop = [column for column in upper.columns if any(upper[column] > 0.95)]

# Drop features
dataframe.drop(dataframe.columns[to_drop], axis=1).head(3)
```

	0	2
0	1	1
1	2	0
2	3	1

Discussion

One problem we often run into in machine learning is highly correlated features. If two features are highly correlated, then the information they contain is very similar, and it is likely redundant to include both features. In the case of simple models like linear regression, failing to remove such features violates the assumptions of linear regression and can result in an artificially inflated R-squared value. The solution to highly correlated features is simple: remove one of them from the feature set. Removing highly correlated features by setting a correlation threshold is another example of filtering.

In our solution, first we create a correlation matrix of all features:

```
# Correlation matrix
dataframe.corr()
```

	0	1	2
0	1.000000	0.976103	0.000000
1	0.976103	1.000000	-0.034503
2	0.000000	-0.034503	1.000000

Second, we look at the upper triangle of the correlation matrix to identify pairs of highly correlated features:

```
# Upper triangle of correlation matrix
upper
```

	0	1	2
0	NaN	0.976103	0.000000
1	NaN	NaN	0.034503
2	NaN	NaN	NaN

Third, we remove one feature from each of those pairs.

10.4 Removing Irrelevant Features for Classification

Problem

You have a categorical target vector and want to remove uninformative features.

Solution

If the features are categorical, calculate a chi-square (χ^2) statistic between each feature and the target vector:

```
# Load libraries
from sklearn.datasets import load_iris
from sklearn.feature_selection import SelectKBest
from sklearn.feature_selection import chi2, f_classif

# Load data
iris = load_iris()
features = iris.data
target = iris.target

# Convert to categorical data by converting data to integers
features = features.astype(int)

# Select two features with highest chi-squared statistics
chi2_selector = SelectKBest(chi2, k=2)
features_kbest = chi2_selector.fit_transform(features, target)

# Show results
print("Original number of features:", features.shape[1])
print("Reduced number of features:", features_kbest.shape[1])

Original number of features: 4
Reduced number of features: 2
```

If the features are quantitative, compute the ANOVA F-value between each feature and the target vector:

```
# Select two features with highest F-values
fvalue_selector = SelectKBest(f_classif, k=2)
features_kbest = fvalue_selector.fit_transform(features, target)

# Show results
```

```
print("Original number of features:", features.shape[1])
print("Reduced number of features:", features_kbest.shape[1])

Original number of features: 4
Reduced number of features: 2
```

Instead of selecting a specific number of features, we can use `SelectPercentile` to select the top *n* percent of features:

```
# Load library
from sklearn.feature_selection import SelectPercentile

# Select top 75% of features with highest F-values
fvalue_selector = SelectPercentile(f_classif, percentile=75)
features_kbest = fvalue_selector.fit_transform(features, target)

# Show results
print("Original number of features:", features.shape[1])
print("Reduced number of features:", features_kbest.shape[1])

Original number of features: 4
Reduced number of features: 3
```

Discussion

Chi-square statistics examine the independence of two categorical vectors. That is, the statistic is the difference between the observed number of observations in each class of a categorical feature and what we would expect if that feature were independent (i.e., no relationship) of the target vector:

$$\chi^2 = \sum_{i=1}^{n} \frac{(O_i - E_i)^2}{E_i}$$

where O_i is the number of observed observations in class i, and E_i is the number of expected observations in class i.

A chi-squared statistic is a single number that tells you how much difference exists between your observed counts and the counts you would expect if there were no relationship at all in the population. By calculating the chi-squared statistic between a feature and the target vector, we obtain a measurement of the independence between the two. If the target is independent of the feature variable, then it is irrelevant for our purposes because it contains no information we can use for classification. On the other hand, if the two features are highly dependent, they likely are very informative for training our model.

To use chi-squared in feature selection, we calculate the chi-squared statistic between each feature and the target vector, then select the features with the best chi-square statistics. In scikit-learn, we can use `SelectKBest` to select them. The parameter k determines the number of features we want to keep and filters out the least informative features.

It is important to note that chi-square statistics can be calculated only between two categorical vectors. For this reason, chi-squared for feature selection requires that both the target vector and the features are categorical. However, if we have a numerical feature we can use the chi-squared technique by first transforming the quantitative feature into a categorical feature. Finally, to use our chi-squared approach, all values need to be nonnegative.

Alternatively, if we have a numerical feature, we can use `f_classif` to calculate the ANOVA F-value statistic with each feature and the target vector. F-value scores examine if, when we group the numerical feature by the target vector, the means for each group are significantly different. For example, if we had a binary target vector, gender, and a quantitative feature, test scores, the F-value score would tell us if the mean test score for men is different than the mean test score for women. If it is not, then test score doesn't help us predict gender and therefore the feature is irrelevant.

10.5 Recursively Eliminating Features

Problem

You want to automatically select the best features to keep.

Solution

Use scikit-learn's RFECV to conduct *recursive feature elimination* (RFE) using cross-validation (CV). That is, use the wrapper feature selection method and repeatedly train a model, each time removing a feature until model performance (e.g., accuracy) becomes worse. The remaining features are the best:

```
# Load libraries
import warnings
from sklearn.datasets import make_regression
from sklearn.feature_selection import RFECV
from sklearn import datasets, linear_model

# Suppress an annoying but harmless warning
warnings.filterwarnings(action="ignore", module="scipy",
                        message="^internal gelsd")

# Generate features matrix, target vector, and the true coefficients
features, target = make_regression(n_samples = 10000,
                                   n_features = 100,
                                   n_informative = 2,
                                   random_state = 1)
```

```
# Create a linear regression
ols = linear_model.LinearRegression()

# Recursively eliminate features
rfecv = RFECV(estimator=ols, step=1, scoring="neg_mean_squared_error")
rfecv.fit(features, target)
rfecv.transform(features)

array([[ 0.00850799,  0.7031277 ,  1.52821875],
       [-1.07500204,  2.56148527, -0.44567768],
       [ 1.37940721, -1.77039484, -0.74675125],
       ...,
       [-0.80331656, -1.60648007,  0.52231601],
       [ 0.39508844, -1.34564911,  0.4228057 ],
       [-0.55383035,  0.82880112,  1.73232647]])
```

Once we have conducted RFE, we can see the number of features we should keep:

```
# Number of best features
rfecv.n_features_

3
```

We can also see which of those features we should keep:

```
# Which categories are best
rfecv.support_

array([False, False, False, False, False,  True, False, False, False,
       False, False, False, False, False, False, False, False, False,
       False, False, False, False, False, False, False, False, False,
       False, False, False, False, False, False, False, False, False,
       False, False, False,  True, False, False, False, False, False,
       False, False, False, False, False, False, False, False, False,
       False, False, False, False, False, False, False, False, False,
       False, False, False, False, False, False, False,  True, False,
       False, False, False, False, False, False, False, False, False,
       False, False, False, False, False, False, False, False, False,
       False, False, False, False, False, False, False, False, False,
       False])
```

We can even view the rankings of the features:

```
# Rank features best (1) to worst
rfecv.ranking_

array([11, 92, 96, 87, 46,  1, 48, 23, 16,  2, 66, 83, 33, 27, 70, 75, 29,
       84, 54, 88, 37, 42, 85, 62, 74, 50, 80, 10, 38, 59, 79, 57, 44,  8,
       82, 45, 89, 69, 94,  1, 35, 47, 39,  1, 34, 72, 19,  4, 17, 91, 90,
       24, 32, 13, 49, 26, 12, 71, 68, 40,  1, 43, 63, 28, 73, 58, 21, 67,
        1, 95, 77, 93, 22, 52, 30, 60, 81, 14, 86, 18, 15, 41,  7, 53, 65,
       51, 64,  6,  9, 20,  5, 55, 56, 25, 36, 61, 78, 31,  3, 76])
```

Discussion

This is likely the most advanced recipe in this book up to this point, combining a number of topics we have yet to address in detail. However, the intuition is straightforward enough that we can address it here rather than holding off until a later chapter. The idea behind RFE is to train a model repeatedly, updating the *weights* or *coefficients* of that model each time. The first time we train the model, we include all the features. Then, we find the feature with the smallest parameter (notice that this assumes the features are either rescaled or standardized), meaning it is less important, and remove that feature from the feature set.

The obvious question then is: how many features should we keep? We can (hypothetically) repeat this loop until we only have one feature left. A better approach requires that we include a new concept called *cross-validation*. We will discuss CV in detail in the next chapter, but here is the general idea.

Given data containing (1) a target we want to predict, and (2) a feature matrix, first we split the data into two groups: a training set and a test set. Second, we train our model using the training set. Third, we pretend that we do not know the target of the test set and apply our model to its features to predict the values of the test set. Finally, we compare our predicted target values with the true target values to evaluate our model.

We can use CV to find the optimum number of features to keep during RFE. Specifically, in RFE with CV, after every iteration we use cross-validation to evaluate our model. If CV shows that our model improved after we eliminated a feature, then we continue on to the next loop. However, if CV shows that our model got worse after we eliminated a feature, we put that feature back into the feature set and select those features as the best.

In scikit-learn, RFE with CV is implemented using RFECV, which contains a number of important parameters. The `estimator` parameter determines the type of model we want to train (e.g., linear regression), the `step` parameter sets the number or proportion of features to drop during each loop, and the `scoring` parameter sets the metric of quality we use to evaluate our model during cross-validation.

See Also

- scikit-learn documentation: Recursive feature elimination with cross-validation (*https://oreil.ly/aV-Fz*)

## CHAPTER 11

Model Evaluation

11.0 Introduction

In this chapter we will examine strategies for evaluating the quality of models created through our learning algorithms. It might appear strange to discuss model evaluation before discussing how to create them, but there is a method to our madness. Models are only as useful as the quality of their predictions, and thus, fundamentally, our goal is not to create models (which is easy) but to create high-quality models (which is hard). Therefore, before we explore the myriad learning algorithms, let's first learn how we can evaluate the models they produce.

11.1 Cross-Validating Models

Problem

You want to evaluate how well your classification model generalizes to unforeseen data.

Solution

Create a pipeline that preprocesses the data, trains the model, and then evaluates it using cross-validation:

```
# Load libraries
from sklearn import datasets
from sklearn import metrics
from sklearn.model_selection import KFold, cross_val_score
from sklearn.pipeline import make_pipeline
from sklearn.linear_model import LogisticRegression
from sklearn.preprocessing import StandardScaler
```

```
# Load digits dataset
digits = datasets.load_digits()

# Create features matrix
features = digits.data

# Create target vector
target = digits.target

# Create standardizer
standardizer = StandardScaler()

# Create logistic regression object
logit = LogisticRegression()

# Create a pipeline that standardizes, then runs logistic regression
pipeline = make_pipeline(standardizer, logit)

# Create k-fold cross-validation
kf = KFold(n_splits=5, shuffle=True, random_state=0)

# Conduct k-fold cross-validation
cv_results = cross_val_score(pipeline, # Pipeline
                             features, # Feature matrix
                             target, # Target vector
                             cv=kf, # Performance metric
                             scoring="accuracy", # Loss function
                             n_jobs=-1) # Use all CPU cores

# Calculate mean
cv_results.mean()

0.969958217270195
```

Discussion

At first consideration, evaluating supervised-learning models might appear straight-forward: train a model and then calculate how well it did using some performance metric (accuracy, squared errors, etc.). However, this approach is fundamentally flawed. If we train a model using our data, and then evaluate how well it did on that data, we are not achieving our desired goal. Our goal is not to evaluate how well the model does on our training data, but how well it does on data it has never seen before (e.g., a new customer, a new crime, a new image). For this reason, our method of evaluation should help us understand how well models are able to make predictions from data they have never seen before.

One strategy might be to hold off a slice of data for testing. This is called *validation* (or *hold-out*). In validation, our observations (features and targets) are split into two sets, traditionally called the *training set* and the *test set*. We take the test set and put it off to the side, pretending that we have never seen it before. Next we train our model using our training set, using the features and target vector to teach the model how to make the best prediction. Finally, we simulate having never-before-seen external data by evaluating how our model performs on our test set. However, the validation approach has two major weaknesses. First, the performance of the model can be highly dependent on which few observations were selected for the test set. Second, the model is not being trained using all the available data, and it's not being evaluated on all the available data.

A better strategy, which overcomes these weaknesses, is called *k-fold cross-validation* (KFCV). In KFCV, we split the data into *k* parts called *folds*. The model is then trained using *k – 1* folds—combined into one training set—and then the last fold is used as a test set. We repeat this *k* times, each time using a different fold as the test set. The performance on the model for each of the *k* iterations is then averaged to produce an overall measurement.

In our solution, we conducted k-fold cross-validation using five folds and outputted the evaluation scores to `cv_results`:

```
# View score for all 5 folds
cv_results
```

```
array([0.96111111, 0.96388889, 0.98050139, 0.97214485, 0.97214485])
```

There are three important points to consider when we are using KFCV. First, KFCV assumes that each observation was created independently from the other (i.e., the data is independent and identically distributed [IID]). If the data is IID, it is a good idea to shuffle observations when assigning to folds. In scikit-learn we can set `shuffle=True` to perform shuffling.

Second, when we are using KFCV to evaluate a classifier, it is often beneficial to have folds containing roughly the same percentage of observations from each of the different target classes (called *stratified k-fold*). For example, if our target vector contained gender and 80% of the observations were male, then each fold would contain 80% male and 20% female observations. In scikit-learn, we can conduct stratified k-fold cross-validation by replacing the `KFold` class with `StratifiedKFold`.

Finally, when we are using validation sets or cross-validation, it is important to preprocess data based on the training set and then apply those transformations to both the training and test set. For example, when we `fit` our standardization object, `standardizer`, we calculate the mean and variance of only the training set. Then we apply that transformation (using `transform`) to both the training and test sets:

```
# Import library
from sklearn.model_selection import train_test_split

# Create training and test sets
features_train, features_test, target_train, target_test = train_test_split(
    features, target, test_size=0.1, random_state=1)
```

```
# Fit standardizer to training set
standardizer.fit(features_train)

# Apply to both training and test sets which can then be used to train models
features_train_std = standardizer.transform(features_train)
features_test_std = standardizer.transform(features_test)
```

The reason for this is because we are pretending that the test set is unknown data. If we fit both our preprocessors using observations from both training and test sets, some of the information from the test set leaks into our training set. This rule applies for any preprocessing step such as feature selection.

scikit-learn's `pipeline` package makes this easy to do while using cross-validation techniques. We first create a pipeline that preprocesses the data (e.g., `standardizer`) and then trains a model (logistic regression, `logit`):

```
# Create a pipeline
pipeline = make_pipeline(standardizer, logit)
```

Then we run KFCV using that pipeline and scikit does all the work for us:

```
# Do k-fold cross-validation
cv_results = cross_val_score(pipeline, # Pipeline
                             features, # Feature matrix
                             target, # Target vector
                             cv=kf, # Performance metric
                             scoring="accuracy", # Loss function
                             n_jobs=-1) # Use all CPU cores
```

`cross_val_score` comes with three parameters we have not discussed, but that are worth noting:

cv

> cv determines our cross-validation technique. K-fold is the most common by far, but there are others, such as leave-one-out cross-validation where the number of folds k equals the number of data points in the set.

scoring

> `scoring` defines the metric for success, a number of which are discussed in other recipes in this chapter.

n_jobs=-1

> `n_jobs=-1` tells scikit-learn to use every core available. For example, if your computer has four cores (a common number for laptops), then scikit-learn will use all four cores at once to speed up the operation.

One small note: when running some of these examples, you may see a warning that says "ConvergenceWarning: lbfgs failed to converge." The configuration used in these examples is designed to prevent this, but should it still occur, you can ignore it for now. We will troubleshoot issues like this later in the book as we dive into specific types of models.

See Also

- Why Every Statistician Should Know About Cross-Validation (*https://oreil.ly/vrGXy*)
- Cross-Validation Gone Wrong (*https://oreil.ly/NE-B8*)

11.2 Creating a Baseline Regression Model

Problem

You want a simple baseline regression model to use as a comparison against other models that you train.

Solution

Use scikit-learn's DummyRegressor to create a simple model to use as a baseline:

```
# Load libraries
from sklearn.datasets import load_wine
from sklearn.dummy import DummyRegressor
from sklearn.model_selection import train_test_split

# Load data
wine = load_wine()

# Create features
features, target = wine.data, wine.target

# Make test and training split
features_train, features_test, target_train, target_test = train_test_split(
    features, target, random_state=0)

# Create a dummy regressor
dummy = DummyRegressor(strategy='mean')

# "Train" dummy regressor
dummy.fit(features_train, target_train)

# Get R-squared score
dummy.score(features_test, target_test)
```

```
-0.0480213580840978
```

To compare, we train our model and evaluate the performance score:

```
# Load library
from sklearn.linear_model import LinearRegression

# Train simple linear regression model
ols = LinearRegression()
ols.fit(features_train, target_train)

# Get R-squared score
ols.score(features_test, target_test)
```

```
0.804353263176954
```

Discussion

DummyRegressor allows us to create a very simple model that we can use as a baseline to compare against any other models that we train. This can often be useful to simulate a "naive" existing prediction process in a product or system. For example, a product might have been originally hardcoded to assume that all new users will spend $100 in the first month, regardless of their features. If we encode that assumption into a baseline model, we are able to concretely state the benefits of using a machine learning approach by comparing the dummy model's score with that of a trained model.

DummyRegressor uses the strategy parameter to set the method of making predictions, including the mean or median value in the training set. Furthermore, if we set strategy to constant and use the constant parameter, we can set the dummy regressor to predict some constant value for every observation:

```
# Create dummy regressor that predicts 1s for everything
clf = DummyRegressor(strategy='constant', constant=1)
clf.fit(features_train, target_train)

# Evaluate score
clf.score(features_test, target_test)
```

```
-0.06299212598425186
```

One small note regarding score. By default, score returns the coefficient of determination (R-squared, R^2) score:

$$R^2 = 1 - \frac{\Sigma_i(y_i - \widehat{y}_i)^2}{\Sigma_i(y_i - \bar{y})^2}$$

where y_i is the true value of the target observation, $\widehat{y}_i$ is the predicted value, and $\bar{y}$ is the mean value for the target vector.

The closer R^2 is to 1, the more of the variance in the target vector that is explained by the features.

11.3 Creating a Baseline Classification Model

Problem

You want a simple baseline classifier to compare against your model.

Solution

Use scikit-learn's DummyClassifier:

```
# Load libraries
from sklearn.datasets import load_iris
from sklearn.dummy import DummyClassifier
from sklearn.model_selection import train_test_split

# Load data
iris = load_iris()

# Create target vector and feature matrix
features, target = iris.data, iris.target

# Split into training and test set
features_train, features_test, target_train, target_test = train_test_split(
    features, target, random_state=0)

# Create dummy classifier
dummy = DummyClassifier(strategy='uniform', random_state=1)

# "Train" model
dummy.fit(features_train, target_train)

# Get accuracy score
dummy.score(features_test, target_test)

0.42105263157894735
```

By comparing the baseline classifier to our trained classifier, we can see the improvement:

```
# Load library
from sklearn.ensemble import RandomForestClassifier

# Create classifier
classifier = RandomForestClassifier()

# Train model
classifier.fit(features_train, target_train)

# Get accuracy score
classifier.score(features_test, target_test)

0.9736842105263158
```

Discussion

A common measure of a classifier's performance is how much better it is than random guessing. scikit-learn's DummyClassifier makes this comparison easy. The strategy parameter gives us a number of options for generating values. There are two particularly useful strategies. First, stratified makes predictions proportional to the class proportions of the training set's target vector (e.g., if 20% of the observations in the training data are women, then DummyClassifier will predict women 20% of the time). Second, uniform will generate predictions uniformly at random between the different classes. For example, if 20% of observations are women and 80% are men, uniform will produce predictions that are 50% women and 50% men.

See Also

- scikit-learn documentation: DummyClassifier (*https://oreil.ly/bwqQU*)

11.4 Evaluating Binary Classifier Predictions

Problem

Given a trained classification model, you want to evaluate its quality.

Solution

Use scikit-learn's cross_val_score to conduct cross-validation while using the scoring parameter to define one of a number of performance metrics, including accuracy, precision, recall, and F_1. *Accuracy* is a common performance metric. It is simply the proportion of observations predicted correctly:

$$Accuracy = \frac{TP + TN}{TP + TN + FP + FN}$$

where:

TP
> The number of true positives. These are observations that are part of the *positive* class (has the disease, purchased the product, etc.) and that we predicted correctly.

TN
> The number of true negatives. These are observations that are part of the *negative* class (does not have the disease, did not purchase the product, etc.) and that we predicted correctly.

FP

The number of false positives, also called a *Type I error*. These are observations that are predicted to be part of the *positive* class but are actually part of the *negative* class.

FN

The number of false negatives, also called a *Type II error*. These are observations that are predicted to be part of the *negative* class but are actually part of the *positive* class.

We can measure accuracy in three-fold (the default number of folds) cross-validation by setting `scoring="accuracy"`:

```
# Load libraries
from sklearn.model_selection import cross_val_score
from sklearn.linear_model import LogisticRegression
from sklearn.datasets import make_classification

# Generate features matrix and target vector
X, y = make_classification(n_samples = 10000,
                           n_features = 3,
                           n_informative = 3,
                           n_redundant = 0,
                           n_classes = 2,
                           random_state = 1)

# Create logistic regression
logit = LogisticRegression()

# Cross-validate model using accuracy
cross_val_score(logit, X, y, scoring="accuracy")
```

```
array([0.9555, 0.95  , 0.9585, 0.9555, 0.956 ])
```

The appeal of accuracy is that it has an intuitive and plain English explanation: the proportion of observations predicted correctly. However, in the real world, often our data has imbalanced classes (e.g., the 99.9% of observations are of class 1 and only 0.1% are class 2). When in the presence of imbalanced classes, accuracy suffers from a paradox where a model is highly accurate but lacks predictive power. For example, imagine we are trying to predict the presence of a very rare cancer that occurs in 0.1% of the population. After training our model, we find the accuracy is at 95%. However, 99.9% of people do not have the cancer: if we simply created a model that "predicted" that nobody had that form of cancer, our naive model would be 4.9% more accurate, but it clearly is not able to *predict* anything. For this reason, we are often motivated to use other metrics such as precision, recall, and the F_1 score.

Precision is the proportion of every observation predicted to be positive that is actually positive. We can think about it as a measurement noise in our predictions—that is, how likely we are to be right when we predict something is positive. Models with high precision are pessimistic in that they predict an observation is of the positive class only when they are very certain about it. Formally, precision is:

$$Precision = \frac{TP}{TP + FP}$$

```
# Cross-validate model using precision
cross_val_score(logit, X, y, scoring="precision")
```

```
array([0.95963673, 0.94820717, 0.9635996 , 0.96149949, 0.96060606])
```

Recall is the proportion of every positive observation that is truly positive. Recall measures the model's ability to identify an observation of the positive class. Models with high recall are optimistic in that they have a low bar for predicting that an observation is in the positive class:

$$Recall = \frac{TP}{TP + FN}$$

```
# Cross-validate model using recall
cross_val_score(logit, X, y, scoring="recall")
```

```
array([0.951, 0.952, 0.953, 0.949, 0.951])
```

If this is the first time you have encountered precision and recall, it is understandable if it takes a little while to fully understand them. This is one of the downsides to accuracy; precision and recall are less intuitive. Almost always we want some kind of balance between precision and recall, and this role is filled by the F_1 score. The F_1 score is the *harmonic mean* (a kind of average used for ratios):

$$F_1 = 2 \times \frac{Precision \times Recall}{Precision + Recall}$$

This score is a measure of correctness achieved in positive prediction—that is, of observations labeled as positive, how many are actually positive:

```
# Cross-validate model using F1
cross_val_score(logit, X, y, scoring="f1")
```

```
array([0.95529884, 0.9500998 , 0.95827049, 0.95520886, 0.95577889])
```

Discussion

As an evaluation metric, accuracy has some valuable properties, especially its intuitiveness. However, better metrics often involve using some balance of precision and recall—that is, a trade-off between the optimism and pessimism of our model. F_1 represents a balance between the recall and precision, where the relative contributions of both are equal.

As an alternative to using `cross_val_score`, if we already have the true y values and the predicted y values, we can calculate the metrics accuracy and recall directly:

```
# Load libraries
from sklearn.model_selection import train_test_split
from sklearn.metrics import accuracy_score

# Create training and test split
X_train, X_test, y_train, y_test = train_test_split(X,
                                                    y,
                                                    test_size=0.1,
                                                    random_state=1)

# Predict values for training target vector
y_hat = logit.fit(X_train, y_train).predict(X_test)

# Calculate accuracy
accuracy_score(y_test, y_hat)
```

```
0.947
```

See Also

- Accuracy paradox, Wikipedia (*https://oreil.ly/vjgZ-*)

11.5 Evaluating Binary Classifier Thresholds

Problem

You want to evaluate a binary classifier and various probability thresholds.

Solution

Use the *receiver operating characteristic* (ROC) curve to evaluate the quality of the binary classifier. In scikit-learn, we can use `roc_curve` to calculate the true and false positives at each threshold, and then plot them:

```
# Load libraries
import matplotlib.pyplot as plt
from sklearn.datasets import make_classification
from sklearn.linear_model import LogisticRegression
from sklearn.metrics import roc_curve, roc_auc_score
from sklearn.model_selection import train_test_split

# Create feature matrix and target vector
features, target = make_classification(n_samples=10000,
                                       n_features=10,
```

```
                                n_classes=2,
                                n_informative=3,
                                random_state=3)

# Split into training and test sets
features_train, features_test, target_train, target_test = train_test_split(
    features, target, test_size=0.1, random_state=1)

# Create classifier
logit = LogisticRegression()

# Train model
logit.fit(features_train, target_train)

# Get predicted probabilities
target_probabilities = logit.predict_proba(features_test)[:,1]

# Create true and false positive rates
false_positive_rate, true_positive_rate, threshold = roc_curve(
  target_test,
  target_probabilities
)

# Plot ROC curve
plt.title("Receiver Operating Characteristic")
plt.plot(false_positive_rate, true_positive_rate)
plt.plot([0, 1], ls="--")
plt.plot([0, 0], [1, 0] , c=".7"), plt.plot([1, 1] , c=".7")
plt.ylabel("True Positive Rate")
plt.xlabel("False Positive Rate")
plt.show()
```

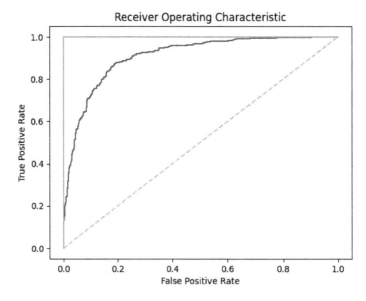

Discussion

The receiver operating characteristic curve is a common method for evaluating the quality of a binary classifier. ROC compares the presence of true positives and false positives at every probability threshold (i.e., the probability at which an observation is predicted to be a class). By plotting the ROC curve, we can see how the model performs. A classifier that predicts every observation correctly would look like the solid light gray line in the ROC output in the previous figure, going straight up to the top immediately. A classifier that predicts at random will appear as the diagonal line. The better the model, the closer it is to the solid line.

Until now we have only examined models based on the values they predict. However, in many learning algorithms, those predicted values are based on probability estimates. That is, each observation is given an explicit probability of belonging in each class. In our solution, we can use `predict_proba` to see the predicted probabilities for the first observation:

```
# Get predicted probabilities
logit.predict_proba(features_test)[0:1]

array([[0.86891533, 0.13108467]])
```

We can see the classes using `classes_`:

```
logit.classes_

array([0, 1])
```

In this example, the first observation has an ~87% chance of being in the negative class (0) and a 13% chance of being in the positive class (1). By default, scikit-learn predicts an observation is part of the positive class if the probability is greater than 0.5 (called the *threshold*). However, instead of a middle ground, we will often want to explicitly bias our model to use a different threshold for substantive reasons. For example, if a false positive is very costly to our company, we might prefer a model that has a high probability threshold. We fail to predict some positives, but when an observation is predicted to be positive, we can be very confident that the prediction is correct. This trade-off is represented in the *true positive rate* (TPR) and the *false positive rate* (FPR). The TPR is the number of observations correctly predicted true divided by all true positive observations:

$$TPR = \frac{TP}{TP+FN}$$

The FPR is the number of incorrectly predicted positives divided by all true negative observations:

$$FPR = \frac{FP}{FP+TN}$$

The ROC curve represents the respective TPR and FPR for every probability threshold. For example, in our solution a threshold of roughly 0.50 has a TPR of ~0.83 and an FPR of ~0.16:

```
print("Threshold:", threshold[124])
print("True Positive Rate:", true_positive_rate[124])
print("False Positive Rate:", false_positive_rate[124])

Threshold: 0.5008252732632008
True Positive Rate: 0.8346938775510204
False Positive Rate: 0.1607843137254902
```

However, if we increase the threshold to ~80% (i.e., increase how certain the model has to be before it predicts an observation as positive) the TPR drops significantly but so does the FPR:

```
print("Threshold:", threshold[49])
print("True Positive Rate:", true_positive_rate[49])
print("False Positive Rate:", false_positive_rate[49])

Threshold: 0.8058575028551827
True Positive Rate: 0.5653061224489796
False Positive Rate: 0.052941176470588235
```

This is because our higher requirement for being predicted to be in the positive class has caused the model to not identify a number of positive observations (the lower TPR) but has also reduced the noise from negative observations being predicted as positive (the lower FPR).

In addition to being able to visualize the trade-off between TPR and FPR, the ROC curve can also be used as a general metric for a model. The better a model is, the higher the curve and thus the greater the area under the curve. For this reason, it is common to calculate the area under the ROC curve (AUC ROC) to judge the overall quality of a model at all possible thresholds. The closer the AUC ROC is to 1, the better the model. In scikit-learn we can calculate the AUC ROC using `roc_auc_score`:

```
# Calculate area under curve
roc_auc_score(target_test, target_probabilities)

0.9073389355742297
```

See Also

- ROC Curves in Python and R (*https://oreil.ly/0qcpZ*)
- The Area Under an ROC Curve (*https://oreil.ly/re7sT*)

11.6 Evaluating Multiclass Classifier Predictions

Problem

You have a model that predicts three or more classes and want to evaluate the model's performance.

Solution

Use cross-validation with an evaluation metric capable of handling more than two classes:

```
# Load libraries
from sklearn.model_selection import cross_val_score
from sklearn.linear_model import LogisticRegression
from sklearn.datasets import make_classification

# Generate features matrix and target vector
features, target = make_classification(n_samples = 10000,
                            n_features = 3,
                            n_informative = 3,
                            n_redundant = 0,
                            n_classes = 3,
                            random_state = 1)

# Create logistic regression
logit = LogisticRegression()

# Cross-validate model using accuracy
cross_val_score(logit, features, target, scoring='accuracy')

array([0.841 , 0.829 , 0.8265, 0.8155, 0.82  ])
```

Discussion

When we have balanced classes (i.e., a roughly equal number of observations in each class of the target vector), accuracy is—just like in the binary class setting—a simple and interpretable choice for an evaluation metric. Accuracy is the number of correct predictions divided by the number of observations and works just as well in the multiclass as in the binary setting. However, when we have imbalanced classes (a common scenario), we should be inclined to use other evaluation metrics.

Many of scikit-learn's built-in metrics are for evaluating binary classifiers. However, many of these metrics can be extended for use when we have more than two classes. Precision, recall, and F_1 scores are useful metrics that we have already covered in detail in previous recipes. While all of them were originally designed for binary classifiers, we can apply them to multiclass settings by treating our data as a set of binary classes. Doing so enables us to apply the metrics to each class as if it were the only class in the data, and then aggregate the evaluation scores for all the classes by averaging them:

```
# Cross-validate model using macro averaged F1 score
cross_val_score(logit, features, target, scoring='f1_macro')

array([0.84061272, 0.82895312, 0.82625661, 0.81515121, 0.81992692])
```

In this code, macro refers to the method used to average the evaluation scores from the classes. The options are macro, weighted, and micro:

macro
  Calculate the mean of metric scores for each class, weighting each class equally.

weighted
  Calculate the mean of metric scores for each class, weighting each class proportional to its size in the data.

micro
  Calculate the mean of metric scores for each observation-class combination.

11.7 Visualizing a Classifier's Performance

Problem

Given predicted classes and true classes of the test data, you want to visually compare the model's quality.

Solution

Use a *confusion matrix*, which compares predicted classes and true classes:

```
# Load libraries
import matplotlib.pyplot as plt
import seaborn as sns
from sklearn import datasets
from sklearn.linear_model import LogisticRegression
from sklearn.model_selection import train_test_split
from sklearn.metrics import confusion_matrix
import pandas as pd

# Load data
iris = datasets.load_iris()

# Create features matrix
features = iris.data

# Create target vector
target = iris.target
```

```
# Create list of target class names
class_names = iris.target_names

# Create training and test set
features_train, features_test, target_train, target_test = train_test_split(
    features, target, random_state=2)

# Create logistic regression
classifier = LogisticRegression()

# Train model and make predictions
target_predicted = classifier.fit(features_train,
    target_train).predict(features_test)

# Create confusion matrix
matrix = confusion_matrix(target_test, target_predicted)

# Create pandas dataframe
dataframe = pd.DataFrame(matrix, index=class_names, columns=class_names)

# Create heatmap
sns.heatmap(dataframe, annot=True, cbar=None, cmap="Blues")
plt.title("Confusion Matrix"), plt.tight_layout()
plt.ylabel("True Class"), plt.xlabel("Predicted Class")
plt.show()
```

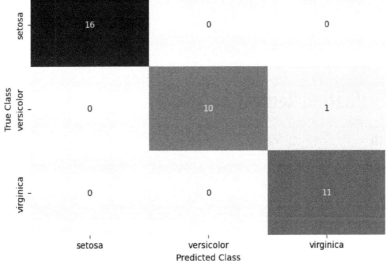

Discussion

Confusion matrices are an easy, effective visualization of a classifier's performance. One of the major benefits of confusion matrices is their interpretability. Each column of the matrix (often visualized as a heatmap) represents predicted classes, while every row shows true classes. The result is that every cell is one possible combination of predicted and true classes. This is probably best explained using an example. In the solution, the top-left cell is the number of observations predicted to be *Iris setosa* (indicated by the column) that are actually *Iris setosa* (indicated by the row). This means the model accurately predicted all *Iris setosa* flowers. However, the model does not do as well at predicting *Iris virginica*. The bottom-right cell indicates that the model successfully predicted eleven observations were *Iris virginica*, but (looking one cell up) predicted one flower to be *virginica* that was actually *Iris versicolor*.

There are three things worth noting about confusion matrices. First, a perfect model will have values along the diagonal and zeros everywhere else. A bad model will have the observation counts spread evenly around cells. Second, a confusion matrix lets us see not only where the model was wrong but also how it was wrong. That is, we can look at patterns of misclassification. For example, our model had an easy time differentiating *Iris virginica* and *Iris setosa*, but a slightly more difficult time classifying *Iris virginica* and *Iris versicolor*. Finally, confusion matrices work with any number of classes (although if we had one million classes in our target vector, the confusion matrix visualization might be difficult to read).

See Also

- Confusion matrix, Wikipedia (*https://oreil.ly/tDWPB*)
- scikit-learn documentation: Confusion Matrix (*https://oreil.ly/fdsTg*)

11.8 Evaluating Regression Models

Problem

You want to evaluate the performance of a regression model.

Solution

Use *mean squared error* (MSE):

```
# Load libraries
from sklearn.datasets import make_regression
from sklearn.model_selection import cross_val_score
from sklearn.linear_model import LinearRegression

# Generate features matrix, target vector
```

```
features, target = make_regression(n_samples = 100,
                                   n_features = 3,
                                   n_informative = 3,
                                   n_targets = 1,
                                   noise = 50,
                                   coef = False,
                                   random_state = 1)

# Create a linear regression object
ols = LinearRegression()

# Cross-validate the linear regression using (negative) MSE
cross_val_score(ols, features, target, scoring='neg_mean_squared_error')

array([-1974.65337976, -2004.54137625, -3935.19355723, -1060.04361386,
       -1598.74104702])
```

Another common regression metric is the coefficient of determination, R^2:

```
# Cross-validate the linear regression using R-squared
cross_val_score(ols, features, target, scoring='r2')

array([0.8622399 , 0.85838075, 0.74723548, 0.91354743, 0.84469331])
```

Discussion

MSE is one of the most common evaluation metrics for regression models. Formally, MSE is:

$$\text{MSE} = \frac{1}{n} \sum_{i=1}^{n} (\widehat{y}_i - y_i)^2$$

where n is the number of observations, y_i is the true value of the target we are trying to predict for observation i, and $\widehat{y}_i$ is the model's predicted value for y_i. MSE is a measurement of the squared sum of all distances between predicted and true values. The higher the value of MSE, the greater the total squared error and thus the worse the model. There are a number of mathematical benefits to squaring the error term, including that it forces all error values to be positive, but one often unrealized implication is that squaring penalizes a few large errors more than many small errors, even if the absolute value of the errors is the same. For example, imagine two models, A and B, each with two observations:

- Model A has errors of 0 and 10, and thus its MSE is $0^2 + 10^2 = 100$.
- Model B has two errors of 5 each, and thus its MSE is $5^2 + 5^2 = 50$.

Both models have the same total errors, 10; however, MSE would consider model A (MSE = 100) worse than model B (MSE = 50). In practice this implication is rarely an issue (and indeed can be theoretically beneficial), and MSE works perfectly fine as an evaluation metric.

One important note: by default, in scikit-learn, arguments of the scoring parameter assume that higher values are better than lower values. However, this is not the case for MSE, where higher values mean a worse model. For this reason, scikit-learn looks at the *negative* MSE using the neg_mean_squared_error argument.

A common alternative regression evaluation metric is the default metric we used in Recipe 11.2, R^2, which measures the amount of variance in the target vector that is explained by the model.

$$R^2 = 1 - \frac{\sum_{i=1}^{n} (y_i - \widehat{y}_i)^2}{\sum_{i=1}^{n} (y_i - \bar{y})^2}$$

where y_i is the true target value of the *i*th observation, $\widehat{y}_i$ is the predicted value for the *i*th observation, and $\bar{y}$ is the mean value of the target vector. The closer that R^2 is to 1.0, the better the model.

See Also

- Mean squared error, Wikipedia (*https://oreil.ly/MWDlR*)
- Coefficient of determination, Wikipedia (*https://oreil.ly/lKKWk*)

11.9 Evaluating Clustering Models

Problem

You have used an unsupervised learning algorithm to cluster your data. Now you want to know how well it did.

Solution

Use *silhouette coefficients* to measure the quality of the clusters (note that this does not measure predictive performance):

```
# Load libraries
import numpy as np
from sklearn.metrics import silhouette_score
from sklearn import datasets
from sklearn.cluster import KMeans
from sklearn.datasets import make_blobs
```

```
# Generate features matrix
features, _ = make_blobs(n_samples = 1000,
                         n_features = 10,
                         centers = 2,
                         cluster_std = 0.5,
                         shuffle = True,
                         random_state = 1)

# Cluster data using k-means to predict classes
model = KMeans(n_clusters=2, random_state=1).fit(features)

# Get predicted classes
target_predicted = model.labels_

# Evaluate model
silhouette_score(features, target_predicted)

0.8916265564072141
```

Discussion

Supervised model evaluation compares predictions (e.g., classes or quantitative values) with the corresponding true values in the target vector. However, the most common motivation for using clustering methods is that your data doesn't have a target vector. A number of clustering evaluation metrics require a target vector, but again, using unsupervised learning approaches like clustering when you have a target vector available to you is probably handicapping yourself unnecessarily.

While we cannot evaluate predictions versus true values if we don't have a target vector, we can evaluate the nature of the clusters themselves. Intuitively, we can imagine "good" clusters having very small distances between observations in the same cluster (i.e., dense clusters) and large distances between the different clusters (i.e., well-separated clusters). Silhouette coefficients provide a single value measuring both traits. Formally, the ith observation's silhouette coefficient is:

$$s_i = \frac{b_i - a_i}{\max(a_i, b_i)}$$

where s_i is the silhouette coefficient for observation i, a_i is the mean distance between i and all observations of the same class, and b_i is the mean distance between i and all observations from the closest cluster of a different class. The value returned by silhouette_score is the mean silhouette coefficient for all observations. Silhouette coefficients range between −1 and 1, with 1 indicating dense, well-separated clusters.

See Also

- scikit-learn documentation: silhouette_score (*https://oreil.ly/gGjQj*)

11.10 Creating a Custom Evaluation Metric

Problem

You want to evaluate a model using a metric you created.

Solution

Create the metric as a function and convert it into a scorer function using scikit-learn's make_scorer:

```
# Load libraries
from sklearn.metrics import make_scorer, r2_score
from sklearn.model_selection import train_test_split
from sklearn.linear_model import Ridge
from sklearn.datasets import make_regression

# Generate features matrix and target vector
features, target = make_regression(n_samples = 100,
                                   n_features = 3,
                                   random_state = 1)

# Create training set and test set
features_train, features_test, target_train, target_test = train_test_split(
    features, target, test_size=0.10, random_state=1)

# Create custom metric
def custom_metric(target_test, target_predicted):
    # Calculate R-squared score
    r2 = r2_score(target_test, target_predicted)
    # Return R-squared score
    return r2

# Make scorer and define that higher scores are better
score = make_scorer(custom_metric, greater_is_better=True)

# Create ridge regression object
classifier = Ridge()

# Train ridge regression model
model = classifier.fit(features_train, target_train)

# Apply custom scorer
score(model, features_test, target_test)
```

```
0.9997906102882058
```

Discussion

While scikit-learn has a number of built-in metrics for evaluating model performance, it is often useful to define our own metrics. scikit-learn makes this easy using `make_scorer`. First, we define a function that takes in two arguments—the ground truth target vector and our predicted values—and outputs some score. Second, we use `make_scorer` to create a scorer object, making sure to specify whether higher or lower scores are desirable (using the `greater_is_better` parameter).

The custom metric in the solution (`custom_metric`) is a toy example since it simply wraps a built-in metric for calculating the R^2 score. In a real-world situation, we would replace the `custom_metric` function with whatever custom metric we wanted. However, we can see that the custom metric that calculates R^2 does work by comparing the results to scikit-learn's `r2_score` built-in method:

```
# Predict values
target_predicted = model.predict(features_test)

# Calculate R-squared score
r2_score(target_test, target_predicted)
```

```
0.9997906102882058
```

See Also

- scikit-learn documentation: make_scorer (*https://oreil.ly/-RqFY*)

11.11 Visualizing the Effect of Training Set Size

Problem

You want to evaluate the effect of the number of observations in your training set on some metric (accuracy, F_1, etc.).

Solution

Plot the accuracy against the training set size:

```
# Load libraries
import numpy as np
import matplotlib.pyplot as plt
from sklearn.ensemble import RandomForestClassifier
from sklearn.datasets import load_digits
from sklearn.model_selection import learning_curve

# Load data
digits = load_digits()
```

```
# Create feature matrix and target vector
features, target = digits.data, digits.target

# Create CV training and test scores for various training set sizes
train_sizes, train_scores, test_scores = learning_curve(# Classifier
                                                        RandomForestClassifier(),
                                                        # Feature matrix
                                                        features,
                                                        # Target vector
                                                        target,
                                                        # Number of folds
                                                        cv=10,
                                                        # Performance metric
                                                        scoring='accuracy',
                                                        # Use all computer cores
                                                        n_jobs=-1,
                                                        # Sizes of 50
                                                        # Training set
                                                        train_sizes=np.linspace(
                                                        0.01,
                                                        1.0,
                                                        50))

# Create means and standard deviations of training set scores
train_mean = np.mean(train_scores, axis=1)
train_std = np.std(train_scores, axis=1)

# Create means and standard deviations of test set scores
test_mean = np.mean(test_scores, axis=1)
test_std = np.std(test_scores, axis=1)

# Draw lines
plt.plot(train_sizes, train_mean, '--', color="#111111",  label="Training score")
plt.plot(train_sizes, test_mean, color="#111111", label="Cross-validation score")

# Draw bands
plt.fill_between(train_sizes, train_mean - train_std,
                 train_mean + train_std, color="#DDDDDD")
plt.fill_between(train_sizes, test_mean - test_std,
                 test_mean + test_std, color="#DDDDDD")

# Create plot
plt.title("Learning Curve")
plt.xlabel("Training Set Size"), plt.ylabel("Accuracy Score"),
plt.legend(loc="best")
plt.tight_layout()
plt.show()
```

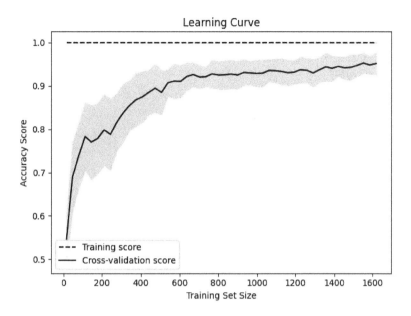

Discussion

Learning curves visualize the performance (e.g., accuracy, recall) of a model on the training set and during cross-validation as the number of observations in the training set increases. They are commonly used to determine if our learning algorithms would benefit from gathering additional training data.

In our solution, we plot the accuracy of a random forest classifier at 50 different training set sizes, ranging from 1% of observations to 100%. The increasing accuracy score of the cross-validated models tell us that we would likely benefit from additional observations (although in practice this might not be feasible).

See Also

- scikit-learn documentation: Learning Curve (*https://oreil.ly/jAKwy*)

11.12 Creating a Text Report of Evaluation Metrics

Problem

You want a quick description of a classifier's performance.

Solution

Use scikit-learn's `classification_report`:

```
# Load libraries
from sklearn import datasets
from sklearn.linear_model import LogisticRegression
from sklearn.model_selection import train_test_split
from sklearn.metrics import classification_report

# Load data
iris = datasets.load_iris()

# Create features matrix
features = iris.data

# Create target vector
target = iris.target

# Create list of target class names
class_names = iris.target_names

# Create training and test set
features_train, features_test, target_train, target_test = train_test_split(
    features, target, random_state=0)

# Create logistic regression
classifier = LogisticRegression()

# Train model and make predictions
model = classifier.fit(features_train, target_train)
target_predicted = model.predict(features_test)

# Create a classification report
print(classification_report(target_test,
                            target_predicted,
                            target_names=class_names))
```

	precision	recall	f1-score	support
setosa	1.00	1.00	1.00	16
versicolor	1.00	0.91	0.95	11
virginica	0.92	1.00	0.96	11
accuracy			0.97	38
macro avg	0.97	0.97	0.97	38
weighted avg	0.98	0.97	0.97	38

Discussion

classification_report provides a quick means for us to see some common evaluation metrics, including precision, recall, and F_1 score (described in Recipe 11.4). Support refers to the number of observations in each class.

See Also

- Precision and recall, Wikipedia (*https://oreil.ly/9mBSF*)

11.13 Visualizing the Effect of Hyperparameter Values

Problem

You want to understand how the performance of a model changes as the value of some hyperparameter changes.

Solution

Plot the hyperparameter against the model accuracy (validation curve):

```
# Load libraries
import matplotlib.pyplot as plt
import numpy as np
from sklearn.datasets import load_digits
from sklearn.ensemble import RandomForestClassifier
from sklearn.model_selection import validation_curve

# Load data
digits = load_digits()

# Create feature matrix and target vector
features, target = digits.data, digits.target

# Create range of values for parameter
param_range = np.arange(1, 250, 2)

# Calculate accuracy on training and test set using range of parameter values
train_scores, test_scores = validation_curve(
    # Classifier
    RandomForestClassifier(),
    # Feature matrix
    features,
    # Target vector
    target,
    # Hyperparameter to examine
    param_name="n_estimators",
    # Range of hyperparameter's values
    param_range=param_range,
    # Number of folds
    cv=3,
    # Performance metric
    scoring="accuracy",
    # Use all computer cores
    n_jobs=-1)
```

```python
# Calculate mean and standard deviation for training set scores
train_mean = np.mean(train_scores, axis=1)
train_std = np.std(train_scores, axis=1)

# Calculate mean and standard deviation for test set scores
test_mean = np.mean(test_scores, axis=1)
test_std = np.std(test_scores, axis=1)

# Plot mean accuracy scores for training and test sets
plt.plot(param_range, train_mean, label="Training score", color="black")
plt.plot(param_range, test_mean, label="Cross-validation score",
         color="dimgrey")

# Plot accuracy bands for training and test sets
plt.fill_between(param_range, train_mean - train_std,
                 train_mean + train_std, color="gray")
plt.fill_between(param_range, test_mean - test_std,
                 test_mean + test_std, color="gainsboro")

# Create plot
plt.title("Validation Curve With Random Forest")
plt.xlabel("Number Of Trees")
plt.ylabel("Accuracy Score")
plt.tight_layout()
plt.legend(loc="best")
plt.show()
```

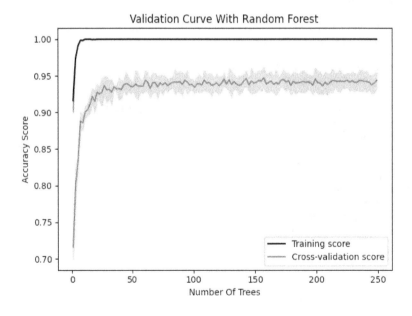

Discussion

Most training algorithms (including many covered in this book) contain hyperparameters that must be chosen before the training process begins. For example, a *random forest classifier* creates a "forest" of decision trees, each of which votes on the predicted class of an observation. One hyperparameter in random forest classifiers is the number of trees in the forest. Most often hyperparameter values are selected during model selection (see Chapter 12). However, it is occasionally useful to visualize how model performance changes as the hyperparameter value changes. In our solution, we plot the changes in accuracy for a random forest classifier for the training set and during cross-validation as the number of trees increases. When we have a small number of trees, both the training and cross-validation score are low, suggesting the model is underfitted. As the number of trees increases to 250, the accuracy of both levels off, suggesting there is probably not much value in the computational cost of training a massive forest.

In scikit-learn, we can calculate the validation curve using `validation_curve`, which contains three important parameters:

`param_name`
: Name of the hyperparameter to vary

`param_range`
: Value of the hyperparameter to use

`scoring`
: Evaluation metric used to judge to model

See Also

- scikit-learn documentation: Validation Curve (*https://oreil.ly/FH_kH*)

## CHAPTER 12

Model Selection

12.0 Introduction

In machine learning, we use training algorithms to learn the parameters of a model by minimizing some loss function. However, many learning algorithms (e.g., support vector classifier and random forests) have additional *hyperparameters* that are defined by the user and affect how the model will learn its parameters. As we mentioned earlier in the book, *parameters* (also sometimes called model weights) are what models learn during the training process, whereas hyperparameters are provided manually by us (the users).

For example, random forests are collections of decision trees (hence the word *forest*); however, the number of decision trees in the forest is not learned by the algorithm and must be set prior to fitting. This is often referred to as *hyperparameter tuning*, *hyperparameter optimization*, or *model selection*. Additionally, we might want to try multiple learning algorithms (for example, trying both support vector classifier and random forests to see which learning method produces the best model).

While there is widespread terminology variation in this area, in this book we refer to selecting both the best learning algorithm and its best hyperparameters as model selection. The reason is straightforward: imagine we have data and want to train a support vector classifier with 10 candidate hyperparameter values and a random forest classifier with 10 candidate hyperparameter values. The result is that we are trying to select the best model from a set of 20 candidate models. In this chapter, we will cover techniques to efficiently select the best model from the set of candidates.

Throughout this chapter we will refer to specific hyperparameters, such as C (the inverse of regularization strength). Don't worry if you don't know what the hyperparameters are. We will cover them in later chapters. Instead, just treat hyperparameters like the settings for the learning algorithm that we must choose before starting training. In general, finding the model and associated hyperparameters that yield the best performance is the result of experimentation—trying a bunch of things out and seeing what works best.

12.1 Selecting the Best Models Using Exhaustive Search

Problem

You want to select the best model by searching over a range of hyperparameters.

Solution

Use scikit-learn's `GridSearchCV`:

```
# Load libraries
import numpy as np
from sklearn import linear_model, datasets
from sklearn.model_selection import GridSearchCV

# Load data
iris = datasets.load_iris()
features = iris.data
target = iris.target

# Create logistic regression
logistic = linear_model.LogisticRegression(max_iter=500, solver='liblinear')

# Create range of candidate penalty hyperparameter values
penalty = ['l1','l2']

# Create range of candidate regularization hyperparameter values
C = np.logspace(0, 4, 10)

# Create dictionary of hyperparameter candidates
hyperparameters = dict(C=C, penalty=penalty)

# Create grid search
gridsearch = GridSearchCV(logistic, hyperparameters, cv=5, verbose=0)

# Fit grid search
best_model = gridsearch.fit(features, target)

# Show the best model
print(best_model.best_estimator_)

LogisticRegression(C=7.742636826811269, max_iter=500, penalty='l1',
                   solver='liblinear')
```

Discussion

GridSearchCV is a brute-force approach to model selection using cross-validation. Specifically, a user defines sets of possible values for one or multiple hyperparameters, and then GridSearchCV trains a model using every value and/or combination of values. The model with the best performance score is selected as the best model.

For example, in our solution we used logistic regression as our learning algorithm and tuned two hyperparameters: C and the regularization penalty. We also specified two other parameters, the solver and max iterations. Don't worry if you don't know what these terms mean; we cover them in the next few chapters. Just realize that C and the regularization penalty can take a range of values, which have to be specified prior to training. For C, we define 10 possible values:

```
np.logspace(0, 4, 10)
```

```
array([1.00000000e+00, 2.78255940e+00, 7.74263683e+00, 2.15443469e+01,
       5.99484250e+01, 1.66810054e+02, 4.64158883e+02, 1.29154967e+03,
       3.59381366e+03, 1.00000000e+04])
```

Similarly, we define two possible values for the regularization penalty: ['l1', 'l2']. For each combination of C and regularization penalty values, we train the model and evaluate it using k-fold cross-validation. In our solution, we have 10 possible values of C, 2 possible values of regularization penalty, and 5 folds. They create $10 \times 2 \times 5 = 100$ candidate models, from which the best is selected.

Once GridSearchCV is complete, we can see the hyperparameters of the best model:

```
# View best hyperparameters
print('Best Penalty:', best_model.best_estimator_.get_params()['penalty'])
print('Best C:', best_model.best_estimator_.get_params()['C'])
```

```
Best Penalty: l1
Best C: 7.742636826811269
```

By default, after identifying the best hyperparameters, GridSearchCV will retrain a model using the best hyperparameters on the entire dataset (rather than leaving a fold out for cross-validation). We can use this model to predict values like any other scikit-learn model:

```
# Predict target vector
best_model.predict(features)
```

```
array([0, 0, 0, 0, 0, 0, 0, 0, 0, 0, 0, 0, 0, 0, 0, 0, 0, 0, 0, 0, 0, 0,
       0, 0, 0, 0, 0, 0, 0, 0, 0, 0, 0, 0, 0, 0, 0, 0, 0, 0, 0, 0, 0, 0,
       0, 0, 0, 0, 0, 0, 1, 1, 1, 1, 1, 1, 1, 1, 1, 1, 1, 1, 1, 1, 1, 1,
       1, 1, 1, 1, 2, 1, 1, 1, 1, 1, 1, 1, 1, 1, 1, 1, 1, 2, 1, 1, 1, 1,
       1, 1, 1, 1, 1, 1, 1, 1, 1, 1, 1, 1, 2, 2, 2, 2, 2, 2, 2, 2, 2, 2,
       2, 2, 2, 2, 2, 2, 2, 2, 2, 2, 2, 2, 2, 2, 2, 2, 2, 2, 2, 2, 2, 2,
       2, 1, 2, 2, 2, 2, 2, 2, 2, 2, 2, 2, 2, 2, 2, 2, 2, 2])
```

One GridSearchCV parameter is worth noting: verbose. While mostly unnecessary, it can be reassuring during long searching processes to receive an indication that the search is progressing. The verbose parameter determines the number of messages outputted during the search, with 0 showing no output, and 1 to 3 outputting additional messages.

See Also

- scikit-learn documentation: GridSearchCV (*https://oreil.ly/XlMPG*)

12.2 Selecting the Best Models Using Randomized Search

Problem

You want a computationally cheaper method than exhaustive search to select the best model.

Solution

Use scikit-learn's RandomizedSearchCV:

```
# Load libraries
from scipy.stats import uniform
from sklearn import linear_model, datasets
from sklearn.model_selection import RandomizedSearchCV

# Load data
iris = datasets.load_iris()
features = iris.data
target = iris.target

# Create logistic regression
logistic = linear_model.LogisticRegression(max_iter=500, solver='liblinear')

# Create range of candidate regularization penalty hyperparameter values
penalty = ['l1', 'l2']

# Create distribution of candidate regularization hyperparameter values
C = uniform(loc=0, scale=4)

# Create hyperparameter options
hyperparameters = dict(C=C, penalty=penalty)

# Create randomized search
randomizedsearch = RandomizedSearchCV(
    logistic, hyperparameters, random_state=1, n_iter=100, cv=5, verbose=0,
    n_jobs=-1)
```

```
# Fit randomized search
best_model = randomizedsearch.fit(features, target)

# Print best model
print(best_model.best_estimator_)

LogisticRegression(C=1.668088018810296, max_iter=500, penalty='l1',
                   solver='liblinear')
```

Discussion

In Recipe 12.1, we used GridSearchCV on a user-defined set of hyperparameter values to search for the best model according to a score function. A more efficient method than GridSearchCV's brute-force search is to search over a specific number of random combinations of hyperparameter values from user-supplied distributions (e.g., normal, uniform). scikit-learn implements this randomized search technique with RandomizedSearchCV.

With RandomizedSearchCV, if we specify a distribution, scikit-learn will randomly sample without replacement hyperparameter values from that distribution. As an example of the general concept, here we randomly sample 10 values from a uniform distribution ranging from 0 to 4:

```
# Define a uniform distribution between 0 and 4, sample 10 values
uniform(loc=0, scale=4).rvs(10)

array([3.95211699, 0.30693116, 2.88237794, 3.00392864, 0.43964702,
       1.46670526, 0.27841863, 2.56541664, 2.66475584, 0.79611958])
```

Alternatively, if we specify a list of values, such as two regularization penalty hyperparameter values ['l1', 'l2'], RandomizedSearchCV will randomly sample with replacement from the list.

Just like with GridSearchCV, we can see the hyperparameter values of the best model:

```
# View best hyperparameters
print('Best Penalty:', best_model.best_estimator_.get_params()['penalty'])
print('Best C:', best_model.best_estimator_.get_params()['C'])

Best Penalty: l1
Best C: 1.668088018810296
```

And just like with GridSearchCV, after the search is complete RandomizedSearchCV fits a new model using the best hyperparameters on the entire dataset. We can use this model like any other in scikit-learn; for example, to make predictions:

```
# Predict target vector
best_model.predict(features)

array([0, 0, 0, 0, 0, 0, 0, 0, 0, 0, 0, 0, 0, 0, 0, 0, 0, 0, 0, 0, 0,
       0, 0, 0, 0, 0, 0, 0, 0, 0, 0, 0, 0, 0, 0, 0, 0, 0, 0, 0, 0, 0,
       0, 0, 0, 0, 0, 0, 1, 1, 1, 1, 1, 1, 1, 1, 1, 1, 1, 1, 1, 1, 1,
```

```
       1, 1, 1, 1, 2, 1, 1, 1, 1, 1, 1, 1, 1, 1, 1, 1, 1, 2, 2, 1, 1, 1,
       1, 1, 1, 1, 1, 1, 1, 1, 1, 1, 1, 1, 2, 2, 2, 2, 2, 2, 2, 2, 2, 2,
       2, 2, 2, 2, 2, 2, 2, 2, 2, 2, 2, 2, 2, 2, 2, 2, 2, 2, 2, 1, 2, 2,
       2, 1, 2, 2, 2, 2, 2, 2, 2, 2, 2, 2, 2, 2, 2, 2, 2, 2])
```

The number of sampled combinations of hyperparameters (i.e., the number of candidate models trained) is specified with the n_iter (number of iterations) setting. It's worth noting that RandomizedSearchCV isn't inherently faster than GridSearchCV, but it often achieves comparable performance to GridSearchCV in less time just by testing fewer combinations.

See Also

- scikit-learn documentation: RandomizedSearchCV (*https://oreil.ly/rpiSs*)
- Random Search for Hyper-Parameter Optimization (*https://oreil.ly/iBcbo*)

12.3 Selecting the Best Models from Multiple Learning Algorithms

Problem

You want to select the best model by searching over a range of learning algorithms and their respective hyperparameters.

Solution

Create a dictionary of candidate learning algorithms and their hyperparameters to use as the search space for GridSearchCV:

```
# Load libraries
import numpy as np
from sklearn import datasets
from sklearn.linear_model import LogisticRegression
from sklearn.ensemble import RandomForestClassifier
from sklearn.model_selection import GridSearchCV
from sklearn.pipeline import Pipeline

# Set random seed
np.random.seed(0)

# Load data
iris = datasets.load_iris()
features = iris.data
target = iris.target

# Create a pipeline
pipe = Pipeline([("classifier", RandomForestClassifier())])
```

```
# Create dictionary with candidate learning algorithms and their hyperparameters
search_space = [{"classifier": [LogisticRegression(max_iter=500,
        solver='liblinear')],
                "classifier__penalty": ['l1', 'l2'],
                "classifier__C": np.logspace(0, 4, 10)},
                {"classifier": [RandomForestClassifier()],
                "classifier__n_estimators": [10, 100, 1000],
                "classifier__max_features": [1, 2, 3]}]

# Create grid search
gridsearch = GridSearchCV(pipe, search_space, cv=5, verbose=0)

# Fit grid search
best_model = gridsearch.fit(features, target)

# Print best model
print(best_model.best_estimator_)

Pipeline(steps=[('classifier',
                LogisticRegression(C=7.742636826811269, max_iter=500,
                                    penalty='l1', solver='liblinear'))])
```

Discussion

In the previous two recipes, we found the best model by searching over possible hyperparameter values of a learning algorithm. However, what if we are not certain which learning algorithm to use? scikit-learn allows us to include learning algorithms as part of the search space. In our solution we define a search space that includes two learning algorithms: logistic regression and random forest classifier. Each learning algorithm has its own hyperparameters, and we define their candidate values using the format classifier__[hyperparameter name]. For example, for our logistic regression, to define the set of possible values for regularization hyperparameter space, C, and potential types of regularization penalties, penalty, we create a dictionary:

```
{'classifier': [LogisticRegression(max_iter=500, solver='liblinear')],
 'classifier__penalty': ['l1', 'l2'],
 'classifier__C': np.logspace(0, 4, 10)}
```

We can also create a similar dictionary for the random forest hyperparameters:

```
{'classifier': [RandomForestClassifier()],
 'classifier__n_estimators': [10, 100, 1000],
 'classifier__max_features': [1, 2, 3]}
```

After the search is complete, we can use best_estimator_ to view the best model's learning algorithm and hyperparameters:

```
# View best model
print(best_model.best_estimator_.get_params()["classifier"])
```

```
LogisticRegression(C=7.742636826811269, max_iter=500, penalty='l1',
                   solver='liblinear')
```

Just like with the last two recipes, once we have fit the model selection search, we can use this best model just like any other scikit-learn model:

```
# Predict target vector
best_model.predict(features)
```

```
array([0, 0, 0, 0, 0, 0, 0, 0, 0, 0, 0, 0, 0, 0, 0, 0, 0, 0, 0, 0, 0,
       0, 0, 0, 0, 0, 0, 0, 0, 0, 0, 0, 0, 0, 0, 0, 0, 0, 0, 0, 0, 0,
       0, 0, 0, 0, 0, 0, 1, 1, 1, 1, 1, 1, 1, 1, 1, 1, 1, 1, 1, 1, 1,
       1, 1, 1, 1, 2, 1, 1, 1, 1, 1, 1, 1, 1, 1, 1, 1, 1, 2, 1, 1, 1, 1,
       1, 1, 1, 1, 1, 1, 1, 1, 1, 1, 1, 1, 2, 2, 2, 2, 2, 2, 2, 2, 2, 2,
       2, 2, 2, 2, 2, 2, 2, 2, 2, 2, 2, 2, 2, 2, 2, 2, 2, 2, 2, 2, 2, 2,
       2, 1, 2, 2, 2, 2, 2, 2, 2, 2, 2, 2, 2, 2, 2, 2, 2, 2])
```

12.4 Selecting the Best Models When Preprocessing

Problem

You want to include a preprocessing step during model selection.

Solution

Create a pipeline that includes the preprocessing step and any of its parameters:

```
# Load libraries
import numpy as np
from sklearn import datasets
from sklearn.linear_model import LogisticRegression
from sklearn.model_selection import GridSearchCV
from sklearn.pipeline import Pipeline, FeatureUnion
from sklearn.decomposition import PCA
from sklearn.preprocessing import StandardScaler

# Set random seed
np.random.seed(0)

# Load data
iris = datasets.load_iris()
features = iris.data
target = iris.target

# Create a preprocessing object that includes StandardScaler features and PCA
preprocess = FeatureUnion([("std", StandardScaler()), ("pca", PCA())])

# Create a pipeline
pipe = Pipeline([("preprocess", preprocess),
                 ("classifier", LogisticRegression(max_iter=1000,
                     solver='liblinear'))])
```

```
# Create space of candidate values
search_space = [{"preprocess__pca__n_components": [1, 2, 3],
                 "classifier__penalty": ["l1", "l2"],
                 "classifier__C": np.logspace(0, 4, 10)}]

# Create grid search
clf = GridSearchCV(pipe, search_space, cv=5, verbose=0, n_jobs=-1)

# Fit grid search
best_model = clf.fit(features, target)

# Print best model
print(best_model.best_estimator_)

Pipeline(steps=[('preprocess',
                 FeatureUnion(transformer_list=[('std', StandardScaler()),
                                                ('pca', PCA(n_components=1))])),
                ('classifier',
                 LogisticRegression(C=7.742636826811269, max_iter=1000,
                                    penalty='l1', solver='liblinear'))])
```

Discussion

Very often we will need to preprocess our data before using it to train a model. We have to be careful to properly handle preprocessing when conducting model selection. First, GridSearchCV uses cross-validation to determine which model has the highest performance. However, in cross-validation, we are in effect pretending that the fold held out as the test set is not seen, and thus not part of fitting any preprocessing steps (e.g., scaling or standardization). For this reason, we cannot preprocess the data and then run GridSearchCV. Rather, the preprocessing steps must be a part of the set of actions taken by GridSearchCV.

This might appear complex, but scikit-learn makes it simple. FeatureUnion allows us to combine multiple preprocessing actions properly. In our solution, we use FeatureUnion to combine two preprocessing steps: standardize the feature values (StandardScaler) and principal component analysis (PCA). This object is called preprocess and contains both of our preprocessing steps. We then include preprocess in a pipeline with our learning algorithm. The result is that this allows us to outsource the proper (and confusing) handling of fitting, transforming, and training the models with combinations of hyperparameters to scikit-learn.

Second, some preprocessing methods have their own parameters, which often have to be supplied by the user. For example, dimensionality reduction using PCA requires the user to define the number of principal components to use to produce the transformed feature set. Ideally, we would choose the number of components that produces a model with the greatest performance for some evaluation test metric.

Luckily, scikit-learn makes this easy. When we include candidate component values in the search space, they are treated like any other hyperparameter to be searched over. In our solution, we defined features__pca__n_components': [1, 2, 3] in the search space to indicate that we want to discover if one, two, or three principal components produce the best model.

After model selection is complete, we can view the preprocessing values that produced the best model. For example, we can see the best number of principal components:

```
# View best n_components
best_model.best_estimator_.get_params()['preprocess__pca__n_components']

1
```

12.5 Speeding Up Model Selection with Parallelization

Problem

You need to speed up model selection.

Solution

Use all the cores in your machine by setting n_jobs=-1, which enables you to train multiple models simultaneously:

```
# Load libraries
import numpy as np
from sklearn import linear_model, datasets
from sklearn.model_selection import GridSearchCV

# Load data
iris = datasets.load_iris()
features = iris.data
target = iris.target

# Create logistic regression
logistic = linear_model.LogisticRegression(max_iter=500, solver='liblinear')

# Create range of candidate regularization penalty hyperparameter values
penalty = ["l1", "l2"]

# Create range of candidate values for C
C = np.logspace(0, 4, 1000)

# Create hyperparameter options
hyperparameters = dict(C=C, penalty=penalty)

# Create grid search
gridsearch = GridSearchCV(logistic, hyperparameters, cv=5, n_jobs=-1, verbose=1)
```

```
# Fit grid search
best_model = gridsearch.fit(features, target)

# Print best model
print(best_model.best_estimator_)

Fitting 5 folds for each of 2000 candidates, totalling 10000 fits
LogisticRegression(C=5.926151812475554, max_iter=500, penalty='l1',
                    solver='liblinear')
```

Discussion

In the recipes in this chapter, we have kept the number of candidate models small to make the code complete quickly. However, in the real world we may have many thousands or tens of thousands of models to train. As a result, it can take many hours to find the best model.

To speed up the process, scikit-learn lets us train multiple models simultaneously. Without going into too much technical detail, scikit-learn can simultaneously train models up to the number of cores on the machine. Most modern laptops have at least four cores, so (assuming you're currently on a laptop) we can potentially train four models at the same time. This will dramatically increase the speed of our model selection process. The parameter n_jobs defines the number of models to train in parallel.

In our solution, we set n_jobs to -1, which tells scikit-learn to use *all* cores. However, by default n_jobs is set to 1, meaning it uses only one core. To demonstrate this, if we run the same GridSearchCV as in the solution, but with n_jobs=1, we can see it takes significantly longer to find the best model (note that exact time will depend on your computer):

```
# Create grid search using one core
clf = GridSearchCV(logistic, hyperparameters, cv=5, n_jobs=1, verbose=1)

# Fit grid search
best_model = clf.fit(features, target)

# Print best model
print(best_model.best_estimator_)

Fitting 5 folds for each of 2000 candidates, totalling 10000 fits
LogisticRegression(C=5.926151812475554, max_iter=500, penalty='l1',
                    solver='liblinear')
```

12.6 Speeding Up Model Selection Using Algorithm-Specific Methods

Problem

You need to speed up model selection without using additional compute power.

Solution

If you are using a select number of learning algorithms, use scikit-learn's model-specific cross-validation hyperparameter tuning, `LogisticRegressionCV`:

```
# Load libraries
from sklearn import linear_model, datasets

# Load data
iris = datasets.load_iris()
features = iris.data
target = iris.target

# Create cross-validated logistic regression
logit = linear_model.LogisticRegressionCV(Cs=100, max_iter=500,
        solver='liblinear')

# Train model
logit.fit(features, target)

# Print model
print(logit)

LogisticRegressionCV(Cs=100, max_iter=500, solver='liblinear')
```

Discussion

Sometimes the characteristics of a learning algorithm allow us to search for the best hyperparameters significantly faster than either brute-force or randomized model search methods. In scikit-learn, many learning algorithms (e.g., ridge, lasso, and elastic net regression) have an algorithm-specific cross-validation method to take advantage of this. For example, `LogisticRegression` is used to conduct a standard logistic regression classifier, while `LogisticRegressionCV` implements an efficient cross-validated logistic regression classifier that can identify the optimum value of the hyperparameter C.

scikit-learn's `LogisticRegressionCV` method includes a parameter `Cs`. If supplied a list, `Cs` contains the candidate hyperparameter values to select from. If supplied an integer, the parameter `Cs` generates a list of that number of candidate values. The candidate values are drawn logarithmically from a range between 0.0001 and 10,0000 (a range of reasonable values for C).

However, a major downside to `LogisticRegressionCV` is that it can only search a range of values for C. In Recipe 12.1 our possible hyperparameter space included both C and another hyperparameter (the regularization penalty norm). This limitation is common to many of scikit-learn's model-specific cross-validated approaches.

See Also

- scikit-learn documentation: LogisticRegressionCV (*https://oreil.ly/uguJi*)
- scikit-learn documentation: Model specific cross-validation (*https://oreil.ly/6xfn6*)

12.7 Evaluating Performance After Model Selection

Problem

You want to evaluate the performance of a model found through model selection.

Solution

Use nested cross-validation to avoid biased evaluation:

```
# Load libraries
import numpy as np
from sklearn import linear_model, datasets
from sklearn.model_selection import GridSearchCV, cross_val_score

# Load data
iris = datasets.load_iris()
features = iris.data
target = iris.target

# Create logistic regression
logistic = linear_model.LogisticRegression(max_iter=500, solver='liblinear')

# Create range of 20 candidate values for C
C = np.logspace(0, 4, 20)

# Create hyperparameter options
hyperparameters = dict(C=C)

# Create grid search
gridsearch = GridSearchCV(logistic, hyperparameters, cv=5, n_jobs=-1, verbose=0)

# Conduct nested cross-validation and output the average score
cross_val_score(gridsearch, features, target).mean()

0.9733333333333334
```

Discussion

Nested cross-validation during model selection is a difficult concept for many people to grasp the first time. Remember that in k-fold cross-validation, we train our model on *k–1* folds of the data, use this model to make predictions on the remaining fold, and then evaluate our model on how well its predictions compare to the true values. We then repeat this process *k* times.

In the model selection searches described in this chapter (i.e., `GridSearchCV` and `RandomizedSearchCV`), we used cross-validation to evaluate which hyperparameter values produced the best models. However, a nuanced and generally underappreciated problem arises: since we used the data to select the best hyperparameter values, we cannot use that same data to evaluate the model's performance. The solution? Wrap the cross-validation used for model search in another cross-validation! In nested cross-validation, the "inner" cross-validation selects the best model, while the "outer" cross-validation provides an unbiased evaluation of the model's performance. In our solution, the inner cross-validation is our `GridSearchCV` object, which we then wrap in an outer cross-validation using `cross_val_score`.

If you are confused, try a simple experiment. First, set `verbose=1` so we can see what is happening:

```
gridsearch = GridSearchCV(logistic, hyperparameters, cv=5, verbose=1)
```

Next, run `gridsearch.fit(features, target)`, which is our inner cross-validation used to find the best model:

```
best_model = gridsearch.fit(features, target)
Fitting 5 folds for each of 20 candidates, totalling 100 fits
```

From the output you can see the inner cross-validation trained 20 candidate models five times, totaling 100 models. Next, nest `clf` inside a new cross-validation, which defaults to five folds:

```
scores = cross_val_score(gridsearch, features, target)
Fitting 5 folds for each of 20 candidates, totalling 100 fits
Fitting 5 folds for each of 20 candidates, totalling 100 fits
Fitting 5 folds for each of 20 candidates, totalling 100 fits
Fitting 5 folds for each of 20 candidates, totalling 100 fits
Fitting 5 folds for each of 20 candidates, totalling 100 fits
```

The output shows that the inner cross-validation trained 20 models five times to find the best model, and this model was evaluated using an outer five-fold cross-validation, creating a total of 500 models trained.

## CHAPTER 13

Linear Regression

13.0 Introduction

Linear regression is one of the simplest supervised learning algorithms in our toolkit. If you have ever taken an introductory statistics course in college, likely the final topic you covered was linear regression. Linear regression and its extensions continue to be a common and useful method of making predictions when the target vector is a quantitative value (e.g., home price, age). In this chapter we will cover a variety of linear regression methods (and some extensions) for creating well-performing prediction models.

13.1 Fitting a Line

Problem

You want to train a model that represents a linear relationship between the feature and target vector.

Solution

Use a linear regression (in scikit-learn, `LinearRegression`):

```
# Load libraries
from sklearn.linear_model import LinearRegression
from sklearn.datasets import make_regression

# Generate features matrix, target vector
features, target = make_regression(n_samples = 100,
                                   n_features = 3,
                                   n_informative = 2,
                                   n_targets = 1,
```

```
                                    noise = 0.2,
                                    coef = False,
                                    random_state = 1)

# Create linear regression
regression = LinearRegression()

# Fit the linear regression
model = regression.fit(features, target)
```

Discussion

Linear regression assumes that the relationship between the features and the target vector is approximately linear. That is, the *effect* (also called *coefficient*, *weight*, or *parameter*) of the features on the target vector is constant. In our solution, for the sake of explanation, we have trained our model using only three features. This means our linear model will be:

$$\widehat{y} = \widehat{\beta}_0 + \widehat{\beta}_1 x_1 + \widehat{\beta}_2 x_2 + \widehat{\beta}_3 x_3 + \epsilon$$

where $\widehat{y}$ is our target, x_i is the data for a single feature, $\widehat{\beta}_1$, $\widehat{\beta}_2$, and $\widehat{\beta}_3$ are the coefficients identified by fitting the model, and ϵ is the error. After we have fit our model, we can view the value of each parameter. For example, $\widehat{\beta}_0$, also called the *bias* or *intercept*, can be viewed using `intercept_`:

```
# View the intercept
model.intercept_
```

```
-0.009650118178816669
```

And $\widehat{\beta}_1$ and $\widehat{\beta}_2$ are shown using `coef_`:

```
# View the feature coefficients
model.coef_
```

```
array([1.95531234e-02, 4.42087450e+01, 5.81494563e+01])
```

In our dataset, the target value is a randomly generated continuous variable:

```
# First value in the target vector
target[0]
```

```
-20.870747595269407
```

Using the `predict` method, we can predict the output based on the input features:

```
# Predict the target value of the first observation
model.predict(features)[0]
```

```
-20.861927709296808
```

Not bad! Our model was off only by about 0.01!

The major advantage of linear regression is its interpretability, in large part because the coefficients of the model are the effect of a one-unit change on the target vector. Our model's coefficient of the first feature was ~–0.02, meaning that we have the change in target for each additional unit change in the first feature.

Using the score function, we can also see how well our model performed on the data:

```
# Print the score of the model on the training data
print(model.score(features, target))
```

```
0.9999901732607787
```

The default score for linear regression in scikit learn is R^2, which ranges from 0.0 (worst) to 1.0 (best). As we can see in this example, we are very close to the perfect value of 1.0. However it's worth noting that we are evaluating this model on data it has already seen (the training data), where typically we'd evaluate on a held-out test set of data instead. Nonetheless, such a high score would bode well for our model in a real setting.

13.2 Handling Interactive Effects

Problem

You have a feature whose effect on the target variable depends on another feature.

Solution

Create an interaction term to capture that dependence using scikit-learn's PolynomialFeatures:

```
# Load libraries
from sklearn.linear_model import LinearRegression
from sklearn.preprocessing import PolynomialFeatures
from sklearn.datasets import make_regression

# Generate features matrix, target vector
features, target = make_regression(n_samples = 100,
                                   n_features = 2,
                                   n_informative = 2,
                                   n_targets = 1,
                                   noise = 0.2,
                                   coef = False,
                                   random_state = 1)

# Create interaction term
interaction = PolynomialFeatures(
    degree=3, include_bias=False, interaction_only=True)
features_interaction = interaction.fit_transform(features)

# Create linear regression
```

```
regression = LinearRegression()

# Fit the linear regression
model = regression.fit(features_interaction, target)
```

Discussion

Sometimes a feature's effect on our target variable is at least partially dependent on another feature. For example, imagine a simple coffee-based example where we have two binary features—the presence of sugar (sugar) and whether or not we have stirred (stirred)—and we want to predict if the coffee tastes sweet. Just putting sugar in the coffee (sugar=1, stirred=0) won't make the coffee taste sweet (all the sugar is at the bottom!) and just stirring the coffee without adding sugar (sugar=0, stirred=1) won't make it sweet either. Instead it is the interaction of putting sugar in the coffee *and* stirring the coffee (sugar=1, stirred=1) that will make a coffee taste sweet. The effects of sugar and stirred on sweetness are dependent on each other. In this case we say there is an *interaction effect* between the features sugar and stirred.

We can account for interaction effects by including a new feature comprising the product of corresponding values from the interacting features:

$$\hat{y} = \hat{\beta}_0 + \hat{\beta}_1 x_1 + \hat{\beta}_2 x_2 + \hat{\beta}_3 x_1 x_2 + \epsilon$$

where x_1 and x_2 are the values of the sugar and stirred, respectively, and $x_1 x_2$ represents the interaction between the two.

In our solution, we used a dataset containing only two features. Here is the first observation's values for each of those features:

```
# View the feature values for first observation
features[0]
```

```
array([0.0465673 , 0.80186103])
```

To create an interaction term, we simply multiply those two values together for every observation:

```
# Import library
import numpy as np

# For each observation, multiply the values of the first and second feature
interaction_term = np.multiply(features[:, 0], features[:, 1])
```

We can then view the interaction term for the first observation:

```
# View interaction term for first observation
interaction_term[0]

0.037340501965846186
```

However, while often we will have a substantive reason for believing there is an interaction between two features, sometimes we will not. In those cases it can be useful to use scikit-learn's `PolynomialFeatures` to create interaction terms for all combinations of features. We can then use model selection strategies to identify the combination of features and interaction terms that produces the best model.

To create interaction terms using `PolynomialFeatures`, there are three important parameters we must set. Most important, `interaction_only=True` tells `PolynomialFeatures` to return only interaction terms (and not polynomial features, which we will discuss in Recipe 13.3). By default, `PolynomialFeatures` will add a feature containing 1s called a *bias*. We can prevent that with `include_bias=False`. Finally, the `degree` parameter determines the maximum number of features to create interaction terms from (in case we wanted to create an interaction term that is the combination of three features). We can see the output of `PolynomialFeatures` from our solution by checking to see if the first observation's feature values and interaction term value match our manually calculated version:

```
# View the values of the first observation
features_interaction[0]

array([0.0465673 , 0.80186103, 0.0373405 ])
```

13.3 Fitting a Nonlinear Relationship

Problem

You want to model a nonlinear relationship.

Solution

Create a polynomial regression by including polynomial features in a linear regression model:

```
# Load library
from sklearn.linear_model import LinearRegression
from sklearn.preprocessing import PolynomialFeatures
from sklearn.datasets import make_regression

# Generate features matrix, target vector
features, target = make_regression(n_samples = 100,
                                   n_features = 3,
                                   n_informative = 2,
                                   n_targets = 1,
                                   noise = 0.2,
```

```
                        coef = False,
                        random_state = 1)

# Create polynomial features x^2 and x^3
polynomial = PolynomialFeatures(degree=3, include_bias=False)
features_polynomial = polynomial.fit_transform(features)

# Create linear regression
regression = LinearRegression()

# Fit the linear regression
model = regression.fit(features_polynomial, target)
```

Discussion

So far we have discussed modeling only linear relationships. An example of a linear relationship would be the number of stories a building has and the building's height. In linear regression, we assume the effect of number of stories and building height is approximately constant, meaning a 20-story building will be roughly twice as high as a 10-story building, which will be roughly twice as high as a 5-story building. Many relationships of interest, however, are not strictly linear.

Often we want to model a nonlinear relationship—for example, the relationship between the number of hours a student studies and the score she gets on a test. Intuitively, we can imagine there is a big difference in test scores between students who study for one hour compared to students who did not study at all. However, there is a much smaller difference in test scores between a student who studied for 99 hours and a student who studied for 100 hours. The effect that one hour of studying has on a student's test score decreases as the number of hours increases.

Polynomial regression is an extension of linear regression that allows us to model nonlinear relationships. To create a polynomial regression, convert the linear function we used in Recipe 13.1:

$$\widehat{y} = \widehat{\beta}_0 + \widehat{\beta}_1 x_1 + \epsilon$$

into a polynomial function by adding polynomial features:

$$\widehat{y} = \widehat{\beta}_0 + \widehat{\beta}_1 x_1 + \widehat{\beta}_2 x_1^2 + \ldots + \widehat{\beta}_d x_1^d + \epsilon$$

where d is the degree of the polynomial. How are we able to use a linear regression for a nonlinear function? The answer is that we do not change how the linear regression fits the model but rather only add polynomial features. That is, the linear regression does not "know" that the x^2 is a quadratic transformation of x. It just considers it one more variable.

A more practical description might be in order. To model nonlinear relationships, we can create new features that raise an existing feature, x, up to some power: x^2, x^3, and so on. The more of these new features we add, the more flexible the "line" created by our model. To make this more explicit, imagine we want to create a polynomial to the third degree. For the sake of simplicity, we will focus on only one observation (the first observation in the dataset), $x[0]$:

```
# View first observation
features[0]
```

```
array([-0.61175641])
```

To create a polynomial feature, we would raise the first observation's value to the second degree, x_1^2:

```
# View first observation raised to the second power, x^2
features[0]**2
```

```
array([0.37424591])
```

This would be our new feature. We would then also raise the first observation's value to the third degree, x_1^3:

```
# View first observation raised to the third power, x^3
features[0]**3
```

```
array([-0.22894734])
```

By including all three features (x, x^2, and x^3) in our feature matrix and then running a linear regression, we have conducted a polynomial regression:

```
# View the first observation's values for x, x^2, and x^3
features_polynomial[0]
```

```
array([-0.61175641,  0.37424591, -0.22894734])
```

PolynomialFeatures has two important parameters. First, degree determines the maximum number of degrees for the polynomial features. For example, degree=3 will generate x^2 and x^3. Second, by default PolynomialFeatures includes a feature containing only 1s (called a bias). We can remove that by setting include_bias=False.

13.4 Reducing Variance with Regularization

Problem

You want to reduce the variance of your linear regression model.

Solution

Use a learning algorithm that includes a *shrinkage penalty* (also called *regularization*) like ridge regression and lasso regression:

```
# Load libraries
from sklearn.linear_model import Ridge
from sklearn.preprocessing import StandardScaler
from sklearn.datasets import make_regression

# Generate features matrix, target vector
features, target = make_regression(n_samples = 100,
                                   n_features = 3,
                                   n_informative = 2,
                                   n_targets = 1,
                                   noise = 0.2,
                                   coef = False,
                                   random_state = 1)

# Standardize features
scaler = StandardScaler()
features_standardized = scaler.fit_transform(features)

# Create ridge regression with an alpha value
regression = Ridge(alpha=0.5)

# Fit the linear regression
model = regression.fit(features_standardized, target)
```

Discussion

In standard linear regression the model trains to minimize the sum of squared error between the true (y_i) and prediction ($\hat{y}_i$) target values, or residual sum of squares (RSS):

$$RSS = \sum_{i=1}^{n} (y_i - \hat{y}_i)^2$$

Regularized regression learners are similar, except they attempt to minimize RSS *and* some penalty for the total size of the coefficient values, called a *shrinkage penalty* because it attempts to "shrink" the model. There are two common types of regularized learners for linear regression: ridge regression and the lasso. The only formal difference is the type of shrinkage penalty used. In *ridge regression*, the shrinkage penalty is a tuning hyperparameter multiplied by the squared sum of all coefficients:

$$RSS + \alpha \sum_{j=1}^{p} \hat{\beta}_j^2$$

where $\widehat{\beta}_j$ is the coefficient of the jth of p features and α is a hyperparameter (discussed next). The *lasso* is similar, except the shrinkage penalty is a tuning hyperparameter multiplied by the sum of the absolute value of all coefficients:

$$\frac{1}{2n}RSS + \alpha \sum_{j=1}^{p} \left|\widehat{\beta}_j\right|$$

where n is the number of observations. So which one should we use? As a very general rule of thumb, ridge regression often produces slightly better predictions than lasso, but lasso (for reasons we will discuss in Recipe 13.5) produces more interpretable models. If we want a balance between ridge and lasso's penalty functions we can use *elastic net*, which is simply a regression model with both penalties included. Regardless of which one we use, both ridge and lasso regressions can penalize large or complex models by including coefficient values in the loss function we are trying to minimize.

The hyperparameter, α, lets us control how much we penalize the coefficients, with higher values of α creating simpler models. The ideal value of α should be tuned like any other hyperparameter. In scikit-learn, α is set using the `alpha` parameter.

scikit-learn includes a `RidgeCV` method that allows us to select the ideal value for α:

```
# Load library
from sklearn.linear_model import RidgeCV

# Create ridge regression with three alpha values
regr_cv = RidgeCV(alphas=[0.1, 1.0, 10.0])

# Fit the linear regression
model_cv = regr_cv.fit(features_standardized, target)

# View coefficients
model_cv.coef_
```
```
array([1.29223201e-02, 4.40972291e+01, 5.38979372e+01])
```

We can then easily view the best model's α value:

```
# View alpha
model_cv.alpha_
```
```
0.1
```

One final note: because in linear regression the value of the coefficients is partially determined by the scale of the feature, and in regularized models all coefficients are summed together, we must make sure to standardize the feature prior to training.

13.5 Reducing Features with Lasso Regression

Problem

You want to simplify your linear regression model by reducing the number of features.

Solution

Use a lasso regression:

```python
# Load library
from sklearn.linear_model import Lasso
from sklearn.preprocessing import StandardScaler
from sklearn.datasets import make_regression

# Generate features matrix, target vector
features, target = make_regression(n_samples = 100,
                                   n_features = 3,
                                   n_informative = 2,
                                   n_targets = 1,
                                   noise = 0.2,
                                   coef = False,
                                   random_state = 1)

# Standardize features
scaler = StandardScaler()
features_standardized = scaler.fit_transform(features)

# Create lasso regression with alpha value
regression = Lasso(alpha=0.5)

# Fit the linear regression
model = regression.fit(features_standardized, target)
```

Discussion

One interesting characteristic of lasso regression's penalty is that it can shrink the coefficients of a model to zero, effectively reducing the number of features in the model. For example, in our solution we set alpha to 0.5, and we can see that many of the coefficients are 0, meaning their corresponding features are not used in the model:

```python
# View coefficients
model.coef_
```

```
array([-0.      , 43.58618393, 53.39523724])
```

However, if we increase α to a much higher value, we see that literally none of the features are being used:

```
# Create lasso regression with a high alpha
regression_a10 = Lasso(alpha=10)
model_a10 = regression_a10.fit(features_standardized, target)
model_a10.coef_
```

```
array([-0.        , 32.92181899, 42.73086731])
```

The practical benefit of this effect is that it means we could include 100 features in our feature matrix and then, through adjusting lasso's α hyperparameter, produce a model that uses only 10 (for instance) of the most important features. This lets us reduce variance while improving the interpretability of our model (since fewer features are easier to explain).

## CHAPTER 14

Trees and Forests

14.0 Introduction

Tree-based learning algorithms are a broad and popular family of related non-parametric, supervised methods for both classification and regression. The basis of tree-based learners is the *decision tree*, wherein a series of decision rules (e.g., "If a person's credit score is greater than 720...") are chained. The result looks vaguely like an upside-down tree, with the first decision rule at the top and subsequent decision rules spreading out below. In a decision tree, every decision rule occurs at a decision node, with the rule creating branches leading to new nodes. A branch without a decision rule at the end is called a *leaf*.

One reason for the popularity of tree-based models is their interpretability. In fact, decision trees can literally be drawn out in their complete form (see Recipe 14.3) to create a highly intuitive model. From this basic tree system comes a wide variety of extensions from random forests to stacking. In this chapter we will cover how to train, handle, adjust, visualize, and evaluate a number of tree-based models.

14.1 Training a Decision Tree Classifier

Problem

You need to train a classifier using a decision tree.

Solution

Use scikit-learn's `DecisionTreeClassifier`:

```
# Load libraries
from sklearn.tree import DecisionTreeClassifier
from sklearn import datasets

# Load data
iris = datasets.load_iris()
features = iris.data
target = iris.target

# Create decision tree classifier object
decisiontree = DecisionTreeClassifier(random_state=0)

# Train model
model = decisiontree.fit(features, target)
```

Discussion

Decision tree learners attempt to find a decision rule that produces the greatest decrease in impurity at a node. While there are a number of measurements of impurity, by default `DecisionTreeClassifier` uses Gini impurity:

$$G(t) = 1 - \sum_{i=1}^{c} p_i^2$$

where $G(t)$ is the Gini impurity at node t, and p_i is the proportion of observations of class c at node t. This process of finding the decision rules that create splits to decrease impurity is repeated recursively until all leaf nodes are pure (i.e., contain only one class) or some arbitrary cutoff is reached.

In scikit-learn, `DecisionTreeClassifier` operates like other learning methods; after the model is trained using `fit`, we can use the model to predict the class of an observation:

```
# Make new observation
observation = [[ 5,  4,  3,  2]]

# Predict observation's class
model.predict(observation)

array([1])
```

We can also see the predicted class probabilities of the observation:

```
# View predicted class probabilities for the three classes
model.predict_proba(observation)

array([[0., 1., 0.]])
```

Finally, if we want to use a different impurity measurement we can use the `criterion` parameter:

```
# Create decision tree classifier object using entropy
decisiontree_entropy = DecisionTreeClassifier(
    criterion='entropy', random_state=0)

# Train model
model_entropy = decisiontree_entropy.fit(features, target)
```

See Also

- Decision Tree Learning, Princeton (*https://oreil.ly/lCPBG*)

14.2 Training a Decision Tree Regressor

Problem

You need to train a regression model using a decision tree.

Solution

Use scikit-learn's `DecisionTreeRegressor`:

```
# Load libraries
from sklearn.tree import DecisionTreeRegressor
from sklearn import datasets

# Load data with only two features
diabetes = datasets.load_diabetes()
features = diabetes.data
target = diabetes.target

# Create decision tree regressor object
decisiontree = DecisionTreeRegressor(random_state=0)

# Train model
model = decisiontree.fit(features, target)
```

Discussion

Decision tree regression works similarly to decision tree classification; however, instead of reducing Gini impurity or entropy, potential splits are by default measured on how much they reduce mean squared error (MSE):

$$\text{MSE} = \frac{1}{n} \sum_{i=1}^{n} (y_i - \bar{y}_i)^2$$

where y_i is the true value of the target and $\bar{y}_i$ is the mean value. In scikit-learn, decision tree regression can be conducted using DecisionTreeRegressor. Once we have trained a decision tree, we can use it to predict the target value for an observation:

```
# Make new observation
observation = [features[0]]

# Predict observation's value
model.predict(observation)

array([151.])
```

Just like with DecisionTreeClassifier we can use the criterion parameter to select the desired measurement of split quality. For example, we can construct a tree whose splits reduce mean absolute error (MAE):

```
# Create decision tree classifier object using MAE
decisiontree_mae = DecisionTreeRegressor(criterion="absolute_error",
    random_state=0)

# Train model
model_mae = decisiontree_mae.fit(features, target)
```

See Also

- scikit-learn documentation: Decision Tree Regression (*https://oreil.ly/EGkU_*)

14.3 Visualizing a Decision Tree Model

Problem

You need to visualize a model created by a decision tree learning algorithm.

Solution

Export the decision tree model into DOT format, then visualize:

```
# Load libraries
import pydotplus
from sklearn.tree import DecisionTreeClassifier
from sklearn import datasets
from IPython.display import Image
from sklearn import tree

# Load data
iris = datasets.load_iris()
features = iris.data
target = iris.target

# Create decision tree classifier object
```

```
decisiontree = DecisionTreeClassifier(random_state=0)

# Train model
model = decisiontree.fit(features, target)

# Create DOT data
dot_data = tree.export_graphviz(decisiontree,
                                out_file=None,
                                feature_names=iris.feature_names,
                                class_names=iris.target_names)

# Draw graph
graph = pydotplus.graph_from_dot_data(dot_data)

# Show graph
Image(graph.create_png())
```

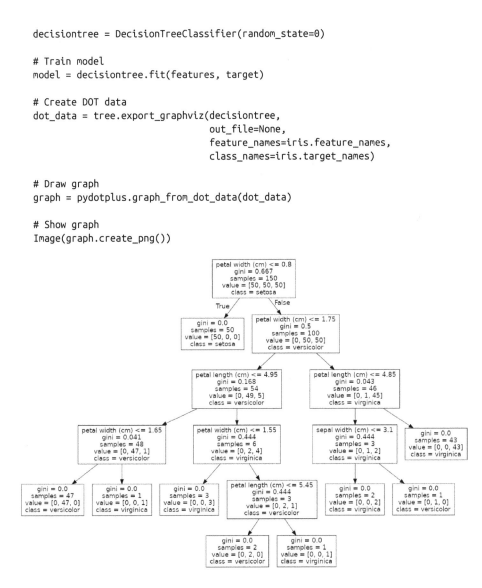

Discussion

One of the advantages of decision tree classifiers is that we can visualize the entire trained model, making decision trees one of the most interpretable models in machine learning. In our solution, we exported our trained model in DOT format (a graph description language) and then used that to draw the graph.

If we look at the root node, we can see the decision rule is that if petal widths are less than or equal to 0.8 cm, then go to the left branch; if not, go to the right branch. We can also see the Gini impurity index (0.667), the number of observations (150), the number of observations in each class ([50,50,50]), and the class the observations would be predicted to be if we stopped at that node (*setosa*). We can also see that at that node the learner found that a single decision rule (`petal width (cm) <= 0.8`) was able to perfectly identify all of the *setosa* class observations. Furthermore, with one more decision rule with the same feature (`petal width (cm) <= 1.75`) the decision tree is able to correctly classify 144 of 150 observations. This makes petal width a very important feature!

If we want to use the decision tree in other applications or reports, we can easily export the visualization into PDF or a PNG image:

```
# Create PDF
graph.write_pdf("iris.pdf")

True

# Create PNG
graph.write_png("iris.png")

True
```

While this solution visualized a decision tree classifier, it can just as easily be used to visualize a decision tree regressor.

Note: macOS users might have to install Graphviz's executable to run the preceding code. This can be done with the Homebrew command `brew install graphviz`. For Homebrew installation instructions, visit Homebrew's website.

See Also

- Homebrew (*https://oreil.ly/GgeNI*)

14.4 Training a Random Forest Classifier

Problem

You want to train a classification model using a "forest" of randomized decision trees.

Solution

Use scikit-learn's `RandomForestClassifier` to train a random forest classification model.

```
# Load libraries
from sklearn.ensemble import RandomForestClassifier
from sklearn import datasets

# Load data
iris = datasets.load_iris()
```

```
features = iris.data
target = iris.target

# Create random forest classifier object
randomforest = RandomForestClassifier(random_state=0, n_jobs=-1)

# Train model
model = randomforest.fit(features, target)
```

Discussion

A common problem with decision trees is that they tend to fit the training data too closely (i.e., overfitting). This has motivated the widespread use of an ensemble learning method called *random forest*. In a random forest, many decision trees are trained, but each tree receives only a bootstrapped sample of observations (i.e., a random sample of observations with replacement that matches the original number of observations), and each node considers only a subset of features when determining the best split. This forest of randomized decision trees (hence the name) votes to determine the predicted class.

As we can see by comparing this solution to Recipe 14.1, scikit-learn's RandomForestClassifier works similarly to DecisionTreeClassifier:

```
# Make new observation
observation = [[ 5,  4,  3,  2]]

# Predict observation's class
model.predict(observation)

array([1])
```

RandomForestClassifier also uses many of the same parameters as DecisionTreeClassifier. For example, we can change the measure of split quality used:

```
# Create random forest classifier object using entropy
randomforest_entropy = RandomForestClassifier(
    criterion="entropy", random_state=0)

# Train model
model_entropy = randomforest_entropy.fit(features, target)
```

However, being a forest rather than an individual decision tree, RandomForestClassifier has certain parameters that are either unique to random forests or particularly important. First, the max_features parameter determines the maximum number of features to be considered at each node and takes a number of arguments including integers (number of features), floats (percentage of features), and sqrt (square root of the number of features). By default, max_features is set to auto, which acts the same as sqrt. Second, the bootstrap parameter allows us to set whether the subset of observations considered for a tree is created using sampling with replacement (the default setting) or without replacement. Third, n_estimators sets the number of decision trees to include in the forest. Finally, while not specific to random forest classifiers, because we are effectively training many decision tree models, it is often useful to use all available cores by setting n_jobs=-1.

See Also

- Random Forests, Berkeley Statistics (*https://oreil.ly/h-LQL*)

14.5 Training a Random Forest Regressor

Problem

You want to train a regression model using a "forest" of randomized decision trees.

Solution

Train a random forest regression model using scikit-learn's RandomForestRegressor:

```
# Load libraries
from sklearn.ensemble import RandomForestRegressor
from sklearn import datasets

# Load data with only two features
diabetes = datasets.load_diabetes()
features = diabetes.data
target = diabetes.target

# Create random forest regressor object
randomforest = RandomForestRegressor(random_state=0, n_jobs=-1)

# Train model
model = randomforest.fit(features, target)
```

Discussion

Just as we can make a forest of decision tree classifiers, we can make a forest of decision tree regressors, where each tree uses a bootstrapped subset of observations and at each node the decision rule considers only a subset of features. As with RandomForestClassifier we have certain important parameters:

max_features
Sets the maximum number of features to consider at each node. Defaults to p features, where p is the total number of features.

```
bootstrap
```
Sets whether or not to sample with replacement. Defaults to `True`.

```
n_estimators
```
Sets the number of decision trees to construct. Defaults to `10`.

See Also

- scikit-learn documentation: RandomForestRegressor (*https://oreil.ly/ksa9Z*)

14.6 Evaluating Random Forests with Out-of-Bag Errors

Problem

You need to evaluate a random forest model without using cross-validation.

Solution

Calculate the model's out-of-bag score:

```
# Load libraries
from sklearn.ensemble import RandomForestClassifier
from sklearn import datasets

# Load data
iris = datasets.load_iris()
features = iris.data
target = iris.target

# Create random forest classifier object
randomforest = RandomForestClassifier(
    random_state=0, n_estimators=1000, oob_score=True, n_jobs=-1)

# Train model
model = randomforest.fit(features, target)

# View out-of-bag-error
randomforest.oob_score_
```

```
0.9533333333333334
```

Discussion

In random forests, each decision tree is trained using a bootstrapped subset of observations. This means that for every tree there is a separate subset of observations not being used to train that tree. These are called out-of-bag (OOB) observations. We can use OOB observations as a test set to evaluate the performance of our random forest.

For every observation, the learning algorithm compares the observation's true value with the prediction from a subset of trees not trained using that observation. The overall score is calculated and provides a single measure of a random forest's performance. OOB score estimation is an alternative to cross-validation.

In scikit-learn, we can compute OOB scores of a random forest by setting oob_score=True in the random forest object (i.e., RandomForestClassifier). The score can be retrieved using oob_score_.

14.7 Identifying Important Features in Random Forests

Problem

You need to know which features are most important in a random forest model.

Solution

Calculate and visualize the importance of each feature by inspecting the model's feature_importances_ attribute:

```
# Load libraries
import numpy as np
import matplotlib.pyplot as plt
from sklearn.ensemble import RandomForestClassifier
from sklearn import datasets

# Load data
iris = datasets.load_iris()
features = iris.data
target = iris.target

# Create random forest classifier object
randomforest = RandomForestClassifier(random_state=0, n_jobs=-1)

# Train model
model = randomforest.fit(features, target)

# Calculate feature importances
importances = model.feature_importances_

# Sort feature importances in descending order
indices = np.argsort(importances)[::-1]

# Rearrange feature names so they match the sorted feature importances
names = [iris.feature_names[i] for i in indices]

# Create plot
plt.figure()
```

```
# Create plot title
plt.title("Feature Importance")

# Add bars
plt.bar(range(features.shape[1]), importances[indices])

# Add feature names as x-axis labels
plt.xticks(range(features.shape[1]), names, rotation=90)

# Show plot
plt.show()
```

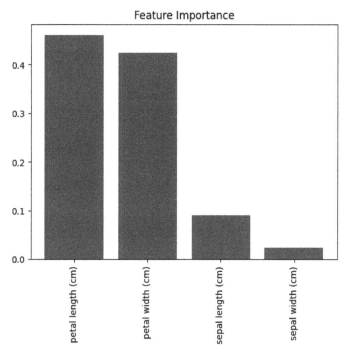

Discussion

One of the major benefits of decision trees is interpretability. Specifically, we can visualize the entire model (see Recipe 14.3). However, a random forest model is composed of tens, hundreds, or even thousands of decision trees. This makes a simple, intuitive visualization of a random forest model impractical. That said, there is another option: we can compare (and visualize) the relative importance of each feature.

In Recipe 14.3, we visualized a decision tree classifier model and saw that decision rules based only on petal width were able to classify many observations correctly. Intuitively, we can say this means that petal width is an important feature in our classifier. More formally, features with splits that have the greater mean decrease in impurity (e.g., Gini impurity or entropy in classifiers and variance in regressors) are considered more important.

However, there are two things to keep in mind regarding feature importance. First, scikit-learn requires that we break up nominal categorical features into multiple binary features. This has the effect of spreading the importance of that feature across all of the binary features and can make each feature appear to be unimportant even when the original nominal categorical feature is highly important. Second, if two features are highly correlated, one feature will claim much of the importance, making the other feature appear to be far less important, which has implications for interpretation if not considered.

In scikit-learn, classification and regression decision trees and random forests can report the relative importance of each feature using the `feature_importances_` method:

```
# View feature importances
model.feature_importances_

array([0.09090795, 0.02453104, 0.46044474, 0.42411627])
```

The higher the number, the more important the feature (all importance scores sum to 1). By plotting these values, we can add interpretability to our random forest models.

14.8 Selecting Important Features in Random Forests

Problem

You need to conduct feature selection on a random forest.

Solution

Identify the importance features and retrain the model using only the most important features:

```
# Load libraries
from sklearn.ensemble import RandomForestClassifier
from sklearn import datasets
from sklearn.feature_selection import SelectFromModel

# Load data
iris = datasets.load_iris()
features = iris.data
target = iris.target

# Create random forest classifier
randomforest = RandomForestClassifier(random_state=0, n_jobs=-1)
```

```
# Create object that selects features with importance greater
# than or equal to a threshold
selector = SelectFromModel(randomforest, threshold=0.3)

# Create new feature matrix using selector
features_important = selector.fit_transform(features, target)

# Train random forest using most important features
model = randomforest.fit(features_important, target)
```

Discussion

There are situations where we might want to reduce the number of features in our model. For example, we might want to reduce the model's variance, or we might want to improve interpretability by including only the most important features.

In scikit-learn we can use a simple two-stage workflow to create a model with reduced features. First, we train a random forest model using all features. Then, we use this model to identify the most important features. Next, we create a new feature matrix that includes only these features. In our solution, we used the SelectFromModel method to create a feature matrix containing only features with an importance greater than or equal to some threshold value. Finally, we created a new model using only those features.

We must note two caveats to this approach. First, nominal categorical features that have been one-hot encoded will see the feature importance diluted across the binary features. Second, the feature importance of highly correlated features will be effectively assigned to one feature and not evenly distributed across both features.

See Also

- Variable Selection Using Random Forests, Robin Genuer, Jean-Michel Poggi, and Christine Tuleau-Malot (*https://oreil.ly/y9k2U*)

14.9 Handling Imbalanced Classes

Problem

You have a target vector with highly imbalanced classes and want to train a random forest model.

Solution

Train a decision tree or random forest model with class_weight="balanced":

```
# Load libraries
import numpy as np
```

```
from sklearn.ensemble import RandomForestClassifier
from sklearn import datasets

# Load data
iris = datasets.load_iris()
features = iris.data
target = iris.target

# Make class highly imbalanced by removing first 40 observations
features = features[40:,:]
target = target[40:]

# Create target vector indicating if class 0, otherwise 1
target = np.where((target == 0), 0, 1)

# Create random forest classifier object
randomforest = RandomForestClassifier(
    random_state=0, n_jobs=-1, class_weight="balanced")

# Train model
model = randomforest.fit(features, target)
```

Discussion

Imbalanced classes are a common problem when we are doing machine learning in the real world. Left unaddressed, the presence of imbalanced classes can reduce the performance of our model. We will discuss handling imbalanced classes during preprocessing in Recipe 17.5. However, many learning algorithms in scikit-learn come with built-in methods for correcting for imbalanced classes. We can set RandomForestClassifier to correct for imbalanced classes using the class_weight parameter. If supplied with a dictionary in the form of class names and their desired weights (e.g., {"male": 0.2, "female": 0.8}), RandomForestClassifier will weight the classes accordingly. However, often a more useful argument is bal anced, wherein classes are automatically weighted inversely proportional to how frequently they appear in the data:

$$w_j = \frac{n}{k n_j}$$

where w_j is the weight of class j, n is the number of observations, n_j is the number of observations in class j, and k is the total number of classes. For example, in our solution we have 2 classes (k), 110 observations (n), and 10 and 100 observations in each class, respectively (n_j). If we weight the classes using class_weight="balanced", then the smaller class is weighted more:

```
# Calculate weight for small class
110/(2*10)
```

```
5.5
```

while the larger class is weighted less:

```
# Calculate weight for large class
110/(2*100)
```

```
0.55
```

14.10 Controlling Tree Size

Problem

You want to manually determine the structure and size of a decision tree.

Solution

Use the tree structure parameters in scikit-learn tree-based learning algorithms:

```
# Load libraries
from sklearn.tree import DecisionTreeClassifier
from sklearn import datasets

# Load data
iris = datasets.load_iris()
features = iris.data
target = iris.target

# Create decision tree classifier object
decisiontree = DecisionTreeClassifier(random_state=0,
                                      max_depth=None,
                                      min_samples_split=2,
                                      min_samples_leaf=1,
                                      min_weight_fraction_leaf=0,
                                      max_leaf_nodes=None,
                                      min_impurity_decrease=0)

# Train model
model = decisiontree.fit(features, target)
```

Discussion

scikit-learn's tree-based learning algorithms have a variety of techniques for controlling the size of decision trees. These are accessed through parameters:

max_depth
    Maximum depth of the tree. If None, the tree is grown until all leaves are pure. If an integer, the tree is effectively "pruned" to that depth.

`min_samples_split`

Minimum number of observations at a node before that node is split. If an integer is supplied as an argument, it determines the raw minimum, while if a float is supplied, the minimum is the percent of total observations.

`min_samples_leaf`

Minimum number of observations required to be at a leaf. Uses the same arguments as `min_samples_split`.

`max_leaf_nodes`

Maximum number of leaves.

`min_impurity_split`

Minimum impurity decrease required before a split is performed.

While it is useful to know these parameters exist, most likely we will only be using `max_depth` and `min_impurity_split` because shallower trees (sometimes called *stumps*) are simpler models and thus have lower variance.

14.11 Improving Performance Through Boosting

Problem

You need a model with better performance than decision trees or random forests.

Solution

Train a boosted model using `AdaBoostClassifier` or `AdaBoostRegressor`:

```
# Load libraries
from sklearn.ensemble import AdaBoostClassifier
from sklearn import datasets

# Load data
iris = datasets.load_iris()
features = iris.data
target = iris.target

# Create adaboost tree classifier object
adaboost = AdaBoostClassifier(random_state=0)

# Train model
model = adaboost.fit(features, target)
```

Discussion

In a random forest, an ensemble (group) of randomized decision trees predicts the target vector. An alternative, and often more powerful, approach is called *boosting*. In one form of boosting called AdaBoost, we iteratively train a series of weak models (most often a shallow decision tree, sometimes called a stump), each iteration giving higher priority to observations the previous model predicted incorrectly. More specifically, in AdaBoost:

1. Assign every observation, x_i, an initial weight value, $w_i = \frac{1}{n}$, where n is the total number of observations in the data.

2. Train a "weak" model on the data.

3. For each observation:

    a. If weak model predicts x_i correctly, w_i is decreased.

    b. If weak model predicts x_i incorrectly, w_i is increased.

4. Train a new weak model where observations with greater w_i are given greater priority.

5. Repeat steps 4 and 5 until the data is perfectly predicted or a preset number of weak models has been trained.

The result is an aggregated model where individual weak models focus on more difficult (from a prediction perspective) observations. In scikit-learn, we can implement AdaBoost using `AdaBoostClassifier` or `AdaBoostRegressor`. The most important parameters are `base_estimator`, `n_estimators`, `learning_rate`, and `loss`:

`base_estimator`
> `base_estimator` is the learning algorithm to use to train the weak models. The most common learner to use with AdaBoost is a decision tree, the parameter's default argument.

`n_estimators`
> `n_estimators` is the number of models to iteratively train.

`learning_rate`
> `learning_rate` is the contribution of each model to the weights, and it defaults to 1. Reducing the learning rate will mean the weights will be increased or decreased to a small degree, forcing the model to train slower (but sometimes resulting in better performance scores).

loss

> loss is exclusive to `AdaBoostRegressor` and sets the loss function to use when updating weights. This defaults to a linear loss function but can be changed to `square` or `exponential`.

See Also

- Explaining AdaBoost, Robert E. Schapire (*https://oreil.ly/5E1v4*)

14.12 Training an XGBoost Model

Problem

You need to train a tree-based model with high predictive power.

Solution

Use the `xgboost` Python library:

```
# Load libraries
import xgboost as xgb
from sklearn import datasets, preprocessing
from sklearn.metrics import classification_report
from numpy import argmax

# Load data
iris = datasets.load_iris()
features = iris.data
target = iris.target

# Create dataset
xgb_train = xgb.DMatrix(features, label=target)

# Define parameters
param = {
    'objective': 'multi:softprob',
    'num_class': 3
}

# Train model
gbm = xgb.train(param, xgb_train)

# Get predictions
predictions = argmax(gbm.predict(xgb_train), axis=1)

# Get a classification report
print(classification_report(target, predictions))
```

```
           precision    recall  f1-score   support

        0       1.00      1.00      1.00        50
        1       1.00      0.96      0.98        50
        2       0.96      1.00      0.98        50

 accuracy                           0.99       150
macro avg        0.99      0.99      0.99       150
weighted avg     0.99      0.99      0.99       150
```

Discussion

XGBoost (which stands for Extreme Gradient Boosting) is a very popular gradient boosting algorithm in the machine learning space. Though it is not always a tree-based model, it is frequently applied to ensembles of decision trees. It gained much of its popularity due to widespread success on the machine learning competition website Kaggle and has since been a reliable algorithm for improving performance beyond that of typical random forests or gradient boosted machines.

Although XGBoost is known for being computationally intensive, computational performance optimizations (such as GPU support) over the last few years have made iterating quickly with XGBoost significantly easier, and it remains a common choice of algorithm when statistical performance is a requirement.

See Also

- XGBoost documentation (*https://oreil.ly/cAuGX*)

14.13 Improving Real-Time Performance with LightGBM

Problem

You need to train a gradient boosted tree-based model that is computationally optimized.

Solution

Use the gradient boosted machine library `lightgbm`:

```
# Load libraries
import lightgbm as lgb
from sklearn import datasets, preprocessing
from sklearn.metrics import classification_report
from numpy import argmax

# Load data
iris = datasets.load_iris()
features = iris.data
```

```
target = iris.target

# Create dataset
lgb_train = lgb.Dataset(features, target)

# Define parameters
params = {
    'objective': 'multiclass',
    'num_class': 3,
    'verbose': -1,
}

# Train model
gbm = lgb.train(params, lgb_train)

# Get predictions
predictions = argmax(gbm.predict(features), axis=1)

# Get a classification report
print(classification_report(target, predictions))
              precision    recall  f1-score   support

           0       1.00      1.00      1.00        50
           1       1.00      1.00      1.00        50
           2       1.00      1.00      1.00        50

    accuracy                           1.00       150
   macro avg       1.00      1.00      1.00       150
weighted avg       1.00      1.00      1.00       150
```

Discussion

The `lightgbm` library is used for gradient boosted machines and is highly optimized for training time, inference, and GPU support. As a result of its computational efficiency, it's often used in production and in large scale settings. Although scikit-learn models are typically easier to use, some libraries, such as `lightgbm`, can be handy when you're limited by large data or strict model training/serving times.

See Also

- LightGBM documentation (*https://oreil.ly/XDcpG*)
- CatBoost documentation (another optimized library for GBMs) (*https://oreil.ly/4Bb8g*)

## CHAPTER 15

K-Nearest Neighbors

15.0 Introduction

The k-nearest neighbors (KNN) classifier is one of the simplest yet most commonly used classifiers in supervised machine learning. KNN is often considered a lazy learner; it doesn't technically train a model to make predictions. Instead an observation is predicted to be the same class as that of the largest proportion of the k nearest observations.

For example, if an observation with an unknown class is surrounded by an observation of class 1, then the observation is classified as class 1. In this chapter we will explore how to use scikit-learn to create and use a KNN classifier.

15.1 Finding an Observation's Nearest Neighbors

Problem

You need to find an observation's k nearest observations (neighbors).

Solution

Use scikit-learn's `NearestNeighbors`:

```
# Load libraries
from sklearn import datasets
from sklearn.neighbors import NearestNeighbors
from sklearn.preprocessing import StandardScaler

# Load data
iris = datasets.load_iris()
features = iris.data
```

```
# Create standardizer
standardizer = StandardScaler()

# Standardize features
features_standardized = standardizer.fit_transform(features)

# Two nearest neighbors
nearest_neighbors = NearestNeighbors(n_neighbors=2).fit(features_standardized)

# Create an observation
new_observation = [ 1,  1,  1,  1]

# Find distances and indices of the observation's nearest neighbors
distances, indices = nearest_neighbors.kneighbors([new_observation])

# View the nearest neighbors
features_standardized[indices]

array([[[1.03800476, 0.55861082, 1.10378283, 1.18556721],
        [0.79566902, 0.32841405, 0.76275827, 1.05393502]]])
```

Discussion

In our solution we used the dataset of iris flowers. We created an observation, new_observation, with some values and then found the two observations that are closest to our observation. indices contains the locations of the observations in our dataset that are closest, so X[indices] displays the values of those observations. Intuitively, distance can be thought of as a measure of similarity, so the two closest observations are the two flowers most similar to the flower we created.

How do we measure distance? scikit-learn offers a wide variety of distance metrics, d, including Euclidean:

$$d_{euclidean} = \sqrt{\sum_{i=1}^{n}(x_i - y_i)^2}$$

and Manhattan distance:

$$d_{manhattan} = \sum_{i=1}^{n}|x_i - y_i|$$

By default, NearestNeighbors uses Minkowski distance:

$$d_{minkowski} = \left(\sum_{i=1}^{n}|x_i - y_i|^p\right)^{1/p}$$

where x_i and y_i are the two observations we are calculating the distance between. Minkowski includes a hyperparameter, p, where $p = 1$ is Manhattan distance and $p = 2$ is Euclidean distance, and so on. By default in scikit-learn $p = 2$.

We can set the distance metric using the `metric` parameter:

```
# Find two nearest neighbors based on Euclidean distance
nearestneighbors_euclidean = NearestNeighbors(
    n_neighbors=2, metric='euclidean').fit(features_standardized)
```

The `distance` variable we created contains the actual distance measurement to each of the two nearest neighbors:

```
# View distances
distances
```

```
array([[0.49140089, 0.74294782]])
```

In addition, we can use `kneighbors_graph` to create a matrix indicating each observation's nearest neighbors:

```
# Find each observation's three nearest neighbors
# based on Euclidean distance (including itself)
nearestneighbors_euclidean = NearestNeighbors(
    n_neighbors=3, metric="euclidean").fit(features_standardized)

# List of lists indicating each observation's three nearest neighbors
# (including itself)
nearest_neighbors_with_self = nearestneighbors_euclidean.kneighbors_graph(
    features_standardized).toarray()

# Remove 1s marking an observation is a nearest neighbor to itself
for i, x in enumerate(nearest_neighbors_with_self):
    x[i] = 0

# View first observation's two nearest neighbors
nearest_neighbors_with_self[0]
```

```
array([0., 0., 0., 0., 0., 0., 0., 0., 0., 0., 0., 0., 0., 0., 0., 0., 0.,
       1., 0., 0., 0., 0., 0., 0., 0., 0., 1., 0., 0., 0., 0., 0., 0.,
       0., 0., 0., 0., 0., 0., 0., 0., 0., 0., 0., 0., 0., 0., 0., 0.,
       0., 0., 0., 0., 0., 0., 0., 0., 0., 0., 0., 0., 0., 0., 0., 0.,
       0., 0., 0., 0., 0., 0., 0., 0., 0., 0., 0., 0., 0., 0., 0., 0.,
       0., 0., 0., 0., 0., 0., 0., 0., 0., 0., 0., 0., 0., 0., 0., 0.,
       0., 0., 0., 0., 0., 0., 0., 0., 0., 0., 0., 0., 0., 0., 0., 0.,
       0., 0., 0., 0., 0., 0., 0., 0., 0., 0., 0., 0., 0., 0., 0., 0.,
       0., 0., 0., 0., 0., 0., 0., 0., 0., 0., 0., 0., 0., 0.])
```

When we are finding nearest neighbors or using any learning algorithm based on distance, it is important to transform features so that they are on the same scale. This is because the distance metrics treat all features as if they were on the same scale, but if one feature is in millions of dollars and a second feature is in percentages, the distance calculated will be biased toward the former. In our solution we addressed this potential issue by standardizing the features using StandardScaler.

15.2 Creating a K-Nearest Neighbors Classifier

Problem

Given an observation of unknown class, you need to predict its class based on the class of its neighbors.

Solution

If the dataset is not very large, use KNeighborsClassifier:

```
# Load libraries
from sklearn.neighbors import KNeighborsClassifier
from sklearn.preprocessing import StandardScaler
from sklearn import datasets

# Load data
iris = datasets.load_iris()
X = iris.data
y = iris.target

# Create standardizer
standardizer = StandardScaler()

# Standardize features
X_std = standardizer.fit_transform(X)

# Train a KNN classifier with 5 neighbors
knn = KNeighborsClassifier(n_neighbors=5, n_jobs=-1).fit(X_std, y)

# Create two observations
new_observations = [[ 0.75,  0.75,  0.75,  0.75],
                    [ 1,  1,  1,  1]]

# Predict the class of two observations
knn.predict(new_observations)

array([1, 2])
```

Discussion

In KNN, given an observation, x_u, with an unknown target class, the algorithm first identifies the k closest observations (sometimes called x_u's *neighborhood*) based on some distance metric (e.g., Euclidean distance), then these k observations "vote" based on their class, and the class that wins the vote is x_u's predicted class. More formally, the probability x_u of some class j is:

$$\frac{1}{k} \sum_{i \in \nu} I(y_i = j)$$

where ν is the k observation in x_u's neighborhood, y_i is the class of the ith observation, and I is an indicator function (i.e., 1 is true, 0 otherwise). In scikit-learn we can see these probabilities using `predict_proba`:

```
# View probability that each observation is one of three classes
knn.predict_proba(new_observations)

array([[0. , 0.6, 0.4],
       [0. , 0. , 1. ]])
```

The class with the highest probability becomes the predicted class. For example, in the preceding output, the first observation should be class 1 ($Pr = 0.6$) while the second observation should be class 2 ($Pr = 1$), and this is just what we see:

```
knn.predict(new_observations)

array([1, 2])
```

KNeighborsClassifier contains a number of important parameters to consider. First, `metric` sets the distance metric used. Second, `n_jobs` determines how many of the computer's cores to use. Because making a prediction requires calculating the distance from a point to every single point in the data, using multiple cores is highly recommended. Third, `algorithm` sets the method used to calculate the nearest neighbors. While there are real differences in the algorithms, by default KNeighborsClassifier attempts to auto-select the best algorithm so you often don't need to worry about this parameter. Fourth, by default KNeighborsClassifier works how we described previously, with each observation in the neighborhood getting one vote; however, if we set the `weights` parameter to `distance`, the closer observations' votes are weighted more than observations farther away. Intuitively this make sense, since more similar neighbors might tell us more about an observation's class than others.

Finally, because distance calculations treat all features as if they are on the same scale, it is important to standardize the features prior to using a KNN classifier.

15.3 Identifying the Best Neighborhood Size

Problem

You want to select the best value for k in a k-nearest neighbors classifier.

Solution

Use model selection techniques like `GridSearchCV`:

```
# Load libraries
from sklearn.neighbors import KNeighborsClassifier
from sklearn import datasets
from sklearn.preprocessing import StandardScaler
from sklearn.pipeline import Pipeline, FeatureUnion
from sklearn.model_selection import GridSearchCV

# Load data
iris = datasets.load_iris()
features = iris.data
target = iris.target

# Create standardizer
standardizer = StandardScaler()

# Create a KNN classifier
knn = KNeighborsClassifier(n_neighbors=5, n_jobs=-1)

# Create a pipeline
pipe = Pipeline([("standardizer", standardizer), ("knn", knn)])

# Create space of candidate values
search_space = [{"knn__n_neighbors": [1, 2, 3, 4, 5, 6, 7, 8, 9, 10]}]

# Create grid search
classifier = GridSearchCV(
    pipe, search_space, cv=5, verbose=0).fit(features_standardized, target)
```

Discussion

The size of k has real implications in KNN classifiers. In machine learning we are trying to find a balance between bias and variance, and in few places is that as explicit as the value of k. If $k = n$, where n is the number of observations, then we have high bias but low variance. If $k = 1$, we will have low bias but high variance. The best model will come from finding the value of k that balances this bias-variance trade-off. In our solution, we used `GridSearchCV` to conduct five-fold cross-validation on KNN classifiers with different values of k. When that is completed, we can see the k that produces the best model:

```
# Best neighborhood size (k)
classifier.best_estimator_.get_params()["knn__n_neighbors"]
```

6

15.4 Creating a Radius-Based Nearest Neighbors Classifier

Problem

Given an observation of unknown class, you need to predict its class based on the class of all observations within a certain distance.

Solution

Use RadiusNeighborsClassifier:

```python
# Load libraries
from sklearn.neighbors import RadiusNeighborsClassifier
from sklearn.preprocessing import StandardScaler
from sklearn import datasets

# Load data
iris = datasets.load_iris()
features = iris.data
target = iris.target

# Create standardizer
standardizer = StandardScaler()

# Standardize features
features_standardized = standardizer.fit_transform(features)

# Train a radius neighbors classifier
rnn = RadiusNeighborsClassifier(
    radius=.5, n_jobs=-1).fit(features_standardized, target)

# Create two observations
new_observations = [[ 1,  1,  1,  1]]

# Predict the class of two observations
rnn.predict(new_observations)

array([2])
```

Discussion

In KNN classification, an observation's class is predicted from the classes of its k neighbors. A less common technique is classification in a *radius-based nearest neighbor* (RNN) classifier, where an observation's class is predicted from the classes of all observations within a given radius r.

In scikit-learn, RadiusNeighborsClassifier is very similar to KNeighbors Classifier, with the exception of two parameters. First, in RadiusNeighbors Classifier we need to specify the radius of the fixed area used to determine if an observation is a neighbor using radius. Unless there is some substantive reason for setting radius to some value, it's best to treat it like any other hyperparameter and tune it during model selection. The second useful parameter is outlier_label, which indicates what label to give an observation that has no observations within the radius—which itself can be a useful tool for identifying outliers.

15.5 Finding Approximate Nearest Neighbors

Problem

You want to fetch nearest neighbors for big data at low latency:

Solution

Use an *approximate nearest neighbors* (ANN) based search with Facebook's faiss library:

```
# Load libraries
import faiss
import numpy as np
from sklearn import datasets
from sklearn.neighbors import NearestNeighbors
from sklearn.preprocessing import StandardScaler

# Load data
iris = datasets.load_iris()
features = iris.data

# Create standardizer
standardizer = StandardScaler()

# Standardize features
features_standardized = standardizer.fit_transform(features)

# Set faiss parameters
n_features = features_standardized.shape[1]
nlist = 3
k = 2

# Create an IVF index
quantizer = faiss.IndexFlatIP(n_features)
index = faiss.IndexIVFFlat(quantizer, n_features, nlist)

# Train the index and add feature vectors
index.train(features_standardized)
```

```
index.add(features_standardized)

# Create an observation
new_observation = np.array([[ 1,  1,  1,  1]])

# Search the index for the 2 nearest neighbors
distances, indices = index.search(new_observation, k)

# Show the feature vectors for the two nearest neighbors
np.array([list(features_standardized[i]) for i in indices[0]])

array([[1.03800476, 0.55861082, 1.10378283, 1.18556721],
       [0.79566902, 0.32841405, 0.76275827, 1.05393502]])
```

Discussion

KNN is a great approach to finding the most similar observations in a set of small data. However, as the size of our data increases, so does the time it takes to compute the distance between any one observation and all other points in our dataset. Large scale ML systems such as search or recommendation engines often use some form of vector similarity measure to retrieve similar observations. But at scale in real time, where we need results in less than 100 ms, KNN becomes infeasible to run.

ANN helps us overcome this problem by sacrificing some of the quality of the exact nearest neighbors search in favor of speed. This is to say that although the order and items in the first 10 nearest neighbors of an ANN search may not match the first 10 results from an exact KNN search, we get those first 10 nearest neighbors much faster.

In this example, we use an ANN approach called inverted file index (IVF). This approach works by using clustering to limit the scope of the search space for our nearest neighbors search. IVF uses Voronoi tessellations to partition our search space into a number of distinct areas (or clusters). And when we go to find nearest neighbors, we visit a limited number of clusters to find similar observations, as opposed to conducting a comparison across every point in our dataset.

How Voronoi tessellations are created from data is best visualized using simple data. Take a scatter plot of random data visualized in two dimensions, as shown in Figure 15-1.

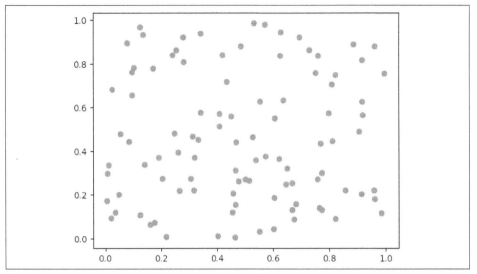

Figure 15-1. A scatter plot of randomly generated two-dimensional data

Using Voronoi tessellations, we can create a number of subspaces, each of which contains only a small subset of the total observations we want to search, as shown in Figure 15-2.

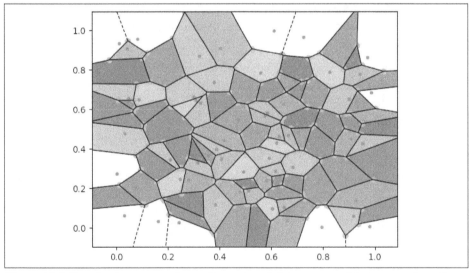

Figure 15-2. Randomly generated two-dimensional data separated into a number of different subspaces

The nlist parameter in the Faiss library lets us define the number of clusters we want to create. An additional parameter, nprobe, can be used at query time to define the number of clusters we want to search to retrieve nearest neighbors for a given observation. Increasing both nlist and nprobe can result in higher quality neighbors at the cost of larger computational effort and thus a longer runtime for IVF indices. Decreasing each of these parameters will have the inverse effect, and your code will run faster but at the risk of returning lower quality results.

Notice this example returns the exact same output as the first recipe in this chapter. This is because we are working with very small data and using only three clusters, which makes it unlikely our ANN results will differ significantly from our KNN results.

See Also

- Nearest Neighbor Indexes for Similarity Search (different ANN index types) (*https://oreil.ly/DVqgn*)

15.6 Evaluating Approximate Nearest Neighbors

Problem

You want to see how your ANN compares to exact nearest neighbors (KNN):

Solution

Compute the recall @k nearest neighbors of the ANN as compared to the KNN:

```
# Load libraries
import faiss
import numpy as np
from sklearn import datasets
from sklearn.neighbors import NearestNeighbors
from sklearn.preprocessing import StandardScaler

# Number of nearest neighbors
k = 10

# Load data
iris = datasets.load_iris()
features = iris.data

# Create standardizer
standardizer = StandardScaler()

# Standardize features
features_standardized = standardizer.fit_transform(features)
```

```
# Create KNN with 10 NN
nearest_neighbors = NearestNeighbors(n_neighbors=k).fit(features_standardized)

# Set faiss parameters
n_features = features_standardized.shape[1]
nlist = 3

# Create an IVF index
quantizer = faiss.IndexFlatIP(n_features)
index = faiss.IndexIVFFlat(quantizer, n_features, nlist)

# Train the index and add feature vectors
index.train(features_standardized)
index.add(features_standardized)
index.nprobe = 1

# Create an observation
new_observation = np.array([[ 1,  1,  1,  1]])

# Find distances and indices of the observation's exact nearest neighbors
knn_distances, knn_indices = nearest_neighbors.kneighbors(new_observation)

# Search the index for the two nearest neighbors
ivf_distances, ivf_indices = index.search(new_observation, k)

# Get the set overlap
recalled_items = set(list(knn_indices[0])) & set(list(ivf_indices[0]))

# Print the recall
print(f"Recall @k={k}: {len(recalled_items)/k * 100}%")

Recall @k=10: 100.0%
```

Discussion

Recall @k is most simply defined as the number of items returned by the ANN at some *k* nearest neighbors that also appear in the exact nearest neighbors at the same *k*, divided by *k*. In this example, at 10 nearest neighbors we have 100% recall, which means that our ANN is returning the same indices as our KNN at k=10 (though not necessarily in the same order).

Recall is a common metric to use when evaluating ANNs against exact nearest neighbors.

See Also

- Google's note on ANN for its Vertex Matching Engine Service (*https://oreil.ly/-COc9*)

## CHAPTER 16

Logistic Regression

16.0 Introduction

Despite being called a regression, *logistic regression* is actually a widely used supervised classification technique. Logistic regression (and its extensions, like multinomial logistic regression) is a straightforward, well-understood approach to predicting the probability that an observation is of a certain class. In this chapter, we will cover training a variety of classifiers using logistic regression in scikit-learn.

16.1 Training a Binary Classifier

Problem

You need to train a simple classifier model.

Solution

Train a logistic regression in scikit-learn using `LogisticRegression`:

```
# Load libraries
from sklearn.linear_model import LogisticRegression
from sklearn import datasets
from sklearn.preprocessing import StandardScaler

# Load data with only two classes
iris = datasets.load_iris()
features = iris.data[:100,:]
target = iris.target[:100]

# Standardize features
scaler = StandardScaler()
features_standardized = scaler.fit_transform(features)
```

```
# Create logistic regression object
logistic_regression = LogisticRegression(random_state=0)

# Train model
model = logistic_regression.fit(features_standardized, target)
```

Discussion

Despite having "regression" in its name, a logistic regression is actually a widely used binary classifier (i.e., the target vector can take only two values). In a logistic regression, a linear model (e.g., $\beta_0 + \beta_1 x$) is included in a logistic (also called sigmoid) function, $\frac{1}{1 + e^{-z}}$, such that:

$$P(y_i = 1 \mid X) = \frac{1}{1 + e^{-(\beta_0 + \beta_1 x)}}$$

where $P(y_i = 1 \mid X)$ is the probability of the ith observation's target value, y_i, being class 1; X is the training data; β_0 and β_1 are the parameters to be learned; and e is Euler's number. The effect of the logistic function is to constrain the value of the function's output to between 0 and 1, so that it can be interpreted as a probability. If $P(y_i = 1 \mid X)$ is greater than 0.5, class 1 is predicted; otherwise, class 0 is predicted.

In scikit-learn, we can train a logistic regression model using `LogisticRegression`. Once it is trained, we can use the model to predict the class of new observations:

```
# Create new observation
new_observation = [[.5, .5, .5, .5]]

# Predict class
model.predict(new_observation)

array([1])
```

In this example, our observation was predicted to be class 1. Additionally, we can see the probability that an observation is a member of each class:

```
# View predicted probabilities
model.predict_proba(new_observation)

array([[0.17738424, 0.82261576]])
```

Our observation had a 17.7% chance of being class 0 and an 82.2% chance of being class 1.

16.2 Training a Multiclass Classifier

Problem

Given more than two classes, you need to train a classifier model.

Solution

Train a logistic regression in scikit-learn with `LogisticRegression` using one-vs-rest or multinomial methods:

```
# Load libraries
from sklearn.linear_model import LogisticRegression
from sklearn import datasets
from sklearn.preprocessing import StandardScaler

# Load data
iris = datasets.load_iris()
features = iris.data
target = iris.target

# Standardize features
scaler = StandardScaler()
features_standardized = scaler.fit_transform(features)

# Create one-vs-rest logistic regression object
logistic_regression = LogisticRegression(random_state=0, multi_class="ovr")

# Train model
model = logistic_regression.fit(features_standardized, target)
```

Discussion

On their own, logistic regressions are only binary classifiers, meaning they cannot handle target vectors with more than two classes. However, two clever extensions to logistic regression do just that. First, in *one-vs-rest* logistic regression (OvR) a separate model is trained for each class predicted, whether an observation is that class or not (thus making it a binary classification problem). It assumes that each classification problem (e.g., class 0 or not) is independent.

Alternatively, in *multinomial logistic regression* (MLR), the logistic function we saw in Recipe 16.1 is replaced with a softmax function:

$$P(y_i = k \mid X) = \frac{e^{\beta_k x_i}}{\sum_{j=1}^{K} e^{\beta_j x_i}}$$

---

where $P(y_i = k \mid X)$ is the probability of the ith observation's target value, y_i, being in class k, and K is the total number of classes. One practical advantage of MLR is that its predicted probabilities using the `predict_proba` method are more reliable (i.e., better calibrated).

When using `LogisticRegression` we can select which of the two techniques we want, with OvR (`ovr`) being the default argument. We can switch to MLR by setting the argument to `multinomial`.

16.3 Reducing Variance Through Regularization

Problem

You need to reduce the variance of your logistic regression model.

Solution

Tune the regularization strength hyperparameter, C:

```
# Load libraries
from sklearn.linear_model import LogisticRegressionCV
from sklearn import datasets
from sklearn.preprocessing import StandardScaler

# Load data
iris = datasets.load_iris()
features = iris.data
target = iris.target

# Standardize features
scaler = StandardScaler()
features_standardized = scaler.fit_transform(features)

# Create decision tree regression object
logistic_regression = LogisticRegressionCV(
    penalty='l2', Cs=10, random_state=0, n_jobs=-1)

# Train model
model = logistic_regression.fit(features_standardized, target)
```

Discussion

Regularization is a method of penalizing complex models to reduce their variance. Specifically, a penalty term is added to the loss function we are trying to minimize, typically the L1 and L2 penalties. In the L1 penalty:

$$\alpha \sum_{j=1}^{p} \left| \widehat{\beta}_j \right|$$

where $\widehat{\beta}_j$ is the parameters of the jth of p features being learned, and α is a hyperparameter denoting the regularization strength. With the L2 penalty:

$$\alpha \sum_{j=1}^{p} \widehat{\beta}_j^{\,2}$$

Higher values of α increase the penalty for larger parameter values (i.e., more complex models). scikit-learn follows the common method of using C instead of α where C is the inverse of the regularization strength: $C = \frac{1}{\alpha}$. To reduce variance while using logistic regression, we can treat C as a hyperparameter to be tuned to find the value of C that creates the best model. In scikit-learn we can use the LogisticRegressionCV class to efficiently tune C. LogisticRegressionCV's parameter Cs can either accept a range of values for C to search over (if a list of floats is supplied as an argument) or, if supplied an integer, will generate a list of that many candidate values drawn from a logarithmic scale between –10,000 and 10,000.

Unfortunately, LogisticRegressionCV does not allow us to search over different penalty terms. To do this we have to use the less efficient model selection techniques discussed in Chapter 12.

16.4 Training a Classifier on Very Large Data

Problem

You need to train a simple classifier model on a very large set of data.

Solution

Train a logistic regression in scikit-learn with LogisticRegression using the *stochastic average gradient* (SAG) solver:

```
# Load libraries
from sklearn.linear_model import LogisticRegression
from sklearn import datasets
from sklearn.preprocessing import StandardScaler

# Load data
iris = datasets.load_iris()
features = iris.data
target = iris.target
```

```
# Standardize features
scaler = StandardScaler()
features_standardized = scaler.fit_transform(features)

# Create logistic regression object
logistic_regression = LogisticRegression(random_state=0, solver="sag")

# Train model
model = logistic_regression.fit(features_standardized, target)
```

Discussion

scikit-learn's `LogisticRegression` offers a number of techniques for training a logistic regression, called *solvers*. Most of the time scikit-learn will select the best solver automatically for us or warn us that we cannot do something with that solver. However, there is one particular case we should be aware of.

While an exact explanation is beyond the bounds of this book (for more information see Mark Schmidt's slides in the "See Also" section of this recipe), stochastic average gradient descent allows us to train a model much faster than other solvers when our data is very large. However, it is also very sensitive to feature scaling, so standardizing our features is particularly important. We can set our learning algorithm to use this solver by setting `solver="sag"`.

See Also

- Minimizing Finite Sums with the Stochastic Average Gradient Algorithm, Mark Schmidt (*https://oreil.ly/K5rEG*)

16.5 Handling Imbalanced Classes

Problem

You need to train a simple classifier model.

Solution

Train a logistic regression in scikit-learn using `LogisticRegression`:

```
# Load libraries
import numpy as np
from sklearn.linear_model import LogisticRegression
from sklearn import datasets
from sklearn.preprocessing import StandardScaler

# Load data
iris = datasets.load_iris()
```

```
features = iris.data
target = iris.target

# Make class highly imbalanced by removing first 40 observations
features = features[40:,:]
target = target[40:]

# Create target vector indicating if class 0, otherwise 1
target = np.where((target == 0), 0, 1)

# Standardize features
scaler = StandardScaler()
features_standardized = scaler.fit_transform(features)

# Create decision tree regression object
logistic_regression = LogisticRegression(random_state=0, class_weight="balanced")

# Train model
model = logistic_regression.fit(features_standardized, target)
```

Discussion

Like many other learning algorithms in scikit-learn, `LogisticRegression` comes with a built-in method of handling imbalanced classes. If we have highly imbalanced classes and have not addressed it during preprocessing, we have the option of using the `class_weight` parameter to weight the classes to make certain we have a balanced mix of each class. Specifically, the `balanced` argument will automatically weigh classes inversely proportional to their frequency:

$$w_j = \frac{n}{kn_j}$$

where w_j is the weight to class j, n is the number of observations, n_j is the number of observations in class j, and k is the total number of classes.

## CHAPTER 17

Support Vector Machines

17.0 Introduction

To understand support vector machines, we must understand hyperplanes. Formally, a *hyperplane* is an *n – 1* subspace in an *n*-dimensional space. While that sounds complex, it actually is pretty simple. For example, if we wanted to divide a two-dimensional space, we'd use a one-dimensional hyperplane (i.e., a line). If we wanted to divide a three-dimensional space, we'd use a two-dimensional hyperplane (i.e., a flat piece of paper or a bed sheet). A hyperplane is simply a generalization of that concept into *n* dimensions.

Support vector machines classify data by finding the hyperplane that maximizes the margin between the classes in the training data. In a two-dimensional example with two classes, we can think of a hyperplane as the widest straight "band" (i.e., line with margins) that separates the two classes.

In this chapter, we cover training support vector machines in a variety of situations and dive under the hood to look at how we can extend the approach to tackle common problems.

17.1 Training a Linear Classifier

Problem

You need to train a model to classify observations.

Solution

Use a *support vector classifier* (SVC) to find the hyperplane that maximizes the margins between the classes:

```
# Load libraries
from sklearn.svm import LinearSVC
from sklearn import datasets
from sklearn.preprocessing import StandardScaler
import numpy as np

# Load data with only two classes and two features
iris = datasets.load_iris()
features = iris.data[:100,:2]
target = iris.target[:100]

# Standardize features
scaler = StandardScaler()
features_standardized = scaler.fit_transform(features)

# Create support vector classifier
svc = LinearSVC(C=1.0)

# Train model
model = svc.fit(features_standardized, target)
```

Discussion

scikit-learn's LinearSVC implements a simple SVC. To get an intuition behind what
an SVC is doing, let's plot out the data and hyperplane. While SVCs work well in
high dimensions, in our solution we loaded only two features and took a subset of
observations so that the data contains only two classes. This will let us visualize the
model. Recall that SVC attempts to find the hyperplane—a line when we have only
two dimensions—with the maximum margin between the classes. In the following
code we plot the two classes on a two-dimensional space, then draw the hyperplane:

```
# Load library
from matplotlib import pyplot as plt

# Plot data points and color using their class
color = ["black" if c == 0 else "lightgrey" for c in target]
plt.scatter(features_standardized[:,0], features_standardized[:,1], c=color)

# Create the hyperplane
w = svc.coef_[0]
a = -w[0] / w[1]
xx = np.linspace(-2.5, 2.5)
yy = a * xx - (svc.intercept_[0]) / w[1]

# Plot the hyperplane
plt.plot(xx, yy)
plt.axis("off"), plt.show();
```

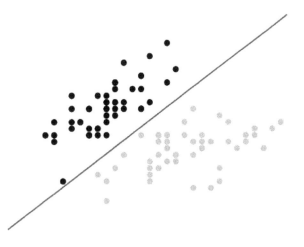

In this visualization, all observations of class 0 are black and observations of class 1 are light gray. The hyperplane is the decision boundary deciding how new observations are classified. Specifically, any observation above the line will by classified as class 0, while any observation below the line will be classified as class 1. We can prove this by creating a new observation in the top-left corner of our visualization, meaning it should be predicted to be class 0:

```
# Create new observation
new_observation = [[ -2,    3]]

# Predict class of new observation
svc.predict(new_observation)

array([0])
```

There are a few things to note about SVCs. First, for the sake of visualization, we limited our example to a binary example (i.e., only two classes); however, SVCs can work well with multiple classes. Second, as our visualization shows, the hyperplane is by definition linear (i.e., not curved). This was okay in this example because the data was linearly separable, meaning there was a hyperplane that could perfectly separate the two classes. Unfortunately, in the real world this is rarely the case.

More typically, we will not be able to perfectly separate classes. In these situations there is a balance between SVC maximizing the margin of the hyperplane and minimizing the misclassification. In SVC, the latter is controlled with the hyperparameter C. C is a parameter of the SVC learner and is the penalty for misclassifying a data point. When C is small, the classifier is okay with misclassified data points (high bias but low variance). When C is large, the classifier is heavily penalized for misclassified data and therefore bends over backward to avoid any misclassified data points (low bias but high variance).

In scikit-learn, C is determined by the parameter C and defaults to C=1.0. We should treat C has a hyperparameter of our learning algorithm, which we tune using model selection techniques in Chapter 12.

17.2 Handling Linearly Inseparable Classes Using Kernels

Problem

You need to train a support vector classifier, but your classes are linearly inseparable.

Solution

Train an extension of a support vector machine using kernel functions to create nonlinear decision boundaries:

```
# Load libraries
from sklearn.svm import SVC
from sklearn import datasets
from sklearn.preprocessing import StandardScaler
import numpy as np

# Set randomization seed
np.random.seed(0)

# Generate two features
features = np.random.randn(200, 2)

# Use an XOR gate (you don't need to know what this is) to generate
# linearly inseparable classes
target_xor = np.logical_xor(features[:, 0] > 0, features[:, 1] > 0)
target = np.where(target_xor, 0, 1)

# Create a support vector machine with a radial basis function kernel
svc = SVC(kernel="rbf", random_state=0, gamma=1, C=1)

# Train the classifier
model = svc.fit(features, target)
```

Discussion

A full explanation of support vector machines is outside the scope of this book. However, a short explanation is likely beneficial for understanding support vector machines and kernels. For reasons best learned elsewhere, a support vector classifier can be represented as:

$$f(x) = \beta_0 + \sum_{i \in S} \alpha_i K(x_i, x_{i'})$$

where β_0 is the bias, S is the set of all support vector observations, α is the model parameters to be learned, and $(x_i, x_{i'})$ are pairs of two support vector observations, x_i and $x_{i'}$. Most importantly, K is a kernel function that compares the similarity between x_i and $x_{i'}$. Don't worry if you don't understand kernel functions. For our purposes, just realize that (1) K determines the type of hyperplane used to separate our classes, and (2) we create different hyperplanes by using different kernels. For example, if we want a basic linear hyperplane like the one we created in Recipe 17.1, we can use the linear kernel:

$$K(x_i, x_{i'}) = \sum_{j=1}^{p} x_{ij} x_{i'j}$$

where p is the number of features. However, if we want a nonlinear decision boundary, we swap the linear kernel with a polynomial kernel:

$$K(x_i, x_{i'}) = \left(r + \gamma \sum_{j=1}^{p} x_{ij} x_{i'j} \right)^d$$

where d is the degree of the polynomial kernel function. Alternatively, we can use one of the most common kernels in support vectors machines, the *radial basis function kernel*:

$$K(x_i, x_{i'}) = e \left(-\gamma \sum_{j=1}^{p} \left(x_{ij} x_{i'j} \right)^2 \right)$$

where γ is a hyperparameter and must be greater than zero. The main point of the preceding explanation is that if we have linearly inseparable data, we can swap out a linear kernel with an alternative kernel to create a nonlinear hyperplane decision boundary.

We can understand the intuition behind kernels by visualizing a simple example. This function, based on one by Sebastian Raschka, plots the observations and decision boundary hyperplane of a two-dimensional space. You do not need to understand how this function works; I have included it here so you can experiment on your own:

```
# Plot observations and decision boundary hyperplane
from matplotlib.colors import ListedColormap
import matplotlib.pyplot as plt

def plot_decision_regions(X, y, classifier):
    cmap = ListedColormap(("red", "blue"))
    xx1, xx2 = np.meshgrid(np.arange(-3, 3, 0.02), np.arange(-3, 3, 0.02))
    Z = classifier.predict(np.array([xx1.ravel(), xx2.ravel()]).T)
    Z = Z.reshape(xx1.shape)
    plt.contourf(xx1, xx2, Z, alpha=0.1, cmap=cmap)
```

```
for idx, cl in enumerate(np.unique(y)):
    plt.scatter(x=X[y == cl, 0], y=X[y == cl, 1],
                alpha=0.8, c=cmap(idx),
                marker="+", label=cl)
```

In our solution, we have data containing two features (i.e., two dimensions) and a target vector with the class of each observation. Importantly, the classes are assigned such that they are *linearly inseparable*. That is, there is no straight line we can draw that will divide the two classes. First, let's create a support vector machine classifier with a linear kernel:

```
# Create support vector classifier with a linear kernel
svc_linear = SVC(kernel="linear", random_state=0, C=1)

# Train model
svc_linear.fit(features, target)

SVC(C=1, kernel='linear', random_state=0)
```

Next, since we have only two features, we are working in a two-dimensional space and can visualize the observations, their classes, and our model's linear hyperplane:

```
# Plot observations and hyperplane
plot_decision_regions(features, target, classifier=svc_linear)
plt.axis("off"), plt.show();
```

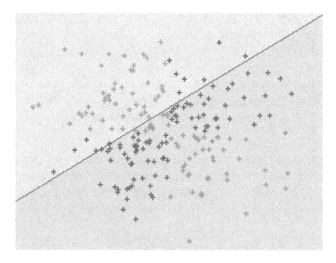

As we can see, our linear hyperplane did very poorly at dividing the two classes! Now, let's swap out the linear kernel with a radial basis function kernel and use it to train a new model:

```
# Create a support vector machine with a radial basis function kernel
svc = SVC(kernel="rbf", random_state=0, gamma=1, C=1)
```

```
# Train the classifier
model = svc.fit(features, target)
```

And then visualize the observations and hyperplane:

```
# Plot observations and hyperplane
plot_decision_regions(features, target, classifier=svc)
plt.axis("off"), plt.show();
```

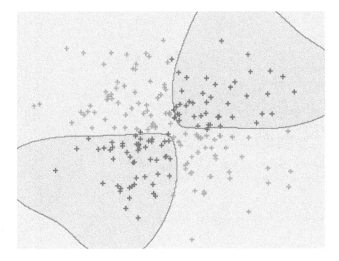

By using the radial basis function kernel we can create a decision boundary that is able to do a much better job of separating the two classes than the linear kernel. This is the motivation behind using kernels in support vector machines.

In scikit-learn, we can select the kernel we want to use by using the kernel parameter. Once we select a kernel, we need to specify the appropriate kernel options, such as the value of d (using the degree parameter) in polynomial kernels, and the value of γ (using the gamma parameter) in radial basis function kernels. We will also need to set the penalty parameter, C. When training the model, in most cases we should treat all of these as hyperparameters and use model selection techniques to identify the combination of their values that produces the model with the best performance.

17.3 Creating Predicted Probabilities

Problem

You need to know the predicted class probabilities for an observation.

Solution

When using scikit-learn's SVC, set `probability=True`, train the model, then use `predict_proba` to see the calibrated probabilities:

```
# Load libraries
from sklearn.svm import SVC
from sklearn import datasets
from sklearn.preprocessing import StandardScaler
import numpy as np

# Load data
iris = datasets.load_iris()
features = iris.data
target = iris.target

# Standardize features
scaler = StandardScaler()
features_standardized = scaler.fit_transform(features)

# Create support vector classifier object
svc = SVC(kernel="linear", probability=True, random_state=0)

# Train classifier
model = svc.fit(features_standardized, target)

# Create new observation
new_observation = [[.4, .4, .4, .4]]

# View predicted probabilities
model.predict_proba(new_observation)

array([[0.00541761, 0.97348825, 0.02109414]])
```

Discussion

Many of the supervised learning algorithms we have covered use probability esti-mates to predict classes. For example, in k-nearest neighbors, an observation's k neighbor's classes were treated as votes to create a probability that an observation was of that class. Then the class with the highest probability was predicted. SVC's use of a hyperplane to create decision regions does not naturally output a probability estimate that an observation is a member of a certain class. However, we can in fact output calibrated class probabilities with a few caveats. In an SVC with two classes, *Platt scal-ing* can be used, wherein first the SVC is trained, and then a separate cross-validated logistic regression is trained to map the SVC outputs into probabilities:

$$P(y = 1 \mid x) = \frac{1}{1 + e^{(A \times f(x) + B)}}$$

where A and B are parameter vectors, and $f(x)$ is the ith observation's signed distance from the hyperplane. When we have more than two classes, an extension of Platt scaling is used.

In more practical terms, creating predicted probabilities has two major issues. First, because we are training a second model with cross-validation, generating predicted probabilities can significantly increase the time it takes to train our model. Second, because the predicted probabilities are created using cross-validation, they might not always match the predicted classes. That is, an observation might be predicted to be class 1 but have a predicted probability of being class 1 of less than 0.5.

In scikit-learn, the predicted probabilities must be generated when the model is being trained. We can do this by setting SVC's `probability` to `True`. After the model is trained, we can output the estimated probabilities for each class using `predict_proba`.

17.4 Identifying Support Vectors

Problem

You need to identify which observations are the support vectors of the decision hyperplane.

Solution

Train the model, then use `support_vectors_`:

```
# Load libraries
from sklearn.svm import SVC
from sklearn import datasets
from sklearn.preprocessing import StandardScaler
import numpy as np

# Load data with only two classes
iris = datasets.load_iris()
features = iris.data[:100,:]
target = iris.target[:100]

# Standardize features
scaler = StandardScaler()
features_standardized = scaler.fit_transform(features)

# Create support vector classifier object
svc = SVC(kernel="linear", random_state=0)

# Train classifier
model = svc.fit(features_standardized, target)
```

```
# View support vectors
model.support_vectors_

array([[-0.5810659 ,  0.42196824, -0.80497402, -0.50860702],
       [-1.52079513, -1.67737625, -1.08231219, -0.86427627],
       [-0.89430898, -1.4674418 ,  0.30437864,  0.38056609],
       [-0.5810659 , -1.25750735,  0.09637501,  0.55840072]])
```

Discussion

Support vector machines get their name from the fact that the hyperplane is being determined by a relatively small number of observations, called the *support vectors*. Intuitively, think of the hyperplane as being "carried" by these support vectors. These support vectors are therefore very important to our model. For example, if we remove an observation that is not a support vector from the data, the model does not change; however, if we remove a support vector, the hyperplane will not have the maximum margin.

After we have trained an SVC, scikit-learn offers a number of options for identifying the support vector. In our solution, we used support_vectors_ to output the actual observations' features of the four support vectors in our model. Alternatively, we can view the indices of the support vectors using support_:

```
model.support_

array([23, 41, 57, 98], dtype=int32)
```

Finally, we can use n_support_ to find the number of support vectors belonging to each class:

```
model.n_support_

array([2, 2], dtype=int32)
```

17.5 Handling Imbalanced Classes

Problem

You need to train a support vector machine classifier in the presence of imbalanced classes.

Solution

Increase the penalty for misclassifying the smaller class using class_weight:

```
# Load libraries
from sklearn.svm import SVC
from sklearn import datasets
from sklearn.preprocessing import StandardScaler
import numpy as np
```

```
# Load data with only two classes
iris = datasets.load_iris()
features = iris.data[:100,:]
target = iris.target[:100]

# Make class highly imbalanced by removing first 40 observations
features = features[40:,:]
target = target[40:]

# Create target vector indicating if class 0, otherwise 1
target = np.where((target == 0), 0, 1)

# Standardize features
scaler = StandardScaler()
features_standardized = scaler.fit_transform(features)

# Create support vector classifier
svc = SVC(kernel="linear", class_weight="balanced", C=1.0, random_state=0)

# Train classifier
model = svc.fit(features_standardized, target)
```

Discussion

In support vector machines, C is a hyperparameter that determines the penalty for misclassifying an observation. One method for handling imbalanced classes in support vector machines is to weight C by classes, so that:

$$C_k = C \times w_j$$

where C is the penalty for misclassification, w_j is a weight inversely proportional to class j's frequency, and C_k is the C value for class k. The general idea is to increase the penalty for misclassifying minority classes to prevent them from being "overwhelmed" by the majority class.

In scikit-learn, when using SVC we can set the values for C_k automatically by setting class_weight="balanced". The balanced argument automatically weighs classes such that:

$$w_j = \frac{n}{kn_j}$$

where w_j is the weight to class j, n is the number of observations, n_j is the number of observations in class j, and k is the total number of classes.

## CHAPTER 18

Naive Bayes

18.0 Introduction

Bayes' theorem is the premier method for understanding the probability of some event, $P(A \mid B)$, given some new information, $P(B \mid A)$, and a prior belief in the probability of the event, $P(A)$:

$$P(A \mid B) = \frac{P(B \mid A)\, P(A)}{P(B)}$$

The Bayesian method's popularity has skyrocketed in the last decade, increasingly rivaling traditional frequentist applications in academia, government, and business. In machine learning, one application of Bayes' theorem to classification comes in the form of the *naive Bayes classifier*. Naive Bayes classifiers combine a number of desirable qualities in practical machine learning into a single classifier. These include:

- An intuitive approach
- The ability to work with small data
- Low computation costs for training and prediction
- Often solid results in a variety of settings

Specifically, a naive Bayes classifier is based on:

$$P\big(y \mid x_1, ..., x_j\big) = \frac{P\big(x_1, ..., x_j \mid y\big)P(y)}{P\big(x_1, ..., x_j\big)}$$

where:

- $P(y \mid x_1, ..., x_j)$ is called the *posterior* and is the probability that an observation is class y given the observation's values for the j features, $x_1, ..., x_j$.

- $P(x_1, ..., x_j \mid y)$ is called *likelihood* and is the likelihood of an observation's values for features $x_1, ..., x_j$ given their class, y.

- $P(y)$ is called the *prior* and is our belief for the probability of class y before looking at the data.

- $P(x_1, ..., x_j)$ is called the *marginal probability*.

In naive Bayes, we compare an observation's posterior values for each possible class. Specifically, because the marginal probability is constant across these comparisons, we compare the numerators of the posterior for each class. For each observation, the class with the greatest posterior numerator becomes the predicted class, $\hat{y}$.

There are two important things to note about naive Bayes classifiers. First, for each feature in the data, we have to assume the statistical distribution of the likelihood, $P(x_j \mid y)$. The common distributions are the normal (Gaussian), multinomial, and Bernoulli distributions. The distribution chosen is often determined by the nature of features (continuous, binary, etc.). Second, naive Bayes gets its name because we assume that each feature, and its resulting likelihood, is independent. This "naive" assumption is frequently wrong yet in practice does little to prevent building high-quality classifiers.

In this chapter we will cover using scikit-learn to train three types of naive Bayes classifiers using three different likelihood distributions. Afterwards, we will learn to calibrate the predictions from naive Bayes models to make them interpretable.

18.1 Training a Classifier for Continuous Features

Problem

You have only continuous features and you want to train a naive Bayes classifier.

Solution

Use a Gaussian naive Bayes classifier in scikit-learn:

```
# Load libraries
from sklearn import datasets
from sklearn.naive_bayes import GaussianNB

# Load data
iris = datasets.load_iris()
features = iris.data
```

```
target = iris.target

# Create Gaussian naive Bayes object
classifer = GaussianNB()

# Train model
model = classifer.fit(features, target)
```

Discussion

The most common type of naive Bayes classifier is the *Gaussian naive Bayes.* In Gaussian naive Bayes, we assume that the likelihood of the feature values x, given an observation is of class y, follows a normal distribution:

$$p(x_j \mid y) = \frac{1}{\sqrt{2\pi\sigma_y^2}}\, e^{-\frac{(x_j - \mu_y)^2}{2\sigma_y^2}}$$

where σ_y^2 and μ_y are the variance and mean values of feature x_j for class y. Because of the assumption of the normal distribution, Gaussian naive Bayes is best used in cases where all our features are continuous.

In scikit-learn, we train a Gaussian naive Bayes like any other model using `fit`, and in turn can then make predictions about the class of an observation:

```
# Create new observation
new_observation = [[ 4,  4,  4,  0.4]]

# Predict class
model.predict(new_observation)

array([1])
```

One of the interesting aspects of naive Bayes classifiers is that they allow us to assign a prior belief over the respected target classes. We can do this using the `GaussianNB` `priors` parameter, which takes in a list of the probabilities assigned to each class of the target vector:

```
# Create Gaussian naive Bayes object with prior probabilities of each class
clf = GaussianNB(priors=[0.25, 0.25, 0.5])

# Train model
model = classifer.fit(features, target)
```

If we do not add any argument to the `priors` parameter, the prior is adjusted based on the data.

Finally, note that the raw predicted probabilities from Gaussian naive Bayes (outputted using `predict_proba`) are not calibrated. That is, they should not be believed. If we want to create useful predicted probabilities, we will need to calibrate them using an isotonic regression or a related method.

See Also

- How the Naive Bayes Classifier Works in Machine Learning (*https://oreil.ly/9yqSw*)

18.2 Training a Classifier for Discrete and Count Features

Problem

Given discrete or count data, you need to train a naive Bayes classifier.

Solution

Use a multinomial naive Bayes classifier:

```
# Load libraries
import numpy as np
from sklearn.naive_bayes import MultinomialNB
from sklearn.feature_extraction.text import CountVectorizer

# Create text
text_data = np.array(['I love Brazil. Brazil!',
                      'Brazil is best',
                      'Germany beats both'])

# Create bag of words
count = CountVectorizer()
bag_of_words = count.fit_transform(text_data)

# Create feature matrix
features = bag_of_words.toarray()

# Create target vector
target = np.array([0,0,1])

# Create multinomial naive Bayes object with prior probabilities of each class
classifer = MultinomialNB(class_prior=[0.25, 0.5])

# Train model
model = classifer.fit(features, target)
```

Discussion

Multinomial naive Bayes works similarly to Gaussian naive Bayes, but the features are assumed to be multinomially distributed. In practice, this means that this classifier is commonly used when we have discrete data (e.g., movie ratings ranging from 1 to 5). One of the most common uses of multinomial naive Bayes is text classification using bags of words or *tf-idf* approaches (see Recipes 6.9 and 6.10).

In our solution, we created a toy text dataset of three observations and converted the text strings into a bag-of-words feature matrix and an accompanying target vector. We then used `MultinomialNB` to train a model while defining the prior probabilities for the two classes (pro-`brazil` and pro-`germany`).

`MultinomialNB` works similarly to `GaussianNB`; models are trained using `fit`, and observations can be predicted using `predict`:

```
# Create new observation
new_observation = [[0, 0, 0, 1, 0, 1, 0]]

# Predict new observation's class
model.predict(new_observation)

array([0])
```

If `class_prior` is not specified, prior probabilities are learned using the data. However, if we want a uniform distribution to be used as the prior, we can set `fit_prior=False`.

Finally, `MultinomialNB` contains an additive smoothing hyperparameter, `alpha`, that should be tuned. The default value is `1.0`, with `0.0` meaning no smoothing takes place.

18.3 Training a Naive Bayes Classifier for Binary Features

Problem

You have binary feature data and need to train a naive Bayes classifier.

Solution

Use a Bernoulli naive Bayes classifier:

```
# Load libraries
import numpy as np
from sklearn.naive_bayes import BernoulliNB

# Create three binary features
features = np.random.randint(2, size=(100, 3))
```

```
# Create a binary target vector
target = np.random.randint(2, size=(100, 1)).ravel()

# Create Bernoulli naive Bayes object with prior probabilities of each class
classifer = BernoulliNB(class_prior=[0.25, 0.5])

# Train model
model = classifer.fit(features, target)
```

Discussion

The *Bernoulli naive Bayes* classifier assumes that all our features are binary, such that
they take only two values (e.g., a nominal categorical feature that has been one-hot
encoded). Like its multinomial cousin, Bernoulli naive Bayes is often used in text
classification, when our feature matrix is simply the presence or absence of a word in
a document. Furthermore, like `MultinomialNB`, `BernoulliNB` has an additive smoothing hyperparameter, `alpha`, we will want to tune using model selection techniques.
Finally, if we want to use priors, we can use the `class_prior` parameter with a list
containing the prior probabilities for each class. If we want to specify a uniform prior,
we can set `fit_prior=False`:

```
model_uniform_prior = BernoulliNB(class_prior=None, fit_prior=False)
```

18.4 Calibrating Predicted Probabilities

Problem

You want to calibrate the predicted probabilities from naive Bayes classifiers so they
are interpretable.

Solution

Use `CalibratedClassifierCV`:

```
# Load libraries
from sklearn import datasets
from sklearn.naive_bayes import GaussianNB
from sklearn.calibration import CalibratedClassifierCV

# Load data
iris = datasets.load_iris()
features = iris.data
target = iris.target

# Create Gaussian naive Bayes object
classifer = GaussianNB()

# Create calibrated cross-validation with sigmoid calibration
```

```
classifer_sigmoid = CalibratedClassifierCV(classifer, cv=2, method='sigmoid')

# Calibrate probabilities
classifer_sigmoid.fit(features, target)

# Create new observation
new_observation = [[ 2.6,  2.6,  2.6,  0.4]]

# View calibrated probabilities
classifer_sigmoid.predict_proba(new_observation)

array([[0.31859969, 0.63663466, 0.04476565]])
```

Discussion

Class probabilities are a common and useful part of machine learning models. In scikit-learn, most learning algorithms allow us to see the predicted probabilities of class membership using predict_proba. This can be extremely useful if, for instance, we want to predict a certain class only if the model predicts the probability that the class is over 90%. However, some models, including naive Bayes classifiers, output probabilities that are not based on the real world. That is, predict_proba might predict an observation has a 0.70 chance of being a certain class, when the reality is that it is 0.10 or 0.99. Specifically in naive Bayes, while the ranking of predicted probabilities for the different target classes is valid, the raw predicted probabilities tend to take on extreme values close to 0 and 1.

To obtain meaningful predicted probabilities we need conduct what is called *calibration*. In scikit-learn we can use the CalibratedClassifierCV class to create well-calibrated predicted probabilities using k-fold cross-validation. In Calibrated ClassifierCV, the training sets are used to train the model, and the test set is used to calibrate the predicted probabilities. The returned predicted probabilities are the average of the k-folds.

Using our solution we can see the difference between raw and well-calibrated predicted probabilities. In our solution, we created a Gaussian naive Bayes classifier. If we train that classifier and then predict the class probabilities for a new observation, we can see very extreme probability estimates:

```
# Train a Gaussian naive Bayes then predict class probabilities
classifer.fit(features, target).predict_proba(new_observation)

array([[2.31548432e-04, 9.99768128e-01, 3.23532277e-07]])
```

However if, after we calibrate the predicted probabilities (which we did in our solution), we get very different results:

```
# View calibrated probabilities
array([[0.31859969, 0.63663466, 0.04476565]])

array([[ 0.31859969,  0.63663466,  0.04476565]])
```

`CalibratedClassifierCV` offers two calibration methods—Platt's sigmoid model and isotonic regression—defined by the `method` parameter. While we don't have the space to go into the specifics, because isotonic regression is nonparametric it tends to overfit when sample sizes are very small (e.g., 100 observations). In our solution we used the Iris dataset with 150 observations and therefore used the Platt's sigmoid model.

Clustering

19.0 Introduction

In much of this book we have looked at supervised machine learning—where we have access to both the features and the target. This is, unfortunately, not always the case. Frequently, we run into situations where we only know the features. For example, imagine we have records of sales from a grocery store and we want to break up sales by whether the shopper is a member of a discount club. This would be impossible using supervised learning because we don't have a target to train and evaluate our models. However, there is another option: unsupervised learning. If the behavior of discount club members and nonmembers in the grocery store is actually disparate, then the average difference in behavior between two members will be smaller than the average difference in behavior between a member and nonmember shopper. Put another way, there will be two clusters of observations.

The goal of clustering algorithms is to identify those latent groupings of observations, which, if done well, allows us to predict the class of observations even without a target vector. There are many clustering algorithms, and they have a wide variety of approaches to identifying the clusters in data. In this chapter, we will cover a selection of clustering algorithms using scikit-learn and how to use them in practice.

19.1 Clustering Using K-Means

Problem

You want to group observations into *k* groups.

Solution

Use *k-means clustering*:

```
# Load libraries
from sklearn import datasets
from sklearn.preprocessing import StandardScaler
from sklearn.cluster import KMeans

# Load data
iris = datasets.load_iris()
features = iris.data

# Standardize features
scaler = StandardScaler()
features_std = scaler.fit_transform(features)

# Create k-means object
cluster = KMeans(n_clusters=3, random_state=0, n_init="auto")

# Train model
model = cluster.fit(features_std)
```

Discussion

K-means clustering is one of the most common clustering techniques. In k-means clustering, the algorithm attempts to group observations into k groups, with each group having roughly equal variance. The number of groups, k, is specified by the user as a hyperparameter. Specifically, in k-means:

1. k cluster "center" points are created at random locations.

2. For each observation:

   a. The distance between each observation and the k center points is calculated.

   b. The observation is assigned to the cluster of the nearest center point.

3. The center points are moved to the means (i.e., centers) of their respective clusters.

4. Steps 2 and 3 are repeated until no observation changes in cluster membership.

At this point the algorithm is considered converged and stops.

It is important to note three things about k-means. First, k-means clustering assumes the clusters are convex shaped (e.g., a circle, a sphere). Second, all features are equally scaled. In our solution, we standardized the features to meet this assumption. Third, the groups are balanced (i.e., have roughly the same number of observations). If we suspect that we cannot meet these assumptions, we might try other clustering approaches.

In scikit-learn, k-means clustering is implemented in the KMeans class. The most important parameter is n_clusters, which sets the number of clusters k. In some situations, the nature of the data will determine the value for k (e.g., data on a school's students will have one cluster per grade), but often we don't know the number of clusters. In these cases, we will want to select k based on using some criteria. For example, silhouette coefficients (see Recipe 11.9) measure the similarity within clusters compared with the similarity between clusters. Furthermore, because k-means clustering is computationally expensive, we might want to take advantage of all the cores on our computer. We can do this by setting n_jobs=-1.

In our solution, we cheated a little and used the iris flower data, which we know contains three classes. Therefore, we set $k = 3$. We can use labels_ to see the predicted classes of each observation:

```
# View predicted class
model.labels_

array([0, 0, 0, 0, 0, 0, 0, 0, 0, 0, 0, 0, 0, 0, 0, 0, 0, 0, 0, 0, 0,
       0, 0, 0, 0, 0, 0, 0, 0, 0, 0, 0, 0, 0, 0, 0, 0, 0, 0, 0, 0, 0,
       0, 0, 0, 0, 0, 0, 2, 2, 2, 1, 1, 1, 2, 1, 1, 1, 1, 1, 1, 1, 1, 2,
       1, 1, 1, 1, 2, 1, 1, 1, 1, 2, 2, 2, 1, 1, 1, 1, 1, 1, 1, 2, 2, 1,
       1, 1, 1, 1, 1, 1, 1, 1, 1, 1, 2, 1, 2, 2, 2, 2, 1, 2, 1, 2,
       2, 1, 2, 1, 1, 2, 2, 2, 2, 1, 2, 1, 2, 1, 2, 2, 1, 1, 2, 2, 2, 2,
       2, 1, 1, 2, 2, 2, 1, 2, 2, 2, 1, 2, 2, 2, 1, 2, 2, 1], dtype=int32)
```

If we compare this to the observation's true class, we can see that, despite the difference in class labels (i.e., 0, 1, and 2), k-means did reasonably well:

```
# View true class
iris.target

array([0, 0, 0, 0, 0, 0, 0, 0, 0, 0, 0, 0, 0, 0, 0, 0, 0, 0, 0, 0, 0,
       0, 0, 0, 0, 0, 0, 0, 0, 0, 0, 0, 0, 0, 0, 0, 0, 0, 0, 0, 0, 0,
       0, 0, 0, 0, 0, 0, 1, 1, 1, 1, 1, 1, 1, 1, 1, 1, 1, 1, 1, 1, 1, 1,
       1, 1, 1, 1, 1, 1, 1, 1, 1, 1, 1, 1, 1, 1, 1, 1, 1, 1, 1, 1, 1, 1,
       1, 1, 1, 1, 1, 1, 1, 1, 1, 1, 2, 2, 2, 2, 2, 2, 2, 2, 2, 2,
       2, 2, 2, 2, 2, 2, 2, 2, 2, 2, 2, 2, 2, 2, 2, 2, 2, 2, 2, 2, 2, 2,
       2, 2, 2, 2, 2, 2, 2, 2, 2, 2, 2, 2, 2, 2, 2, 2])
```

However, as you might imagine, the performance of k-means drops considerably, even critically, if we select the wrong number of clusters.

Finally, as with other scikit-learn models, we can use the trained cluster to predict the value of new observations:

```
# Create new observation
new_observation = [[0.8, 0.8, 0.8, 0.8]]

# Predict observation's cluster
model.predict(new_observation)

array([2], dtype=int32)
```

The observation is predicted to belong to the cluster whose center point is closest. We can even use cluster_centers_ to see those center points:

```
# View cluster centers
model.cluster_centers_

array([[-1.01457897,  0.85326268, -1.30498732, -1.25489349],
       [-0.01139555, -0.87600831,  0.37707573,  0.31115341],
       [ 1.16743407,  0.14530299,  1.00302557,  1.0300019 ]])
```

See Also

- Introduction to K-means Clustering (*https://oreil.ly/HDfUz*)

19.2 Speeding Up K-Means Clustering

Problem

You want to group observations into *k* groups, but k-means takes too long.

Solution

Use mini-batch k-means:

```
# Load libraries
from sklearn import datasets
from sklearn.preprocessing import StandardScaler
from sklearn.cluster import MiniBatchKMeans

# Load data
iris = datasets.load_iris()
features = iris.data

# Standardize features
scaler = StandardScaler()
features_std = scaler.fit_transform(features)

# Create k-mean object
cluster = MiniBatchKMeans(n_clusters=3, random_state=0, batch_size=100,
        n_init="auto")

# Train model
model = cluster.fit(features_std)
```

Discussion

Mini-batch k-means works similarly to the k-means algorithm discussed in Recipe 19.1. Without going into too much detail, the difference is that in mini-batch k-means the most computationally costly step is conducted on only a random sample of observations as opposed to all observations. This approach can significantly reduce the time required for the algorithm to find convergence (i.e., fit the data) with only a small cost in quality.

`MiniBatchKMeans` works similarly to `KMeans`, with one significant difference: the `batch_size` parameter. `batch_size` controls the number of randomly selected observations in each batch. The larger the size of the batch, the more computationally costly the training process.

19.3 Clustering Using Mean Shift

Problem

You want to group observations without assuming the number of clusters or their shape.

Solution

Use mean shift clustering:

```
# Load libraries
from sklearn import datasets
from sklearn.preprocessing import StandardScaler
from sklearn.cluster import MeanShift

# Load data
iris = datasets.load_iris()
features = iris.data

# Standardize features
scaler = StandardScaler()
features_std = scaler.fit_transform(features)

# Create mean shift object
cluster = MeanShift(n_jobs=-1)

# Train model
model = cluster.fit(features_std)
```

Discussion

One of the disadvantages of k-means clustering we discussed previously is that we needed to set the number of clusters, *k*, prior to training, and the method made assumptions about the shape of the clusters. One clustering algorithm without these limitations is mean shift.

Mean shift is a simple concept, but it's somewhat difficult to explain. Therefore, an analogy might be the best approach. Imagine a very foggy football field (i.e., a two-dimensional feature space) with 100 people standing on it (i.e., our observations). Because it is foggy, a person can see only a short distance. Every minute each person looks around and takes a step in the direction of the most people they can see. As time goes on, people start to group together as they repeatedly take steps toward larger and larger crowds. The end result is clusters of people around the field. People are assigned to the clusters in which they end up.

scikit-learn's actual implementation of mean shift, MeanShift, is more complex but follows the same basic logic. MeanShift has two important parameters we should be aware of. First, bandwidth sets the radius of the area (i.e., kernel) an observation uses to determine the direction to shift. In our analogy, bandwidth is how far a person can see through the fog. We can set this parameter manually, but by default a reasonable bandwidth is estimated automatically (with a significant increase in computational cost). Second, sometimes in mean shift there are no other observations within an observation's kernel. That is, a person on our football field cannot see a single other person. By default, MeanShift assigns all these "orphan" observations to the kernel of the nearest observation. However, if we want to leave out these orphans, we can set cluster_all=False, wherein orphan observations are given the label of -1.

See Also

- The mean shift clustering algorithm, EFAVDB (*https://oreil.ly/Gb3VG*)

19.4 Clustering Using DBSCAN

Problem

You want to group observations into clusters of high density.

Solution

Use DBSCAN clustering:

```
# Load libraries
from sklearn import datasets
from sklearn.preprocessing import StandardScaler
from sklearn.cluster import DBSCAN

# Load data
iris = datasets.load_iris()
features = iris.data

# Standardize features
scaler = StandardScaler()
```

```
features_std = scaler.fit_transform(features)

# Create DBSCAN object
cluster = DBSCAN(n_jobs=-1)

# Train model
model = cluster.fit(features_std)
```

Discussion

DBSCAN is motivated by the idea that clusters will be areas where many observations are densely packed together and makes no assumptions of cluster shape. Specifically, in DBSCAN:

1. A random observation, x_i, is chosen.

2. If x_i has a minimum number of close neighbors, we consider it to be part of a cluster.

3. Step 2 is repeated recursively for all of x_i's neighbors, then neighbor's neighbor, and so on. These are the cluster's core observations.

4. Once step 3 runs out of nearby observations, a new random point is chosen (i.e., restart at step 1).

Once this is complete, we have a set of core observations for a number of clusters. Finally, any observation close to a cluster but not a core sample is considered part of a cluster, while any observation not close to the cluster is labeled an outlier.

DBSCAN has three main parameters to set:

eps
> The maximum distance from an observation for another observation to be considered its neighbor.

min_samples
> The minimum number of observations less than eps distance from an observation for it to be considered a core observation.

metric
> The distance metric used by eps—for example, minkowski or euclidean (note that if Minkowski distance is used, the parameter p can be used to set the power of the Minkowski metric).

If we look at the clusters in our training data we can see two clusters have been identified, 0 and 1, while outlier observations are labeled -1:

```
# Show cluster membership
model.labels_
```

```
array([ 0,  0,  0,  0,  0,  0,  0,  0,  0,  0,  0,  0,  0,  0, -1, -1,  0,
        0,  0,  0,  0,  0,  0,  0,  0,  0,  0,  0,  0,  0,  0, -1, -1,
        0,  0,  0,  0,  0,  0,  0, -1,  0,  0,  0,  0,  0,  0,  0,  0,  1,
        1,  1,  1,  1, -1, -1,  1, -1, -1,  1, -1,  1,  1,  1,  1,  1,
       -1,  1,  1,  1, -1,  1,  1,  1,  1,  1,  1,  1,  1,  1,  1,  1,  1,
       -1,  1, -1,  1,  1,  1,  1,  1, -1,  1,  1,  1,  1, -1,  1, -1,  1,
        1,  1,  1, -1, -1, -1, -1, -1,  1,  1,  1,  1, -1,  1,  1, -1, -1,
       -1,  1,  1, -1,  1,  1, -1,  1,  1,  1, -1, -1, -1,  1,  1,  1, -1,
       -1,  1,  1,  1,  1,  1,  1,  1,  1,  1,  1,  1, -1,  1])
```

See Also

- DBSCAN, Wikipedia (*https://oreil.ly/QBx3a*)

19.5 Clustering Using Hierarchical Merging

Problem

You want to group observations using a hierarchy of clusters.

Solution

Use agglomerative clustering:

```
# Load libraries
from sklearn import datasets
from sklearn.preprocessing import StandardScaler
from sklearn.cluster import AgglomerativeClustering

# Load data
iris = datasets.load_iris()
features = iris.data

# Standardize features
scaler = StandardScaler()
features_std = scaler.fit_transform(features)

# Create agglomerative clustering object
cluster = AgglomerativeClustering(n_clusters=3)

# Train model
model = cluster.fit(features_std)
```

Discussion

Agglomerative clustering is a powerful, flexible hierarchical clustering algorithm. In agglomerative clustering, all observations start as their own clusters. Next, clusters meeting some criteria are merged. This process is repeated, growing clusters until some end point is reached. In scikit-learn, AgglomerativeClustering uses the link age parameter to determine the merging strategy to minimize:

- Variance of merged clusters (ward)
- Average distance between observations from pairs of clusters (average)
- Maximum distance between observations from pairs of clusters (complete)

Two other parameters are useful to know. First, the affinity parameter determines the distance metric used for linkage (minkowski, euclidean, etc.). Second, n_clusters sets the number of clusters the clustering algorithm will attempt to find. That is, clusters are successively merged until only n_clusters remain.

As with other clustering algorithms we have covered, we can use labels_ to see the cluster in which every observation is assigned:

```
# Show cluster membership
model.labels_
```

```
array([1, 1, 1, 1, 1, 1, 1, 1, 1, 1, 1, 1, 1, 1, 1, 1, 1, 1, 1, 1, 1, 1,
       1, 1, 1, 1, 1, 1, 1, 1, 1, 1, 1, 1, 1, 1, 1, 1, 1, 1, 2, 1, 1,
       1, 1, 1, 1, 1, 1, 0, 0, 0, 2, 0, 2, 0, 2, 0, 2, 2, 0, 2, 0, 2, 0,
       2, 2, 2, 2, 0, 0, 0, 0, 0, 0, 0, 0, 0, 2, 2, 2, 2, 0, 2, 0, 0, 2,
       2, 2, 2, 0, 2, 2, 2, 2, 2, 0, 2, 2, 0, 0, 0, 0, 0, 0, 2, 0, 0, 0,
       0, 0, 0, 0, 0, 0, 0, 0, 0, 2, 0, 0, 0, 0, 0, 0, 0, 0, 0, 0, 0, 0,
       0, 0, 0, 0, 0, 0, 0, 0, 0, 0, 0, 0, 0, 0, 0, 0, 0, 0])
```

## CHAPTER 20

Tensors with PyTorch

20.0 Introduction

Just as NumPy is a foundational tool for data manipulation in the machine learning stack, PyTorch is a foundational tool for working with tensors in the deep learning stack. Before moving on to deep learning itself, we should familiarize ourselves with PyTorch tensors and create many operations analogous to those performed with NumPy in Chapter 1.

Although PyTorch is just one of multiple deep learning libraries, it is significantly popular both within academia and industry. PyTorch tensors are *very* similar to NumPy arrays. However, they also allow us to perform tensor operations on GPUs (hardware specialized for deep learning). In this chapter, we'll familiarize ourselves with the basics of PyTorch tensors and many common low-level operations.

20.1 Creating a Tensor

Problem

You need to create a tensor.

Solution

Use Pytorch to create a tensor:

```
# Load library
import torch

# Create a vector as a row
tensor_row = torch.tensor([1, 2, 3])
```

```
# Create a vector as a column
tensor_column = torch.tensor(
    [
        [1],
        [2],
        [3]
    ]
)
```

Discussion

The main data structure within PyTorch is a tensor, and in many ways tensors are exactly like the multidimensional NumPy arrays used in Chapter 1. Just like vectors and arrays, these tensors can be represented horizontally (i.e., rows) or vertically (i.e., columns).

See Also

- PyTorch documentation: Tensors (*https://oreil.ly/utaTD*)

20.2 Creating a Tensor from NumPy

Problem

You need to create PyTorch tensors from NumPy arrays.

Solution

Use the PyTorch from_numpy function:

```
# Import libraries
import numpy as np
import torch

# Create a NumPy array
vector_row = np.array([1, 2, 3])

# Create a tensor from a NumPy array
tensor_row = torch.from_numpy(vector_row)
```

Discussion

As we can see, PyTorch is very similar to NumPy syntactically. In addition, it easily allows us to convert NumPy arrays to PyTorch tensors that we can use on GPUs and other accelerated hardware. At the time of writing, NumPy is mentioned frequently in the PyTorch documentation, and PyTorch itself even offers a way that PyTorch tensors and NumPy arrays can share the same memory to reduce overhead.

See Also

- PyTorch documentation: Bridge with NumPy (*https://oreil.ly/zEJo6*)

20.3 Creating a Sparse Tensor

Problem

Given data with very few nonzero values, you want to efficiently represent it with a tensor.

Solution

Use the PyTorch `to_sparse` function:

```
# Import libraries
import torch

# Create a tensor
tensor = torch.tensor(
[
[0, 0],
[0, 1],
[3, 0]
]
)

# Create a sparse tensor from a regular tensor
sparse_tensor = tensor.to_sparse()
```

Discussion

Sparse tensors are memory-efficient ways to represent data composed of mostly 0s. In Chapter 1 we used `scipy` to create a compressed sparse row (CSR) matrix that was no longer a NumPy array.

The `torch.Tensor` class allows us to create both regular and sparse matrices using the same object. If we inspect the types of the two tensors we just created, we can see they're actually both of the same class:

```
print(type(tensor))
print(type(sparse_tensor))

<class 'torch.Tensor'>
<class 'torch.Tensor'>
```

See Also

- PyTorch documentation: Sparse Tensor (*https://oreil.ly/8J3IO*)

20.4 Selecting Elements in a Tensor

Problem

We need to select specific elements of a tensor.

Solution

Use NumPy-like indexing and slicing to return elements:

```
# Load library
import torch

# Create vector tensor
vector = torch.tensor([1, 2, 3, 4, 5, 6])

# Create matrix tensor
matrix = torch.tensor(
    [
        [1, 2, 3],
        [4, 5, 6],
        [7, 8, 9]
    ]
)

# Select third element of vector
vector[2]

tensor(3)

# Select second row, second column
matrix[1,1]

tensor(5)
```

Discussion

Like NumPy arrays and most everything in Python, PyTorch tensors are zero-indexed. Both indexing and slicing are supported as well. One key difference is that indexing a PyTorch tensor to return a single element still returns a tensor as opposed to the value of the object itself (which would be in the form of an integer or float). Slicing syntax also has parity with NumPy and will return objects of type tensor in PyTorch:

```
# Select all elements of a vector
vector[:]

array([1, 2, 3, 4, 5, 6])

# Select everything up to and including the third element
vector[:3]
```

```
tensor([1, 2, 3])

# Select everything after the third element
vector[3:]

tensor([4, 5, 6])

# Select the last element
vector[-1]

tensor(6)

# Select the first two rows and all columns of a matrix
matrix[:2,:]

tensor([[1, 2, 3],
        [4, 5, 6]])

# Select all rows and the second column
matrix[:,1:2]

tensor([[2],
        [5],
        [8]])
```

One key difference is that PyTorch tensors do not yet support negative steps when slicing. Therefore, attempting to reverse a tensor using slicing yields an error:

```
# Reverse the vector
vector[::-1]

ValueError: step must be greater than zero
```

Instead, if we wish to reverse a tensor we can use the flip method:

```
vector.flip(dims=(-1,))

tensor([6, 5, 4, 3, 2, 1])
```

See Also

- PyTorch documentation: Operations on Tensors (*https://oreil.ly/8-xj7*)

20.5 Describing a Tensor

Problem

You want to describe the shape, data type, and format of a tensor along with the hardware it's using.

Solution

Inpect the shape, dtype, layout, and device attributes of the tensor:

```
# Load library
import torch

# Create a tensor
tensor = torch.tensor([[1,2,3], [1,2,3]])

# Get the shape of the tensor
tensor.shape

torch.Size([2, 3])
# Get the data type of items in the tensor
tensor.dtype

torch.int64
# Get the layout of the tensor
tensor.layout

torch.strided
# Get the device being used by the tensor
tensor.device

device(type='cpu')
```

Discussion

PyTorch tensors provide a number of helpful attributes for gathering information about a given tensor, including:

Shape
    Returns the dimensions of the tensor

Dtype
    Returns the data type of objects within the tensor

Layout
    Returns the memory layout (most common is `strided` used for dense tensors)

Device
    Returns the hardware the tensor is being stored on (CPU/GPU)

Again, the key differentiator between tensors and arrays is an attribute like *device*, because tensors provide us with hardware-accelerated options like GPUs.

20.6 Applying Operations to Elements

Problem

You want to apply an operation to all elements in a tensor.

Solution

Take advantage of *broadcasting* with PyTorch:

```
# Load library
import torch

# Create a tensor
tensor = torch.tensor([1, 2, 3])

# Broadcast an arithmetic operation to all elements in a tensor
tensor * 100

tensor([100, 200, 300])
```

Discussion

Basic operations in PyTorch will take advantage of broadcasting to parallelize them using accelerated hardware such as GPUs. This is true for supported mathematical operators in Python (+, -, ×, /) and other functions inherent to PyTorch. Unlike NumPy, PyTorch doesn't include a `vectorize` method for applying a function over all elements in a tensor. However, PyTorch comes equipped with all of the mathematical tools necessary to distribute and accelerate the usual operations required for deep learning workflows.

See Also

- PyTorch documentation: Broadcasting Semantics (*https://oreil.ly/NsPpa*)
- Vectorization and Broadcasting with PyTorch (*https://oreil.ly/dfzIJ*)

20.7 Finding the Maximum and Minimum Values

Problem

You need to find the maximum or minimum value in a tensor.

Solution

Use the PyTorch `max` and `min` methods:

```
# Load library
import torch

# Create a tensor
torch.tensor([1,2,3])

# Find the largest value
tensor.max()

tensor(3)
```

```
# Find the smallest value
tensor.min()

tensor(1)
```

Discussion

The max and min methods of a tensor help us find the largest or smallest values in that tensor. These methods work the same across multidimensional tensors as well:

```
# Create a multidimensional tensor
tensor = torch.tensor([[1,2,3],[1,2,5]])

# Find the largest value
tensor.max()

tensor(5)
```

20.8 Reshaping Tensors

Problem

You want to change the shape (number of rows and columns) of a tensor without changing the element values.

Solution

Use the PyTorch reshape method:

```
# Load library
import torch

# Create 4x3 tensor
tensor = torch.tensor([[1, 2, 3],
                       [4, 5, 6],
                       [7, 8, 9],
                       [10, 11, 12]])

# Reshape tensor into 2x6 tensor
tensor.reshape(2, 6)

tensor([[ 1,  2,  3,  4,  5,  6],
        [ 7,  8,  9, 10, 11, 12]])
```

Discussion

Manipulating the shape of a tensor can be common in the field of deep learning, as neurons in a neural network often require tensors of a very specific shape. Since the required shape of a tensor can change between neurons in a given neural network, it is good to have a low-level understanding of our inputs and outputs in deep learning.

20.9 Transposing a Tensor

Problem

You need to transpose a tensor.

Solution

Use the mT method:

```
# Load library
import torch

# Create a two-dimensional tensor
tensor = torch.tensor([[[1,2,3]]])

# Transpose it
tensor.mT

tensor([[1],
        [2],
        [3]])
```

Discussion

Transposing with PyTorch is slightly different from NumPy. The T method used for NumPy arrays is supported in PyTorch only with tensors of two dimensions and at the time of writing is deprecated for tensors of other shapes. The mT method used to transpose batches of tensors is preferred, as it scales to greater than two dimensions.

An additional way to transpose PyTorch tensors of any shape is to use the permute method:

```
tensor.permute(*torch.arange(tensor.ndim - 1, -1, -1))

tensor([[1],
        [2],
        [3]])
```

This method also works for one-dimensional tensors (for which the value of the tranposed tensor is the same as the original tensor).

20.10 Flattening a Tensor

Problem

You need to transform a tensor into one dimension.

Solution

Use the `flatten` method:

```python
# Load library
import torch

# Create tensor
tensor = torch.tensor([[1, 2, 3],
                       [4, 5, 6],
                       [7, 8, 9]])

# Flatten tensor
tensor.flatten()

tensor([1, 2, 3, 4, 5, 6, 7, 8, 9])
```

Discussion

Flattening a tensor is a useful technique for reducing a multidimensional tensor into one dimension.

20.11 Calculating Dot Products

Problem

You need to calculate the dot product of two tensors.

Solution

Use the dot method:

```python
# Load library
import torch

# Create one tensor
tensor_1 = torch.tensor([1, 2, 3])

# Create another tensor
tensor_2 = torch.tensor([4, 5, 6])

# Calculate the dot product of the two tensors
tensor_1.dot(tensor_2)

tensor(32)
```

Discussion

Calculating the dot product of two tensors is a common operation useful in the deep learning space as well as the information retrieval space. You may remember earlier in the book where we used the dot product of two vectors to perform a cosine similarity-based search. Doing this in PyTorch on GPU (instead of with NumPy or scikit-learn on CPU) can yield impressive performance benefits on information retrieval problems.

See Also

- Vectorization and Broadcasting with PyTorch (*https://oreil.ly/lIjtB*)

20.12 Multiplying Tensors

Problem

You need to multiply two tensors.

Solution

Use basic Python arithmetic operators:

```
# Load library
import torch

# Create one tensor
tensor_1 = torch.tensor([1, 2, 3])

# Create another tensor
tensor_2 = torch.tensor([4, 5, 6])

# Multiply the two tensors
tensor_1 * tensor_2

tensor([ 4, 10, 18])
```

Discussion

PyTorch supports basic arithmetic operators such as ×, +, - and /. Although multiplying tensors is probably one of the most common operations used in deep learning, it's useful to know tensors can also be added, subtracted, and divided.

Add one tensor to another:

```
tensor_1+tensor_2

tensor([5, 7, 9])
```

Subtract one tensor from another:

```
tensor_1-tensor_2
tensor([-3, -3, -3])
```

Divide one tensor by another:

```
tensor_1/tensor_2
tensor([0.2500, 0.4000, 0.5000])
```

## CHAPTER 21

Neural Networks

21.0 Introduction

At the heart of basic neural networks is the *unit* (also called a *node* or *neuron*). A unit takes in one or more inputs, multiplies each input by a parameter (also called a *weight*), sums the weighted input's values along with some bias value (typically 0), and then feeds the value into an activation function. This output is then sent forward to the other neurons deeper in the neural network (if they exist).

Neural networks can be visualized as a series of connected layers that form a network connecting an observation's feature values at one end and the target value (e.g., observation's class) at the other end. *Feedforward* neural networks—also called *multilayer perceptron*—are the simplest artificial neural networks used in any real-world setting. The name "feedforward" comes from the fact that an observation's feature values are fed "forward" through the network, with each layer successively transforming the feature values with the goal that the output is the same as (or close to) the target's value.

Specifically, feedforward neural networks contain three types of layers. At the start of the neural network is an input layer, where each unit contains an observation's value for a single feature. For example, if an observation has 100 features, the input layer has 100 units. At the end of the neural network is the output layer, which transforms the output of intermediate layers (called *hidden layers*) into values useful for the task at hand. For example, if our goal is binary classification, we can use an output layer with a single unit that uses a sigmoid function to scale its own output to between 0 and 1, representing a predicted class probability.

Between the input and output layers are the so-called hidden layers. These hidden layers successively transform the feature values from the input layer to something that, once processed by the output layer, resembles the target class. Neural networks with many hidden layers (e.g., 10, 100, 1,000) are considered "deep" networks. Training deep neural networks is a process known as *deep learning*.

Neural networks are typically created with all parameters initialized as small random values from a Gaussian or normal uniform distribution. Once an observation (or more often a set number of observations called a *batch*) is fed through the network, the outputted value is compared with the observation's true value using a loss function. This is called *forward propagation*. Next an algorithm goes "backward" through the network identifying how much each parameter contributed to the error between the predicted and true values, a process called *back propagation*. At each parameter, the optimization algorithm determines how much each weight should be adjusted to improve the output.

Neural networks learn by repeating this process of forward propagation and back propagation for every observation in the training data multiple times (each time all observations have been sent through the network is called an *epoch* and training typically consists of multiple epochs), iteratively updating the values of the parameters utilizing a process called *gradient descent* to slowly optimize the values of the parameters for the given output.

In this chapter, we will use the same Python library used in the last chapter, PyTorch, to build, train, and evaluate a variety of neural networks. PyTorch is a popular tool within the deep learning space due to its well-written APIs and intuitive representation of the low-level tensor operations that power neural networks. One key feature of PyTorch is called *autograd*, which automatically computes and stores the gradients used to optimize the parameters of the network after undergoing forward propagation and back propagation.

Neural networks created using PyTorch code can be trained using both CPUs (i.e., on your laptop) and GPUs (i.e., on a specialized deep learning computer). In the real world with real data, it is often necessary to train neural networks using GPUs, as the training process on large data for complex networks runs orders of magnitude faster on GPUs than CPUs. However, all the neural networks in this book are small and simple enough to be trained on a CPU-only laptop in only a few minutes. Just be aware that when we have larger networks and more training data, training using CPUs is *significantly* slower than training using GPUs.

21.1 Using Autograd with PyTorch

Problem

You want to use PyTorch's autograd features to compute and store the gradients after undergoing forward propagation and back propagation.

Solution

Create tensors with the `requires_grad` option set to True:

```
# Import libraries
import torch

# Create a torch tensor that requires gradients
t = torch.tensor([1.0, 2.0, 3.0], requires_grad=True)

# Perform a tensor operation simulating "forward propagation"
tensor_sum = t.sum()

# Perform back propagation
tensor_sum.backward()

# View the gradients
t.grad

tensor([1., 1., 1.])
```

Discussion

Autograd is one of the core features of PyTorch and a big factor in its popularity as a deep learning library. The ability to easily compute, store, and visualize gradients makes PyTorch very intuitive for researchers and enthusiasts building neural networks from scratch.

PyTorch uses a directed acyclic graph (DAG) to keep a record of all data and computational operations being performed on that data. This is incredibly useful, but it also means we need to be careful with what operations we try to apply on our PyTorch data that requires gradients. When working with autograd, we can't easily convert our tensors to NumPy arrays and back without "breaking the graph," a phrase used to describe operations that don't support autograd:

```
import torch

tensor = torch.tensor([1.0,2.0,3.0], requires_grad=True)
tensor.numpy()

RuntimeError: Can't call numpy() on Tensor that requires grad. Use
    tensor.detach().numpy() instead.
```

To convert this tensor into a NumPy array, we need to call the `detach()` method on it, which will break the graph and thus our ability to automatically compute gradients. While this can definitely be useful, it's worth knowing that detaching the tensor will prevent PyTorch from automatically computing the gradient.

See Also

- PyTorch Autograd Tutorial (*https://oreil.ly/mOWSw*)

21.2 Preprocessing Data for Neural Networks

Problem

You want to preprocess data for use in a neural network.

Solution

Standardize each feature using scikit-learn's `StandardScaler`:

```
# Load libraries
from sklearn import preprocessing
import numpy as np

# Create feature
features = np.array([[-100.1, 3240.1],
                     [-200.2, -234.1],
                     [5000.5, 150.1],
                     [6000.6, -125.1],
                     [9000.9, -673.1]])

# Create scaler
scaler = preprocessing.StandardScaler()

# Convert to a tensor
features_standardized_tensor = torch.from_numpy(features)

# Show features
features_standardized_tensor
```

```
tensor([[-100.1000, 3240.1000],
        [-200.2000, -234.1000],
        [5000.5000,  150.1000],
        [6000.6000, -125.1000],
        [9000.9000, -673.1000]], dtype=torch.float64)
```

Discussion

While this recipe is very similar to Recipe 4.2, it is worth repeating because of how important it is for neural networks. Typically, a neural network's parameters are initialized (i.e., created) as small random numbers. Neural networks often behave poorly when the feature values are much larger than the parameter values. Furthermore, since an observation's feature values are combined as they pass through individual units, it is important that all features have the same scale.

For these reasons, it is best practice (although not always necessary; for example, when we have all binary features) to standardize each feature such that the feature's values have the mean of 0 and the standard deviation of 1. This can be accomplished easily with scikit-learn's `StandardScaler`.

However, if you need to perform this operation after having created tensors with `requires_grad=True`, you'll need to do this natively in PyTorch, so as not to break the graph. While you'll typically standardize features prior to starting to train the network, it's worth knowing how to accomplish the same thing in PyTorch:

```
# Load library
import torch

# Create features
torch_features = torch.tensor([[-100.1, 3240.1],
                               [-200.2, -234.1],
                               [5000.5, 150.1],
                               [6000.6, -125.1],
                               [9000.9, -673.1]], requires_grad=True)

# Compute the mean and standard deviation
mean = torch_features.mean(0, keepdim=True)
standard_deviation = torch_features.std(0, unbiased=False, keepdim=True)

# Standardize the features using the mean and standard deviation
torch_features_standardized = torch_features - mean
torch_features_standardized /= standard_deviation

# Show standardized features
torch_features_standardized

tensor([[-1.1254,  1.9643],
        [-1.1533, -0.5007],
        [ 0.2953, -0.2281],
        [ 0.5739, -0.4234],
        [ 1.4096, -0.8122]], grad_fn=<DivBackward0>)
```

21.3 Designing a Neural Network

Problem

You want to design a neural network.

Solution

Use the PyTorch `nn.Module` class to define a simple neural network architecture:

```
# Import libraries
import torch
import torch.nn as nn
```

```
# Define a neural network
class SimpleNeuralNet(nn.Module):
    def __init__(self):
        super(SimpleNeuralNet, self).__init__()
        self.fc1 = nn.Linear(10, 16)
        self.fc2 = nn.Linear(16, 16)
        self.fc3 = nn.Linear(16, 1)

    def forward(self, x):
        x = nn.functional.relu(self.fc1(x))
        x = nn.functional.relu(self.fc2(x))
        x = nn.functional.sigmoid(self.fc3(x))
        return x

# Initialize the neural network
network = SimpleNeuralNet()

# Define loss function, optimizer
loss_criterion = nn.BCELoss()
optimizer = torch.optim.RMSprop(network.parameters())

# Show the network
network

SimpleNeuralNet(
  (fc1): Linear(in_features=10, out_features=16, bias=True)
  (fc2): Linear(in_features=16, out_features=16, bias=True)
  (fc3): Linear(in_features=16, out_features=1, bias=True)
)
```

Discussion

Neural networks consist of layers of units. However, there's incredible variety in the types of layers and how they are combined to form the network's architecture. While there are commonly used architecture patterns (which we'll cover in this chapter), the truth is that selecting the right architecture is mostly an art and the topic of much research.

To construct a feedforward neural network in PyTorch, we need to make a number of choices about both the network architecture and training process. Remember that each unit in the hidden layers:

1. Receives a number of inputs.

2. Weights each input by a parameter value.

3. Sums together all weighted inputs along with some bias (typically 0).

4. Most often then applies some function (called an *activation function*).

5. Sends the output on to units in the next layer.

First, for each layer in the hidden and output layers we must define the number of units to include in the layer and the activation function. Overall, the more units we have in a layer, the more complex patterns our network is able to learn. However, more units might make our network overfit the training data in a way detrimental to the performance on the test data.

For hidden layers, a popular activation function is the *rectified linear unit* (ReLU):

$$f(z) = \max(0, z)$$

where z is the sum of the weighted inputs and bias. As we can see, if z is greater than 0, the activation function returns z; otherwise, the function returns 0. This simple activation function has a number of desirable properties (a discussion of which is beyond the scope of this book), and this has made it a popular choice in neural networks. We should be aware, however, that many dozens of activation functions exist.

Second, we need to define the number of hidden layers to use in the network. More layers allow the network to learn more complex relationships, but with a computational cost.

Third, we have to define the structure of the activation function (if any) of the output layer. The nature of the output function is often determined by the goal of the network. Here are some common output layer patterns:

Binary classification
    One unit with a sigmoid activation function

Multiclass classification
    k units (where k is the number of target classes) and a softmax activation function

Regression
    One unit with no activation function

Fourth, we need to define a loss function (the function that measures how well a predicted value matches the true value); again, this is often determined by the problem type:

Binary classification
    Binary cross-entropy

Multiclass classification
    Categorical cross-entropy

Regression
    Mean square error

Fifth, we have to define an optimizer, which intuitively can be thought of as our strategy "walking around" the loss function to find the parameter values that produce the lowest error. Common choices for optimizers are stochastic gradient descent, stochastic gradient descent with momentum, root mean square propagation, and adaptive moment estimation (for more information on these optimizers, see "See Also" on page 333).

Sixth, we can select one or more metrics to use to evaluate the performance, such as accuracy.

In our example, we use the torch.nn.Module namespace to compose a simple, sequential neural network that can make binary classifications. The standard PyTorch approach for this is to create a child class that inherits from the torch.nn.Module class, instantiating a network architecture in the __init__ method, and defining the mathematical operations we want to perform upon each forward pass in the forward method of the class. There are many ways to define networks in PyTorch, and although in this case we use functional methods for our activation functions (such as nn.functional.relu) we can also define these activation functions as layers. If we wanted to compose everything in the network as a layer, we could use the Sequential class:

```
# Import libraries
import torch

# Define a neural network using `Sequential`
class SimpleNeuralNet(nn.Module):
    def __init__(self):
        super(SimpleNeuralNet, self).__init__()
        self.sequential = torch.nn.Sequential(
            torch.nn.Linear(10, 16),
            torch.nn.ReLU(),
            torch.nn.Linear(16,16),
            torch.nn.ReLU(),
            torch.nn.Linear(16, 1),
            torch.nn.Sigmoid()
        )

    def forward(self, x):
        x = self.sequential(x)
        return x

# Instantiate and view the network
SimpleNeuralNet()

SimpleNeuralNet(
  (sequential): Sequential(
    (0): Linear(in_features=10, out_features=16, bias=True)
    (1): ReLU()
    (2): Linear(in_features=16, out_features=16, bias=True)
```

```
    (3): ReLU()
    (4): Linear(in_features=16, out_features=1, bias=True)
    (5): Sigmoid()
  )
)
```

In both cases, the network itself is a two-layer neural network (when counting layers we don't include the input layer because it does not have any parameters to learn) defined using PyTorch's sequential model. Each layer is "dense" (also called "fully connected"), meaning that all the units in the previous layer are connected to all the units in the next layer.

In the first hidden layer we set `out_features=16`, meaning that layer contains 16 units. These units have ReLU activation functions as defined in the `forward` method of our class: `x = nn.functional.relu(self.fc1(x))`. The first layer of our network has the size `(10, 16)`, which tells the first layer to expect each observation from our input data to have 10 feature values. This network is designed for binary classification so the output layer contains only one unit with a sigmoid activation function, which constrains the output to between 0 and 1 (representing the probability an observation is class 1).

See Also

- PyTorch tutorial: Build the Neural Network (*https://oreil.ly/iT8iv*)
- Loss functions for classification, Wikipedia (*https://oreil.ly/4bPXv*)
- On Loss Functions for Deep Neural Networks in Classification, Katarzyna Janocha and Wojciech Marian Czarnecki (*https://oreil.ly/pplP-*)

21.4 Training a Binary Classifier

Problem

You want to train a binary classifier neural network.

Solution

Use PyTorch to construct a feedforward neural network and train it:

```
# Import libraries
import torch
import torch.nn as nn
import numpy as np
from torch.utils.data import DataLoader, TensorDataset
from torch.optim import RMSprop
from sklearn.datasets import make_classification
from sklearn.model_selection import train_test_split
```

```python
# Create training and test sets
features, target = make_classification(n_classes=2, n_features=10,
    n_samples=1000)
features_train, features_test, target_train, target_test = train_test_split(
    features, target, test_size=0.1, random_state=1)

# Set random seed
torch.manual_seed(0)
np.random.seed(0)

# Convert data to PyTorch tensors
x_train = torch.from_numpy(features_train).float()
y_train = torch.from_numpy(target_train).float().view(-1, 1)
x_test = torch.from_numpy(features_test).float()
y_test = torch.from_numpy(target_test).float().view(-1, 1)

# Define a neural network using `Sequential`
class SimpleNeuralNet(nn.Module):
    def __init__(self):
        super(SimpleNeuralNet, self).__init__()
        self.sequential = torch.nn.Sequential(
            torch.nn.Linear(10, 16),
            torch.nn.ReLU(),
            torch.nn.Linear(16,16),
            torch.nn.ReLU(),
            torch.nn.Linear(16, 1),
            torch.nn.Sigmoid()
        )

    def forward(self, x):
        x = self.sequential(x)
        return x

# Initialize neural network
network = SimpleNeuralNet()

# Define loss function, optimizer
criterion = nn.BCELoss()
optimizer = RMSprop(network.parameters())

# Define data loader
train_data = TensorDataset(x_train, y_train)
train_loader = DataLoader(train_data, batch_size=100, shuffle=True)

# Compile the model using torch 2.0's optimizer
network = torch.compile(network)

# Train neural network
epochs = 3
for epoch in range(epochs):
    for batch_idx, (data, target) in enumerate(train_loader):
```

```
    optimizer.zero_grad()
    output = network(data)
    loss = criterion(output, target)
    loss.backward()
    optimizer.step()
print("Epoch:", epoch+1, "\tLoss:", loss.item())

# Evaluate neural network
with torch.no_grad():
    output = network(x_test)
    test_loss = criterion(output, y_test)
    test_accuracy = (output.round() == y_test).float().mean()
    print("Test Loss:", test_loss.item(), "\tTest Accuracy:",
        test_accuracy.item())

Epoch: 1        Loss: 0.19006995856761932
Epoch: 2        Loss: 0.14092367887496948
Epoch: 3        Loss: 0.03935524448752403
Test Loss: 0.06877756118774414  Test Accuracy: 0.9700000286102295
```

Discussion

In Recipe 21.3, we discussed how to construct a neural network using PyTorch's sequential model. In this recipe we train that neural network using 10 features and 1,000 observations of fake classification generated from scikit-learn's `make_classification` function.

The neural network we are using is the same as the one in Recipe 21.3 (see that recipe for a detailed explanation). The difference there is that we only created the neural network; we didn't train it.

At the end, we use `with torch.no_grad()` to evaluate the network. This says that we should not compute gradients for any tensor operations conducted in this section of code. Since we use gradients only during the model training process, we don't want to store new gradients for operations that occur outside of it (such as prediction or evaluation).

The `epochs` variable defines how many epochs to use when training the data. `batch_size` sets the number of observations to propagate through the network before updating the parameters.

We then iterate over the number of epochs, making forward passes through the network using the `forward` method, and then backward passes to update the gradients. The result is a trained model.

21.5 Training a Multiclass Classifier

Problem

You want to train a multiclass classifier neural network.

Solution

Use PyTorch to construct a feedforward neural network with an output layer with softmax activation functions:

```
# Import libraries
import torch
import torch.nn as nn
import numpy as np
from torch.utils.data import DataLoader, TensorDataset
from torch.optim import RMSprop
from sklearn.datasets import make_classification
from sklearn.model_selection import train_test_split

N_CLASSES=3
EPOCHS=3

# Create training and test sets
features, target = make_classification(n_classes=N_CLASSES, n_informative=9,
    n_redundant=0, n_features=10, n_samples=1000)
features_train, features_test, target_train, target_test = train_test_split(
    features, target, test_size=0.1, random_state=1)

# Set random seed
torch.manual_seed(0)
np.random.seed(0)

# Convert data to PyTorch tensors
x_train = torch.from_numpy(features_train).float()
y_train = torch.nn.functional.one_hot(torch.from_numpy(target_train).long(),
    num_classes=N_CLASSES).float()
x_test = torch.from_numpy(features_test).float()
y_test = torch.nn.functional.one_hot(torch.from_numpy(target_test).long(),
    num_classes=N_CLASSES).float()

# Define a neural network using `Sequential`
class SimpleNeuralNet(nn.Module):
    def __init__(self):
        super(SimpleNeuralNet, self).__init__()
        self.sequential = torch.nn.Sequential(
            torch.nn.Linear(10, 16),
            torch.nn.ReLU(),
            torch.nn.Linear(16,16),
            torch.nn.ReLU(),
            torch.nn.Linear(16,3),
```

```
            torch.nn.Softmax()
        )

    def forward(self, x):
        x = self.sequential(x)
        return x

# Initialize neural network
network = SimpleNeuralNet()

# Define loss function, optimizer
criterion = nn.CrossEntropyLoss()
optimizer = RMSprop(network.parameters())

# Define data loader
train_data = TensorDataset(x_train, y_train)
train_loader = DataLoader(train_data, batch_size=100, shuffle=True)

# Compile the model using torch 2.0's optimizer
network = torch.compile(network)

# Train neural network
for epoch in range(EPOCHS):
    for batch_idx, (data, target) in enumerate(train_loader):
        optimizer.zero_grad()
        output = network(data)
        loss = criterion(output, target)
        loss.backward()
        optimizer.step()
    print("Epoch:", epoch+1, "\tLoss:", loss.item())

# Evaluate neural network
with torch.no_grad():
    output = network(x_test)
    test_loss = criterion(output, y_test)
    test_accuracy = (output.round() == y_test).float().mean()
    print("Test Loss:", test_loss.item(), "\tTest Accuracy:",
        test_accuracy.item())

Epoch: 1       Loss: 0.8022041916847229
Epoch: 2       Loss: 0.775616466999054
Epoch: 3       Loss: 0.7751263380050659
Test Loss: 0.8105319142341614   Test Accuracy: 0.8199999928474426
```

Discussion

In this solution we created a similar neural network to the binary classifier from
the last recipe, but with some notable changes. In the classification data we
generated, we set N_CLASSES=3. To handle multiclass classification, we also use
nn.CrossEntropyLoss(), which expects the target to be one-hot encoded. To accomplish this, we use the torch.nn.functional.one_hot function and end up with

a one-hot encoded array where the position of 1. indicates the class for a given observation:

```
# View target matrix
y_train

tensor([[1., 0., 0.],
        [0., 1., 0.],
        [1., 0., 0.],
        ...,
        [0., 1., 0.],
        [1., 0., 0.],
        [0., 0., 1.]])
```

Since this is a multiclass classification problem, we used an output layer of size 3 (one per class) containing a softmax activation function. The softmax activation function will return an array of 3 values summing to 1. These 3 values represent an observation's probability of being a member of each of the 3 classes.

As mentioned in this recipe, we used a loss function suited to multiclass classification, the categorical cross-entropy loss function: nn.CrossEntropyLoss().

21.6 Training a Regressor

Problem

You want to train a neural network for regression.

Solution

Use PyTorch to construct a feedforward neural network with a single output unit that has no activation function:

```
# Import libraries
import torch
import torch.nn as nn
import numpy as np
from torch.utils.data import DataLoader, TensorDataset
from torch.optim import RMSprop
from sklearn.datasets import make_regression
from sklearn.model_selection import train_test_split

EPOCHS=5

# Create training and test sets
features, target = make_regression(n_features=10, n_samples=1000)
features_train, features_test, target_train, target_test = train_test_split(
    features, target, test_size=0.1, random_state=1)

# Set random seed
```

```python
torch.manual_seed(0)
np.random.seed(0)

# Convert data to PyTorch tensors
x_train = torch.from_numpy(features_train).float()
y_train = torch.from_numpy(target_train).float().view(-1,1)
x_test = torch.from_numpy(features_test).float()
y_test = torch.from_numpy(target_test).float().view(-1,1)

# Define a neural network using `Sequential`
class SimpleNeuralNet(nn.Module):
    def __init__(self):
        super(SimpleNeuralNet, self).__init__()
        self.sequential = torch.nn.Sequential(
            torch.nn.Linear(10, 16),
            torch.nn.ReLU(),
            torch.nn.Linear(16,16),
            torch.nn.ReLU(),
            torch.nn.Linear(16,1),
        )

    def forward(self, x):
        x = self.sequential(x)
        return x

# Initialize neural network
network = SimpleNeuralNet()

# Define loss function, optimizer
criterion = nn.MSELoss()
optimizer = RMSprop(network.parameters())

# Define data loader
train_data = TensorDataset(x_train, y_train)
train_loader = DataLoader(train_data, batch_size=100, shuffle=True)

# Compile the model using torch 2.0's optimizer
network = torch.compile(network)

# Train neural network
for epoch in range(EPOCHS):
    for batch_idx, (data, target) in enumerate(train_loader):
        optimizer.zero_grad()
        output = network(data)
        loss = criterion(output, target)
        loss.backward()
        optimizer.step()
    print("Epoch:", epoch+1, "\tLoss:", loss.item())

# Evaluate neural network
with torch.no_grad():
    output = network(x_test)
```

```
    test_loss = float(criterion(output, y_test))
    print("Test MSE:", test_loss)
Epoch: 1        Loss: 10764.02734375
Epoch: 2        Loss: 1356.510009765625
Epoch: 3        Loss: 504.9664306640625
Epoch: 4        Loss: 199.11314392089844
Epoch: 5        Loss: 191.20834350585938
Test MSE: 162.24497985839844
```

Discussion

It's completely possible to create a neural network to predict continuous values instead of class probabilities. In the case of our binary classifier (Recipe 21.4) we used an output layer with a single unit and a sigmoid activation function to produce a probability that an observation was class 1. Importantly, the sigmoid activation function constrained the outputted value to between 0 and 1. If we remove that constraint by having no activation function, we allow the output to be a continuous value.

Furthermore, because we are training a regression, we should use an appropriate loss function and evaluation metric, in our case the mean square error:

$$\text{MSE} = \frac{1}{n} \sum_{i=1}^{n} \left(\widehat{y}_i - y_i \right)^2$$

where n is the number of observations; y_i is the true value of the target we are trying to predict, y, for observation i; and $\widehat{y}_i$ is the model's predicted value for y_i.

Finally, because we are using simulated data using scikit-learn `make_regression`, we didn't have to standardize the features. It should be noted, however, that in almost all real-world cases, standardization would be necessary.

21.7 Making Predictions

Problem

You want to use a neural network to make predictions.

Solution

Use PyTorch to construct a feedforward neural network, then make predictions using `forward`:

```
# Import libraries
import torch
import torch.nn as nn
import numpy as np
```

```
from torch.utils.data import DataLoader, TensorDataset
from torch.optim import RMSprop
from sklearn.datasets import make_classification
from sklearn.model_selection import train_test_split

# Create training and test sets
features, target = make_classification(n_classes=2, n_features=10,
    n_samples=1000)
features_train, features_test, target_train, target_test = train_test_split(
    features, target, test_size=0.1, random_state=1)

# Set random seed
torch.manual_seed(0)
np.random.seed(0)

# Convert data to PyTorch tensors
x_train = torch.from_numpy(features_train).float()
y_train = torch.from_numpy(target_train).float().view(-1, 1)
x_test = torch.from_numpy(features_test).float()
y_test = torch.from_numpy(target_test).float().view(-1, 1)

# Define a neural network using `Sequential`
class SimpleNeuralNet(nn.Module):
    def __init__(self):
        super(SimpleNeuralNet, self).__init__()
        self.sequential = torch.nn.Sequential(
            torch.nn.Linear(10, 16),
            torch.nn.ReLU(),
            torch.nn.Linear(16,16),
            torch.nn.ReLU(),
            torch.nn.Linear(16, 1),
            torch.nn.Sigmoid()
        )

    def forward(self, x):
        x = self.sequential(x)
        return x

# Initialize neural network
network = SimpleNeuralNet()

# Define loss function, optimizer
criterion = nn.BCELoss()
optimizer = RMSprop(network.parameters())

# Define data loader
train_data = TensorDataset(x_train, y_train)
train_loader = DataLoader(train_data, batch_size=100, shuffle=True)

# Compile the model using torch 2.0's optimizer
network = torch.compile(network)
```

```
# Train neural network
epochs = 3
for epoch in range(epochs):
    for batch_idx, (data, target) in enumerate(train_loader):
        optimizer.zero_grad()
        output = network(data)
        loss = criterion(output, target)
        loss.backward()
        optimizer.step()
    print("Epoch:", epoch+1, "\tLoss:", loss.item())

# Evaluate neural network
with torch.no_grad():
    predicted_class = network.forward(x_train).round()

predicted_class[0]

Epoch: 1        Loss: 0.19006995856761932
Epoch: 2        Loss: 0.14092367887496948
Epoch: 3        Loss: 0.03935524448752403
tensor([1.])
```

Discussion

Making predictions is easy in PyTorch. Once we have trained our neural network we can use the `forward` method (already used as part of the training process), which takes as input a set of features and does a forward pass through the network. In our solution the neural network is set up for binary classification, so the predicted output is the probability of being class 1. Observations with predicted values very close to 1 are highly likely to be class 1, while observations with predicted values very close to 0 are highly likely to be class 0. Hence, we use the `round` method to convert these values to 1s and 0s for our binary classifier.

21.8 Visualize Training History

Problem

You want to find the "sweet spot" in a neural network's loss and/or accuracy score.

Solution

Use Matplotlib to visualize the loss of the test and training set over each epoch:

```
# Load libraries
import torch
import torch.nn as nn
from torch.utils.data import DataLoader, TensorDataset
from torch.optim import RMSprop
from sklearn.datasets import make_classification
```

```
from sklearn.model_selection import train_test_split

import numpy as np
import matplotlib.pyplot as plt

# Create training and test sets
features, target = make_classification(n_classes=2, n_features=10,
    n_samples=1000)
features_train, features_test, target_train, target_test = train_test_split(
    features, target, test_size=0.1, random_state=1)

# Set random seed
torch.manual_seed(0)
np.random.seed(0)

# Convert data to PyTorch tensors
x_train = torch.from_numpy(features_train).float()
y_train = torch.from_numpy(target_train).float().view(-1, 1)
x_test = torch.from_numpy(features_test).float()
y_test = torch.from_numpy(target_test).float().view(-1, 1)

# Define a neural network using `Sequential`
class SimpleNeuralNet(nn.Module):
    def __init__(self):
        super(SimpleNeuralNet, self).__init__()
        self.sequential = torch.nn.Sequential(
            torch.nn.Linear(10, 16),
            torch.nn.ReLU(),
            torch.nn.Linear(16,16),
            torch.nn.ReLU(),
            torch.nn.Linear(16, 1),
            torch.nn.Sigmoid()
        )

    def forward(self, x):
        x = self.sequential(x)
        return x

# Initialize neural network
network = SimpleNeuralNet()

# Define loss function, optimizer
criterion = nn.BCELoss()
optimizer = RMSprop(network.parameters())

# Define data loader
train_data = TensorDataset(x_train, y_train)
train_loader = DataLoader(train_data, batch_size=100, shuffle=True)

# Compile the model using torch 2.0's optimizer
network = torch.compile(network)
```

```
# Train neural network
epochs = 8
train_losses = []
test_losses = []
for epoch in range(epochs):
    for batch_idx, (data, target) in enumerate(train_loader):
        optimizer.zero_grad()
        output = network(data)
        loss = criterion(output, target)
        loss.backward()
        optimizer.step()

    with torch.no_grad():
        train_output = network(x_train)
        train_loss = criterion(output, target)
        train_losses.append(train_loss.item())

        test_output = network(x_test)
        test_loss = criterion(test_output, y_test)
        test_losses.append(test_loss.item())

# Visualize loss history
epochs = range(0, epochs)
plt.plot(epochs, train_losses, "r--")
plt.plot(epochs, test_losses, "b-")
plt.legend(["Training Loss", "Test Loss"])
plt.xlabel("Epoch")
plt.ylabel("Loss")
plt.show();
```

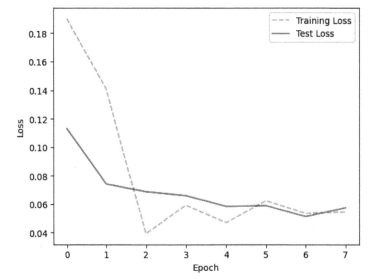

Discussion

When our neural network is new, it will have poor performance. As the neural network learns on the training data, the model's error on both the training and test set will tend to decrease. However, at a certain point, a neural network can start "memorizing" the training data and overfit. When this starts happening, the training error may decrease while the test error starts increasing. Therefore, in many cases, there is a "sweet spot" where the test error (which is the error we mainly care about) is at its lowest point. This effect can be seen in the solution, where we visualize the training and test loss at each epoch. Note that the test error is lowest around epoch 6, after which the training loss plateaus while the test loss starts increasing. From this point onward, the model is overfitting.

21.9 Reducing Overfitting with Weight Regularization

Problem

You want to reduce overfitting by regularizing the weights of your network.

Solution

Try penalizing the parameters of the network, also called *weight regularization*:

```
# Import libraries
import torch
import torch.nn as nn
import numpy as np
from torch.utils.data import DataLoader, TensorDataset
from torch.optim import RMSprop
from sklearn.datasets import make_classification
from sklearn.model_selection import train_test_split

# Create training and test sets
features, target = make_classification(n_classes=2, n_features=10,
    n_samples=1000)
features_train, features_test, target_train, target_test = train_test_split(
    features, target, test_size=0.1, random_state=1)

# Set random seed
torch.manual_seed(0)
np.random.seed(0)

# Convert data to PyTorch tensors
x_train = torch.from_numpy(features_train).float()
y_train = torch.from_numpy(target_train).float().view(-1, 1)
x_test = torch.from_numpy(features_test).float()
y_test = torch.from_numpy(target_test).float().view(-1, 1)
```

```python
# Define a neural network using `Sequential`
class SimpleNeuralNet(nn.Module):
    def __init__(self):
        super(SimpleNeuralNet, self).__init__()
        self.sequential = torch.nn.Sequential(
            torch.nn.Linear(10, 16),
            torch.nn.ReLU(),
            torch.nn.Linear(16,16),
            torch.nn.ReLU(),
            torch.nn.Linear(16, 1),
            torch.nn.Sigmoid()
        )

    def forward(self, x):
        x = self.sequential(x)
        return x

# Initialize neural network
network = SimpleNeuralNet()

# Define loss function, optimizer
criterion = nn.BCELoss()
optimizer = torch.optim.Adam(network.parameters(), lr=1e-4, weight_decay=1e-5)

# Define data loader
train_data = TensorDataset(x_train, y_train)
train_loader = DataLoader(train_data, batch_size=100, shuffle=True)

# Compile the model using torch 2.0's optimizer
network = torch.compile(network)

# Train neural network
epochs = 100
for epoch in range(epochs):
    for batch_idx, (data, target) in enumerate(train_loader):
        optimizer.zero_grad()
        output = network(data)
        loss = criterion(output, target)
        loss.backward()
        optimizer.step()

# Evaluate neural network
with torch.no_grad():
    output = network(x_test)
    test_loss = criterion(output, y_test)
    test_accuracy = (output.round() == y_test).float().mean()
    print("Test Loss:", test_loss.item(), "\tTest Accuracy:",
        test_accuracy.item())

Test Loss: 0.4030887186527252    Test Accuracy: 0.9599999785423279
```

Discussion

One strategy to combat overfitting neural networks is by penalizing the parameters (i.e., weights) of the neural network such that they are driven to be small values, creating a simpler model less prone to overfit. This method is called weight regularization or weight decay. More specifically, in weight regularization a penalty is added to the loss function, such as the L2 norm.

In PyTorch, we can add weight regularization by including `weight_decay=1e-5` in the optimizer where regularization happens. In this example, `1e-5` determines how much we penalize higher parameter values. Values greater than 0 indicate L2 regularization in PyTorch.

21.10 Reducing Overfitting with Early Stopping

Problem

You want to reduce overfitting by stopping training when your train and test scores diverge.

Solution

Use PyTorch Lightning to implement a strategy called *early stopping*:

```
# Import libraries
import torch
import torch.nn as nn
import numpy as np
from torch.utils.data import DataLoader, TensorDataset
from torch.optim import RMSprop
import lightning as pl
from lightning.pytorch.callbacks.early_stopping import EarlyStopping
from sklearn.datasets import make_classification
from sklearn.model_selection import train_test_split

# Create training and test sets
features, target = make_classification(n_classes=2, n_features=10,
    n_samples=1000)
features_train, features_test, target_train, target_test = train_test_split(
    features, target, test_size=0.1, random_state=1)

# Set random seed
torch.manual_seed(0)
np.random.seed(0)

# Convert data to PyTorch tensors
x_train = torch.from_numpy(features_train).float()
y_train = torch.from_numpy(target_train).float().view(-1, 1)
x_test = torch.from_numpy(features_test).float()
```

```python
y_test = torch.from_numpy(target_test).float().view(-1, 1)

# Define a neural network using `Sequential`
class SimpleNeuralNet(nn.Module):
    def __init__(self):
        super(SimpleNeuralNet, self).__init__()
        self.sequential = torch.nn.Sequential(
            torch.nn.Linear(10, 16),
            torch.nn.ReLU(),
            torch.nn.Linear(16,16),
            torch.nn.ReLU(),
            torch.nn.Linear(16, 1),
            torch.nn.Sigmoid()
        )

    def forward(self, x):
        x = self.sequential(x)
        return x

class LightningNetwork(pl.LightningModule):
    def __init__(self, network):
        super().__init__()
        self.network = network
        self.criterion = nn.BCELoss()
        self.metric = nn.functional.binary_cross_entropy

    def training_step(self, batch, batch_idx):
        # training_step defines the train loop.
        data, target = batch
        output = self.network(data)
        loss = self.criterion(output, target)
        self.log("val_loss", loss)
        return loss

    def configure_optimizers(self):
        return torch.optim.Adam(self.parameters(), lr=1e-3)

# Define data loader
train_data = TensorDataset(x_train, y_train)
train_loader = DataLoader(train_data, batch_size=100, shuffle=True)

# Initialize neural network
network = LightningNetwork(SimpleNeuralNet())

# Train network
trainer = pl.Trainer(callbacks=[EarlyStopping(monitor="val_loss", mode="min",
    patience=3)], max_epochs=1000)
trainer.fit(model=network, train_dataloaders=train_loader)

GPU available: False, used: False
TPU available: False, using: 0 TPU cores
IPU available: False, using: 0 IPUs
HPU available: False, using: 0 HPUs
```

```
| Name         | Type          | Params
-------------------------------------------------
0 | network   | SimpleNeuralNet | 465
1 | criterion | BCELoss        | 0
-------------------------------------------------
465       Trainable params
0         Non-trainable params
465       Total params
0.002     Total estimated model params size (MB)
/usr/local/lib/python3.10/site-packages/lightning/pytorch/trainer/
    connectors/data_connector.py:224: PossibleUserWarning:
    The dataloader, train_dataloader, does not have many workers which
    may be a bottleneck. Consider increasing the value of the `num_workers`
    argument (try 7 which is the number of cpus on this machine)
    in the `DataLoader` init to improve performance.
  rank_zero_warn(
/usr/local/lib/python3.10/site-packages/lightning/pytorch/trainer/
    trainer.py:1609: PossibleUserWarning: The number of training batches (9)
    is smaller than the logging interval Trainer(log_every_n_steps=50).
    Set a lower value for log_every_n_steps if you want to see logs
    for the training epoch.
  rank_zero_warn(
Epoch 23: 100%|██████████████| 9/9 [00:00<00:00, 59.29it/s, loss=0.147, v_num=5]
```

Discussion

As we discussed in Recipe 21.8, typically in the first several training epochs, both the training and test errors will decrease, but at some point the network will start "memorizing" the training data, causing the training error to continue to decrease even while the test error starts increasing. Because of this phenomenon, one of the most common and very effective methods to counter overfitting is to monitor the training process and stop training when the test error starts to increase. This strategy is called *early stopping*.

In PyTorch, we can implement early stopping as a callback function. Callbacks are functions that can be applied at certain stages of the training process, such as at the end of each epoch. However, PyTorch itself does not define an early stopping class for you, so here we use the popular library lightning (known as PyTorch Lightning) to use an out-of-the-box one. PyTorch Lightning is a high-level library for PyTorch that provides a lot of useful features. In our solution, we included PyTorch Lightning's EarlyStopping(monitor="val_loss", mode="min", patience=3) to define that we wanted to monitor the test (validation) loss at each epoch, and if the test loss has not improved after three epochs (the default), training is interrupted.

If we did not include the EarlyStopping callback, the model would train for the full 1,000 max epochs without stopping on its own:

```
# Train network
trainer = pl.Trainer(max_epochs=1000)
trainer.fit(model=network, train_dataloaders=train_loader)

GPU available: False, used: False
TPU available: False, using: 0 TPU cores
IPU available: False, using: 0 IPUs
HPU available: False, using: 0 HPUs

  | Name      | Type          | Params
-----------------------------------------------
0 | network   | SimpleNeuralNet | 465
1 | criterion | BCELoss        | 0
-----------------------------------------------
465       Trainable params
0         Non-trainable params
465       Total params
0.002     Total estimated model params size (MB)
Epoch 999: 100%|███████████| 9/9 [00:01<00:00,  7.95it/s, loss=0.00188, v_num=6]
`Trainer.fit` stopped: `max_epochs=1000` reached.
Epoch 999: 100%|███████████| 9/9 [00:01<00:00,  7.80it/s, loss=0.00188, v_num=6]
```

21.11 Reducing Overfitting with Dropout

Problem

You want to reduce overfitting.

Solution

Introduce noise into your network's architecture using dropout:

```
# Load libraries
import torch
import torch.nn as nn
import numpy as np
from torch.utils.data import DataLoader, TensorDataset
from torch.optim import RMSprop
from sklearn.datasets import make_classification
from sklearn.model_selection import train_test_split

# Create training and test sets
features, target = make_classification(n_classes=2, n_features=10,
    n_samples=1000)
features_train, features_test, target_train, target_test = train_test_split(
    features, target, test_size=0.1, random_state=1)

# Set random seed
torch.manual_seed(0)
np.random.seed(0)
```

```python
# Convert data to PyTorch tensors
x_train = torch.from_numpy(features_train).float()
y_train = torch.from_numpy(target_train).float().view(-1, 1)
x_test = torch.from_numpy(features_test).float()
y_test = torch.from_numpy(target_test).float().view(-1, 1)

# Define a neural network using `Sequential`
class SimpleNeuralNet(nn.Module):
    def __init__(self):
        super(SimpleNeuralNet, self).__init__()
        self.sequential = torch.nn.Sequential(
            torch.nn.Linear(10, 16),
            torch.nn.ReLU(),
            torch.nn.Linear(16,16),
            torch.nn.ReLU(),
            torch.nn.Linear(16, 1),
            torch.nn.Dropout(0.1), # Drop 10% of neurons
            torch.nn.Sigmoid(),
        )

    def forward(self, x):
        x = self.sequential(x)
        return x

# Initialize neural network
network = SimpleNeuralNet()

# Define loss function, optimizer
criterion = nn.BCELoss()
optimizer = RMSprop(network.parameters())

# Define data loader
train_data = TensorDataset(x_train, y_train)
train_loader = DataLoader(train_data, batch_size=100, shuffle=True)

# Compile the model using torch 2.0's optimizer
network = torch.compile(network)

# Train neural network
epochs = 3
for epoch in range(epochs):
    for batch_idx, (data, target) in enumerate(train_loader):
        optimizer.zero_grad()
        output = network(data)
        loss = criterion(output, target)
        loss.backward()
        optimizer.step()
    print("Epoch:", epoch+1, "\tLoss:", loss.item())

# Evaluate neural network
with torch.no_grad():
    output = network(x_test)
```

```
        test_loss = criterion(output, y_test)
        test_accuracy = (output.round() == y_test).float().mean()
        print("Test Loss:", test_loss.item(), "\tTest Accuracy:",
            test_accuracy.item())

Epoch: 1         Loss: 0.18791493773460388
Epoch: 2         Loss: 0.17331615090370178
Epoch: 3         Loss: 0.1384529024362564
Test Loss: 0.12702330946922302  Test Accuracy: 0.9100000262260437
```

Discussion

Dropout is a fairly common method for regularizing smaller neural networks. In dropout, every time a batch of observations is created for training, a proportion of the units in one or more layers is multiplied by zero (i.e., dropped). In this setting, every batch is trained on the same network (e.g., the same parameters), but each batch is confronted by a slightly different version of that network's *architecture*.

Dropout is thought to be effective because by constantly and randomly dropping units in each batch, it forces units to learn parameter values able to perform under a wide variety of network architectures. That is, they learn to be robust to disruptions (i.e., noise) in the other hidden units, and this prevents the network from simply memorizing the training data.

It is possible to add dropout to both the hidden and input layers. When an input layer is dropped, its feature value is not introduced into the network for that batch.

In PyTorch, we can implement dropout by adding an nn.Dropout layer into our network architecture. Each nn.Dropout layer will drop a user-defined hyperparameter of units in the previous layer every batch.

21.12 Saving Model Training Progress

Problem

Given a neural network that will take a long time to train, you want to save your progress in case the training process is interrupted.

Solution

Use the torch.save function to save the model after every epoch:

```
# Load libraries
import torch
import torch.nn as nn
import numpy as np
from torch.utils.data import DataLoader, TensorDataset
from torch.optim import RMSprop
```

```
from sklearn.datasets import make_classification
from sklearn.model_selection import train_test_split

# Create training and test sets
features, target = make_classification(n_classes=2, n_features=10,
    n_samples=1000)
features_train, features_test, target_train, target_test = train_test_split(
    features, target, test_size=0.1, random_state=1)

# Set random seed
torch.manual_seed(0)
np.random.seed(0)

# Convert data to PyTorch tensors
x_train = torch.from_numpy(features_train).float()
y_train = torch.from_numpy(target_train).float().view(-1, 1)
x_test = torch.from_numpy(features_test).float()
y_test = torch.from_numpy(target_test).float().view(-1, 1)

# Define a neural network using `Sequential`
class SimpleNeuralNet(nn.Module):
    def __init__(self):
        super(SimpleNeuralNet, self).__init__()
        self.sequential = torch.nn.Sequential(
            torch.nn.Linear(10, 16),
            torch.nn.ReLU(),
            torch.nn.Linear(16,16),
            torch.nn.ReLU(),
            torch.nn.Linear(16, 1),
            torch.nn.Dropout(0.1), # Drop 10% of neurons
            torch.nn.Sigmoid(),
        )

    def forward(self, x):
        x = self.sequential(x)
        return x

# Initialize neural network
network = SimpleNeuralNet()

# Define loss function, optimizer
criterion = nn.BCELoss()
optimizer = RMSprop(network.parameters())

# Define data loader
train_data = TensorDataset(x_train, y_train)
train_loader = DataLoader(train_data, batch_size=100, shuffle=True)

# Compile the model using torch 2.0's optimizer
network = torch.compile(network)

# Train neural network
```

```
epochs = 5
for epoch in range(epochs):
    for batch_idx, (data, target) in enumerate(train_loader):
        optimizer.zero_grad()
        output = network(data)
        loss = criterion(output, target)
        loss.backward()
        optimizer.step()
        # Save the model at the end of every epoch
        torch.save(
            {
                'epoch': epoch,
                'model_state_dict': network.state_dict(),
                'optimizer_state_dict': optimizer.state_dict(),
                'loss': loss,
            },
            "model.pt"
        )
    print("Epoch:", epoch+1, "\tLoss:", loss.item())

Epoch: 1        Loss: 0.18791493773460388
Epoch: 2        Loss: 0.17331615090370178
Epoch: 3        Loss: 0.1384529024362564
Epoch: 4        Loss: 0.1435958743095398
Epoch: 5        Loss: 0.17967987060546875
```

Discussion

In the real world, it is common for neural networks to train for hours or even days. During that time a lot can go wrong: computers can lose power, servers can crash, or inconsiderate graduate students can close your laptop.

We can use `torch.save` to alleviate this problem by saving the model after every epoch. Specifically, after every epoch, we save a model to the location `model.pt`, the second argument to the `torch.save` function. If we include only a filename (e.g., *model.pt*) that file will be overridden with the latest model every epoch.

As you can imagine, we can introduce additional logic to save the model every few epochs, only save a model if the loss goes down, etc. We could even combine this approach with the early stopping approach in PyTorch Lightning to ensure we save a model no matter at what epoch the training ends.

21.13 Tuning Neural Networks

Problem

You want to automatically select the best hyperparameters for your neural network.

Solution

Use the `ray` tuning library with PyTorch:

```
# Load libraries
from functools import partial
import numpy as np
import os
import torch
import torch.nn as nn
import torch.nn.functional as F
import torch.optim as optim
from torch.optim import RMSprop
from torch.utils.data import random_split, DataLoader, TensorDataset
from ray import tune
from ray.tune import CLIReporter
from ray.tune.schedulers import ASHAScheduler
from sklearn.datasets import make_classification
from sklearn.model_selection import train_test_split

# Create training and test sets
features, target = make_classification(n_classes=2, n_features=10,
    n_samples=1000)
features_train, features_test, target_train, target_test = train_test_split(
    features, target, test_size=0.1, random_state=1)

# Set random seed
torch.manual_seed(0)
np.random.seed(0)

# Convert data to PyTorch tensors
x_train = torch.from_numpy(features_train).float()
y_train = torch.from_numpy(target_train).float().view(-1, 1)
x_test = torch.from_numpy(features_test).float()
y_test = torch.from_numpy(target_test).float().view(-1, 1)

# Define a neural network using `Sequential`
class SimpleNeuralNet(nn.Module):
    def __init__(self, layer_size_1=10, layer_size_2=10):
        super(SimpleNeuralNet, self).__init__()
        self.sequential = torch.nn.Sequential(
            torch.nn.Linear(10, layer_size_1),
            torch.nn.ReLU(),
            torch.nn.Linear(layer_size_1, layer_size_2),
            torch.nn.ReLU(),
```

```python
            torch.nn.Linear(layer_size_2, 1),
            torch.nn.Sigmoid()
        )

    def forward(self, x):
        x = self.sequential(x)
        return x

config = {
    "layer_size_1": tune.sample_from(lambda _: 2 ** np.random.randint(2, 9)),
    "layer_size_2": tune.sample_from(lambda _: 2 ** np.random.randint(2, 9)),
    "lr": tune.loguniform(1e-4, 1e-1),
}

scheduler = ASHAScheduler(
    metric="loss",
    mode="min",
    max_t=1000,
    grace_period=1,
    reduction_factor=2
)

reporter = CLIReporter(
    parameter_columns=["layer_size_1", "layer_size_2", "lr"],
    metric_columns=["loss"]
)

# # Train neural network
def train_model(config, epochs=3):
    network = SimpleNeuralNet(config["layer_size_1"], config["layer_size_2"])

    criterion = nn.BCELoss()
    optimizer = optim.SGD(network.parameters(), lr=config["lr"], momentum=0.9)

    train_data = TensorDataset(x_train, y_train)
    train_loader = DataLoader(train_data, batch_size=100, shuffle=True)

    # Compile the model using torch 2.0's optimizer
    network = torch.compile(network)

    for epoch in range(epochs):
        for batch_idx, (data, target) in enumerate(train_loader):
            optimizer.zero_grad()
            output = network(data)
            loss = criterion(output, target)
            loss.backward()
            optimizer.step()
            tune.report(loss=(loss.item()))

result = tune.run(
    train_model,
    resources_per_trial={"cpu": 2},
```

```
        config=config,
        num_samples=1,
        scheduler=scheduler,
        progress_reporter=reporter
    )

    best_trial = result.get_best_trial("loss", "min", "last")
    print("Best trial config: {}".format(best_trial.config))
    print("Best trial final validation loss: {}".format(
        best_trial.last_result["loss"]))

    best_trained_model = SimpleNeuralNet(best_trial.config["layer_size_1"],
        best_trial.config["layer_size_2"])

== Status ==
Current time: 2023-03-05 23:31:33 (running for 00:00:00.07)
Memory usage on this node: 1.7/15.6 GiB
Using AsyncHyperBand: num_stopped=0
Bracket: Iter 512.000: None | Iter 256.000: None | Iter 128.000: None |
    Iter 64.000: None | Iter 32.000: None | Iter 16.000: None |
    Iter 8.000: None | Iter 4.000: None | Iter 2.000: None |
    Iter 1.000: None
Resources requested: 2.0/7 CPUs, 0/0 GPUs, 0.0/8.95 GiB heap,
    0.0/4.48 GiB objects
Result logdir: /root/ray_results/train_model_2023-03-05_23-31-33
Number of trials: 1/1 (1 RUNNING)
...
```

Discussion

In Recipes 12.1 and 12.2, we covered using scikit-learn's model selection techniques to identify the best hyperparameters of a scikit-learn model. While in general the scikit-learn approach can also be applied to neural networks, the ray tuning library provides a sophisticated API that allows you to schedule experiments on both CPUs and GPUs.

The hyperparameters of a model *are* important and should be selected with care. However, running experiments to select hyperparameters can be both cost and time prohibitive. Therefore, automatic hyperparameter tuning of neural networks is not the silver bullet, but it is a useful tool to have in certain circumstances.

In our solution we conducted a search of different parameters for layer sizes and the learning rate of our optimizer. The best_trial.config shows the parameters in our ray tuning configuration that led to the lowest loss and best experiment outcome.

21.14 Visualizing Neural Networks

Problem

You want to quickly visualize a neural network's architecture.

Solution

Use the make_dot function from torch_viz:

```
# Load libraries
import torch
import torch.nn as nn
import numpy as np
from torch.utils.data import DataLoader, TensorDataset
from torch.optim import RMSprop
from torchviz import make_dot
from sklearn.datasets import make_classification
from sklearn.model_selection import train_test_split

# Create training and test sets
features, target = make_classification(n_classes=2, n_features=10,
    n_samples=1000)
features_train, features_test, target_train, target_test = train_test_split(
    features, target, test_size=0.1, random_state=1)

# Set random seed
torch.manual_seed(0)
np.random.seed(0)

# Convert data to PyTorch tensors
x_train = torch.from_numpy(features_train).float()
y_train = torch.from_numpy(target_train).float().view(-1, 1)
x_test = torch.from_numpy(features_test).float()
y_test = torch.from_numpy(target_test).float().view(-1, 1)

# Define a neural network using Sequential
class SimpleNeuralNet(nn.Module):
    def __init__(self):
        super(SimpleNeuralNet, self).__init__()
        self.sequential = torch.nn.Sequential(
            torch.nn.Linear(10, 16),
            torch.nn.ReLU(),
            torch.nn.Linear(16,16),
            torch.nn.ReLU(),
            torch.nn.Linear(16, 1),
            torch.nn.Sigmoid()
        )

    def forward(self, x):
        x = self.sequential(x)
```

```
        return x

# Initialize neural network
network = SimpleNeuralNet()

# Define loss function, optimizer
criterion = nn.BCELoss()
optimizer = RMSprop(network.parameters())

# Define data loader
train_data = TensorDataset(x_train, y_train)
train_loader = DataLoader(train_data, batch_size=100, shuffle=True)

# Compile the model using torch 2.0's optimizer
network = torch.compile(network)

# Train neural network
epochs = 3
for epoch in range(epochs):
    for batch_idx, (data, target) in enumerate(train_loader):
        optimizer.zero_grad()
        output = network(data)
        loss = criterion(output, target)
        loss.backward()
        optimizer.step()

make_dot(output.detach(), params=dict(
    list(
        network.named_parameters()
        )
    )
    ).render(
        "simple_neural_network",
        format="png"
)

'simple_neural_network.png'
```

If we open the image that was saved to our machine, we can see the following:

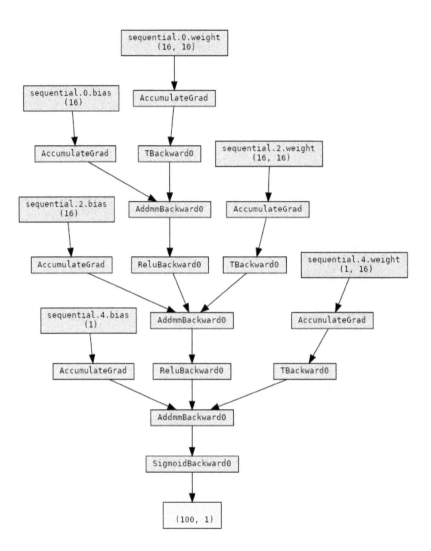

Discussion

The `torchviz` library provides easy utility functions to quickly visualize our neural networks and write them out as images.

## CHAPTER 22

Neural Networks for Unstructured Data

22.0 Introduction

In the previous chapter, we focused on neural network recipes for *structured* data, i.e., tabular data. Most of the largest advances in the past few years have actually involved using neural networks and deep learning for *unstructured* data, such as text or images. Working with these unstructured datasets is a bit different than working with structured sources of data.

Deep learning is particularly powerful in the unstructured data space, where "classic" machine learning techniques (such as boosted trees) typically fail to capture all the complexity and nuance present in text data, audio, images, videos, etc. In this chapter, we will explore using deep learning specifically for text and image data.

In a supervised learning space for text and images, there are many subtasks or "types" of learning. The following are a few examples (though this is not a comprehensive list):

- Text or image classification (example: classifying whether or not an image is a picture of a hotdog)
- Transfer learning (example: using a pretrained contextual model like BERT and fine-tuning it on a task to predict whether or not an email is spam)
- Object detection (example: identifying and classifying specific objects within an image)
- Generative models (example: models that generate text based on a given input such as the GPT models)

As deep learning has grown in popularity and become increasingly commoditized, both the open source and enterprise solutions for dealing with these use cases have become more easily accessible. In this chapter, we'll leverage a few key libraries as our entry point into performing these deep learning tasks. In particular, we'll use PyTorch, Torchvision, and the Transformers Python libraries to accomplish a set of tasks across both text and image ML data.

22.1 Training a Neural Network for Image Classification

Problem

You need to train an image classification neural network.

Solution

Use a convolutional neural network in PyTorch:

```python
# Import libraries
import torch
import torch.nn as nn
import torch.optim as optim
from torchvision import datasets, transforms

# Define the convolutional neural network architecture
class Net(nn.Module):
    def __init__(self):
        super(Net, self).__init__()
        self.conv1 = nn.Conv2d(1, 32, kernel_size=3, padding=1)
        self.conv2 = nn.Conv2d(32, 64, kernel_size=3, padding=1)
        self.dropout1 = nn.Dropout2d(0.25)
        self.dropout2 = nn.Dropout2d(0.5)
        self.fc1 = nn.Linear(64 * 14 * 14, 128)
        self.fc2 = nn.Linear(128, 10)

    def forward(self, x):
        x = nn.functional.relu(self.conv1(x))
        x = nn.functional.relu(self.conv2(x))
        x = nn.functional.max_pool2d(self.dropout1(x), 2)
        x = torch.flatten(x, 1)
        x = nn.functional.relu(self.fc1(self.dropout2(x)))
        x = self.fc2(x)
        return nn.functional.log_softmax(x, dim=1)

# Set the device to run on
device = torch.device("cuda" if torch.cuda.is_available() else "cpu")

# Define the data preprocessing steps
transform = transforms.Compose([
    transforms.ToTensor(),
    transforms.Normalize((0.1307,), (0.3081,))
])
```

```python
# Load the MNIST dataset
train_dataset = datasets.MNIST('./data', train=True, download=True,
    transform=transform)
test_dataset = datasets.MNIST('./data', train=False, transform=transform)

# Create data loaders
batch_size = 64
train_loader = torch.utils.data.DataLoader(train_dataset, batch_size=batch_size,
    shuffle=True)
test_loader = torch.utils.data.DataLoader(test_dataset, batch_size=batch_size,
    shuffle=True)

# Initialize the model and optimizer
model = Net().to(device)
optimizer = optim.Adam(model.parameters())

# Compile the model using torch 2.0's optimizer
model = torch.compile(model)

# Define the training loop
model.train()
for batch_idx, (data, target) in enumerate(train_loader):
    data, target = data.to(device), target.to(device)
    optimizer.zero_grad()
    output = model(data)
    loss = nn.functional.nll_loss(output, target)
    loss.backward()
    optimizer.step()

# Define the testing loop
model.eval()
test_loss = 0
correct = 0
with torch.no_grad():
    for data, target in test_loader:
        data, target = data.to(device), target.to(device)
        output = model(data)

        # get the index of the max log-probability
        test_loss += nn.functional.nll_loss(
            output, target, reduction='sum'
        ).item()  # sum up batch loss
        pred = output.argmax(dim=1, keepdim=True)
        correct += pred.eq(target.view_as(pred)).sum().item()

test_loss /= len(test_loader.dataset)
```

Discussion

Convolutional neural networks are typically used for tasks in image recognition and computer vision. They typically consist of convolutional layers, pooling layers, and a fully connected layer.

The purpose of the *convolutional layers* is to learn important image features that can be used for the task at hand. Convolutional layers work by applying a filter to a particular area of an image (the size of the convolution). The weights of this layer then learn to recognize specific image features critical in the classification task. For instance, if we're training a model that recognizes a person's hand, the filter may learn to recognize fingers.

The purpose of the *pooling layer* is typically to reduce the dimensionality of the inputs from the previous layer. This layer also uses a filter applied to a portion of the input, but it has no activation. Instead, it reduces dimensionality of the input by performing *max pooling* (where it selects the pixel in the filter with the highest value) or *average pooling* (where it takes an average of the input pixels to use instead).

Finally, the *fully connected layer* can be used with something like a softmax activation function to create a binary classification task.

See Also

- Convolutional Neural Networks (*https://oreil.ly/HoO9g*)

22.2 Training a Neural Network for Text Classification

Problem

You need to train a neural network to classify text data.

Solution

Use a PyTorch neural network whose first layer is the size of your vocabulary:

```
# Import libraries
import torch
import torch.nn as nn
import torch.optim as optim
import numpy as np
from sklearn.datasets import fetch_20newsgroups
from sklearn.feature_extraction.text import CountVectorizer
from sklearn.model_selection import train_test_split
from sklearn.metrics import accuracy_score

# Load the 20 newsgroups dataset
```

```python
cats = ['alt.atheism', 'sci.space']
newsgroups_data = fetch_20newsgroups(subset='all', shuffle=True,
    random_state=42, categories=cats)

# Split the dataset into training and test sets
X_train, X_test, y_train, y_test = train_test_split(newsgroups_data.data,
    newsgroups_data.target, test_size=0.2, random_state=42)

# Vectorize the text data using a bag-of-words approach
vectorizer = CountVectorizer(stop_words='english')
X_train = vectorizer.fit_transform(X_train).toarray()
X_test = vectorizer.transform(X_test).toarray()

# Convert the data to PyTorch tensors
X_train = torch.tensor(X_train, dtype=torch.float32)
y_train = torch.tensor(y_train, dtype=torch.long)
X_test = torch.tensor(X_test, dtype=torch.float32)
y_test = torch.tensor(y_test, dtype=torch.long)

# Define the model
class TextClassifier(nn.Module):
    def __init__(self, num_classes):
        super(TextClassifier, self).__init__()
        self.fc1 = nn.Linear(X_train.shape[1], 128)
        self.fc2 = nn.Linear(128, num_classes)

    def forward(self, x):
        x = nn.functional.relu(self.fc1(x))
        x = self.fc2(x)
        return nn.functional.log_softmax(x, dim=1)

# Instantiate the model and define the loss function and optimizer
model = TextClassifier(num_classes=len(cats))
loss_function = nn.CrossEntropyLoss()
optimizer = optim.Adam(model.parameters(), lr=0.01)

# Compile the model using torch 2.0's optimizer
model = torch.compile(model)

# Train the model
num_epochs = 1
batch_size = 10
num_batches = len(X_train) // batch_size
for epoch in range(num_epochs):
    total_loss = 0.0
    for i in range(num_batches):
        # Prepare the input and target data for the current batch
        start_idx = i * batch_size
        end_idx = (i + 1) * batch_size
        inputs = X_train[start_idx:end_idx]
        targets = y_train[start_idx:end_idx]
```

```
# Zero the gradients for the optimizer
optimizer.zero_grad()

# Forward pass through the model and compute the loss
outputs = model(inputs)
loss = loss_function(outputs, targets)

# Backward pass through the model and update the parameters
loss.backward()
optimizer.step()

# Update the total loss for the epoch
total_loss += loss.item()

# Compute the accuracy on the test set for the epoch
test_outputs = model(X_test)
test_predictions = torch.argmax(test_outputs, dim=1)
test_accuracy = accuracy_score(y_test, test_predictions)

# Print the epoch number, average loss, and test accuracy
print(f"Epoch: {epoch+1}, Loss: {total_loss/num_batches}, Test Accuracy:"
    "{test_accuracy}")
```

Discussion

Unlike images, text data is inherently nonnumeric. Before training a model, we need to convert the text into a numeric representation that the model can use to learn which words and word combinations are important for the classification task at hand. In this example, we use scikit-learn's CountVectorizer to encode the vocabulary as a vector the size of the entire vocabulary, where each word is assigned to a specific index in the vector, and the value at that location is the number of times that word appears in a given paragraph. In this case, we can see the vocabulary size by looking at our training set:

```
X_train.shape[1]
```

```
25150
```

We use this same value in the first layer of our neural network to determine the size of the input layer: self.fc1 = nn.Linear(X_train.shape[1], 128). This allows our network to learn what are called *word embeddings*, vector representations of individual words learned from a supervised learning task like the one in this recipe. This task will allow us to learn word embeddings of size 128, though these embeddings will primarily be useful for this specific task and vocabulary.

22.3 Fine-Tuning a Pretrained Model for Image Classification

Problem

You want to train an image classification model using learnings from a pretrained model.

Solution

Use the `transformers` library with `torchvision` to fine-tune a pretrained model on your data:

```
# Import libraries
import torch
from torchvision.transforms import(
    RandomResizedCrop, Compose, Normalize, ToTensor
    )
from transformers import Trainer, TrainingArguments, DefaultDataCollator
from transformers import ViTFeatureExtractor, ViTForImageClassification
from datasets import load_dataset, load_metric, Image

# Define a helper function to convert the images into RGB
def transforms(examples):
    examples["pixel_values"] = [_transforms(img.convert("RGB")) for img in
        examples["image"]]
    del examples["image"]
    return examples

# Define a helper function to compute metrics
def compute_metrics(p):
    return metric.compute(predictions=np.argmax(p.predictions, axis=1),
        references=p.label_ids)

# Load the fashion mnist dataset
dataset = load_dataset("fashion_mnist")

# Load the processor from the VIT model
image_processor = ViTFeatureExtractor.from_pretrained(
    "google/vit-base-patch16-224-in21k"
)

# Set the labels from the dataset
labels = dataset['train'].features['label'].names

# Load the pretrained model
model = ViTForImageClassification.from_pretrained(
    "google/vit-base-patch16-224-in21k",
    num_labels=len(labels),
    id2label={str(i): c for i, c in enumerate(labels)},
```

```python
        label2id={c: str(i) for i, c in enumerate(labels)}
    )

    # Define the collator, normalizer, and transforms
    collate_fn = DefaultDataCollator()
    normalize = Normalize(mean=image_processor.image_mean,
        std=image_processor.image_std)
    size = (
        image_processor.size["shortest_edge"]
        if "shortest_edge" in image_processor.size
        else (image_processor.size["height"], image_processor.size["width"])
    )
    _transforms = Compose([RandomResizedCrop(size), ToTensor(), normalize])

    # Load the dataset we'll use with transformations
    dataset = dataset.with_transform(transforms)

    # Use accuracy as our metric
    metric = load_metric("accuracy")

    # Set the training args
    training_args = TrainingArguments(
        output_dir="fashion_mnist_model",
        remove_unused_columns=False,
        evaluation_strategy="epoch",
        save_strategy="epoch",
        learning_rate=0.01,
        per_device_train_batch_size=16,
        gradient_accumulation_steps=4,
        per_device_eval_batch_size=16,
        num_train_epochs=1,
        warmup_ratio=0.1,
        logging_steps=10,
        load_best_model_at_end=True,
        metric_for_best_model="accuracy",
        push_to_hub=False,
    )

    # Instantiate a trainer
    trainer = Trainer(
        model=model,
        args=training_args,
        data_collator=collate_fn,
        compute_metrics=compute_metrics,
        train_dataset=dataset["train"],
        eval_dataset=dataset["test"],
        tokenizer=image_processor,
    )

    # Train the model, log and save metrics
    train_results = trainer.train()
    trainer.save_model()
```

```
trainer.log_metrics("train", train_results.metrics)
trainer.save_metrics("train", train_results.metrics)
trainer.save_state()
```

Discussion

In the realm of unstructured data like text and images, it is extremely common to start from pretrained models trained on large datasets, instead of starting from scratch, especially in cases where we don't have access to as much labeled data. Using embeddings and other information from the larger model, we can then fine-tune our own model for a new task without the need for as much labeled information. In addition, the pretrained model may have information not captured at all in our training dataset, resulting in an overall performance improvement. This process is known as *transfer learning*.

In this example, we load the weights from Google's ViT (Vision Transformer) model. Then, we use the `transformers` library to fine-tune it for a classification task on the fashion MNIST dataset, a simple dataset of clothing items. This approach can be applied to increase performance on any computer vision dataset, and the `transformers` library provides a high-level interface we can use to fine-tune our own model from larger, pretrained ones without writing an egregious amount of code.

See Also

- Hugging Face website and documentation (*https://oreil.ly/5F3Rf*)

22.4 Fine-Tuning a Pretrained Model for Text Classification

Problem

You want to train a text classification model using learnings from a pretrained model.

Solution

Use the `transformers` library:

```
# Import libraries
from datasets import load_dataset
from transformers import AutoTokenizer, DataCollatorWithPadding
from transformers import (
    AutoModelForSequenceClassification, TrainingArguments, Trainer
    )
import evaluate
import numpy as np
```

```
# Load the imdb dataset
imdb = load_dataset("imdb")

# Create a tokenizer and collator
tokenizer = AutoTokenizer.from_pretrained("distilbert-base-uncased")
data_collator = DataCollatorWithPadding(tokenizer=tokenizer)

# Tokenize the imdb dataset
tokenized_imdb = imdb.map(
    lambda example: tokenizer(
        example["text"], padding="max_length", truncation=True
    ),
    batched=True,
)

# User the accuracy metric
accuracy = evaluate.load("accuracy")

# Define a helper function to produce metrics
def compute_metrics(eval_pred):
    predictions, labels = eval_pred
    predictions = np.argmax(predictions, axis=1)
    return accuracy.compute(predictions=predictions, references=labels)

# Create dictionaries to map indices to labels and vice versa
id2label = {0: "NEGATIVE", 1: "POSITIVE"}
label2id = {"NEGATIVE": 0, "POSITIVE": 1}

# Load a pretrained model
model = AutoModelForSequenceClassification.from_pretrained(
    "distilbert-base-uncased", num_labels=2, id2label=id2label,
        label2id=label2id
)

# Specify the training arguments
training_args = TrainingArguments(
    output_dir="my_awesome_model",
    learning_rate=2e-5,
    per_device_train_batch_size=16,
    per_device_eval_batch_size=16,
    num_train_epochs=2,
    weight_decay=0.01,
    evaluation_strategy="epoch",
    save_strategy="epoch",
    load_best_model_at_end=True,
)

# Instantiate a trainer
trainer = Trainer(
    model=model,
    args=training_args,
    train_dataset=tokenized_imdb["train"],
```

```
        eval_dataset=tokenized_imdb["test"],
        tokenizer=tokenizer,
        data_collator=data_collator,
        compute_metrics=compute_metrics,
)

# Train the model
trainer.train()
```

Discussion

Just like using pretrained image models, pretrained language models hold a massive amount of context about language, as they're typically trained on a wide variety of open internet sources. When we start from a pretrained model base, what we're typically doing is swapping out the classification layer of the existing network for one of our own. This allows us to alter the network weights already learned to fit our specific task.

In this example, we're fine-tuning a DistilBERT model to recognize whether IMDB movie reviews were positive (1) or negative (0). The pretrained DistilBERT model provides a large corpus of words and context on each one, in addition to neural network weights learned from a previous training task. Transfer learning allows us to take advantage of all the initial work done training the DistilBERT model and repurpose it for our use case, which in this instance is classifying movie reviews.

See Also

- Text classification in transformers (*https://oreil.ly/uhrjI*)

## CHAPTER 23

Saving, Loading, and Serving Trained Models

23.0 Introduction

In the last 22 chapters and around 200 recipes, we have covered how to take raw data and use machine learning to create well-performing predictive models. However, for all our work to be worthwhile, we eventually need to *do something* with our model, such as integrate it with an existing software application. To accomplish this goal, we need to be able to save our models after training, load them when they are needed by an application, and then make requests to that application to get predictions.

ML models are typically deployed in simple web servers and designed to take input data and return predictions. This makes the model available to any client on the same network, so other services (such as UIs, users, etc.) can use the ML model to make predictions wherever they are in real time. An example use case would be using ML for item search on an ecommerce website, where an ML model would be served that takes in data about users and listings, and returns a likelihood of the user purchasing that listing. The search results need to be available in real time and available to the ecommerce application that is responsible for taking user searches and coordinating results for the user.

23.1 Saving and Loading a scikit-learn Model

Problem

You have a trained scikit-learn model and want to save it and load it elsewhere.

Solution

Save the model as a pickle file:

```
# Load libraries
import joblib
from sklearn.ensemble import RandomForestClassifier
from sklearn import datasets

# Load data
iris = datasets.load_iris()
features = iris.data
target = iris.target

# Create decision tree classifer object
classifer = RandomForestClassifier()

# Train model
model = classifer.fit(features, target)

# Save model as pickle file
joblib.dump(model, "model.pkl")

['model.pkl']
```

Once the model is saved, we can use scikit-learn in our destination application (e.g., web application) to load the model:

```
# Load model from file
classifer = joblib.load("model.pkl")
```

And use it to make predictions:

```
# Create new observation
new_observation = [[ 5.2,  3.2,  1.1,  0.1]]

# Predict observation's class
classifer.predict(new_observation)

array([0])
```

Discussion

The first step in using a model in production is to save that model as a file that can be loaded by another application or workflow. We can accomplish this by saving the model as a pickle file, a Python-specific data format that enables us to serialize Python objects and write them out to files. Specifically, to save the model we use `joblib`, which is a library extending pickle for cases when we have large NumPy arrays—a common occurrence for trained models in scikit-learn.

When saving scikit-learn models, be aware that saved models might not be compatible between versions of scikit-learn; therefore, it can be helpful to include the version of scikit-learn used in the model in the filename:

```
# Import library
import sklearn

# Get scikit-learn version
scikit_version = sklearn.__version__

# Save model as pickle file
joblib.dump(model, "model_{version}.pkl".format(version=scikit_version))

['model_1.2.0.pkl']
```

23.2 Saving and Loading a TensorFlow Model

Problem

You have a trained TensorFlow model and want to save it and load it elsewhere.

Solution

Save the model using the TensorFlow `saved_model` format:

```
# Load libraries
import numpy as np
from tensorflow import keras

# Set random seed
np.random.seed(0)

# Create model with one hidden layer
input_layer = keras.Input(shape=(10,))
hidden_layer = keras.layers.Dense(10)(input_layer)
output_layer = keras.layers.Dense(1)(input_layer)
model = keras.Model(input_layer, output_layer)
model.compile(optimizer="adam", loss="mean_squared_error")

# Train the model
x_train = np.random.random((1000, 10))
y_train = np.random.random((1000, 1))
model.fit(x_train, y_train)

# Save the model to a directory called `save_model`
model.save("saved_model")

32/32 [==============================] - 1s 8ms/step - loss: 0.2056
INFO:tensorflow:Assets written to: saved_model/assets
```

We can then load the model either in another application or for additional training:

```
# Load neural network
model = keras.models.load_model("saved_model")
```

Discussion

Although we didn't use TensorFlow significantly throughout the course of this book, it is useful to know how to save and load TensorFlow models. Unlike scikit-learn, which uses the Python-native `pickle` format, TensorFlow provides its own method of saving and loading models. The `saved_model` format creates a directory that stores the model and all information necessary to load it back in and make predictions in protocol buffer format (which uses the *.pb* file extension):

```
ls saved_model

assets  fingerprint.pb  keras_metadata.pb  saved_model.pb  variables
```

While we won't go into this format in depth, it is the standard way of saving, loading, and serving models trained in TensorFlow.

See Also

- Serialization and Saving Keras Models (*https://oreil.ly/CDPvo*)
- TensorFlow Saved Model Format (*https://oreil.ly/StpSL*)

23.3 Saving and Loading a PyTorch Model

Problem

You have a trained PyTorch model and want to save it and load it elsewhere.

Solution

Use the `torch.save` and `torch.load` functions:

```
# Load libraries
import torch
import torch.nn as nn
import numpy as np
from torch.utils.data import DataLoader, TensorDataset
from torch.optim import RMSprop
from sklearn.datasets import make_classification
from sklearn.model_selection import train_test_split

# Create training and test sets
features, target = make_classification(n_classes=2, n_features=10,
    n_samples=1000)
features_train, features_test, target_train, target_test = train_test_split(
    features, target, test_size=0.1, random_state=1)
```

```python
# Set random seed
torch.manual_seed(0)
np.random.seed(0)

# Convert data to PyTorch tensors
x_train = torch.from_numpy(features_train).float()
y_train = torch.from_numpy(target_train).float().view(-1, 1)
x_test = torch.from_numpy(features_test).float()
y_test = torch.from_numpy(target_test).float().view(-1, 1)

# Define a neural network using `Sequential`
class SimpleNeuralNet(nn.Module):
    def __init__(self):
        super(SimpleNeuralNet, self).__init__()
        self.sequential = torch.nn.Sequential(
            torch.nn.Linear(10, 16),
            torch.nn.ReLU(),
            torch.nn.Linear(16,16),
            torch.nn.ReLU(),
            torch.nn.Linear(16, 1),
            torch.nn.Dropout(0.1), # Drop 10% of neurons
            torch.nn.Sigmoid(),
        )

    def forward(self, x):
        x = self.sequential(x)
        return x

# Initialize neural network
network = SimpleNeuralNet()

# Define loss function, optimizer
criterion = nn.BCELoss()
optimizer = RMSprop(network.parameters())

# Define data loader
train_data = TensorDataset(x_train, y_train)
train_loader = DataLoader(train_data, batch_size=100, shuffle=True)

# Compile the model using torch 2.0's optimizer
network = torch.compile(network)

# Train neural network
epochs = 5
for epoch in range(epochs):
    for batch_idx, (data, target) in enumerate(train_loader):
        optimizer.zero_grad()
        output = network(data)
        loss = criterion(output, target)
        loss.backward()
        optimizer.step()
```

```
# Save the model after it's been trained
torch.save(
    {
        'epoch': epoch,
        'model_state_dict': network.state_dict(),
        'optimizer_state_dict': optimizer.state_dict(),
        'loss': loss,
    },
    "model.pt"
)

# Reinitialize neural network
network = SimpleNeuralNet()
state_dict = torch.load(
    "model.pt",
    map_location=torch.device('cpu')
    )["model_state_dict"]
network.load_state_dict(state_dict, strict=False)
network.eval()

SimpleNeuralNet(
  (sequential): Sequential(
    (0): Linear(in_features=10, out_features=16, bias=True)
    (1): ReLU()
    (2): Linear(in_features=16, out_features=16, bias=True)
    (3): ReLU()
    (4): Linear(in_features=16, out_features=1, bias=True)
    (5): Dropout(p=0.1, inplace=False)
    (6): Sigmoid()
  )
)
```

Discussion

Though we used a similar formula in Chapter 21 to checkpoint our training progress, here we see how the same approach can be used to load a model back into memory to make predictions. The model.pt that we save the model in is actually just a dictionary that contains the model parameters. We saved the model state in the dictionary key model_state_dict; to load the model back in, we re-initialize our network and load the state of the model using network.load_state_dict.

See Also

- PyTorch tutorial: Saving and Loading Models (*https://oreil.ly/WO3X1*)

23.4 Serving scikit-learn Models

Problem

You want to serve your trained scikit-learn model using a web server.

Solution

Build a Python Flask application that loads the model trained earlier in this chapter:

```
# Import libraries
import joblib
from flask import Flask, request

# Instantiate a flask app
app = Flask(__name__)

# Load the model from disk
model = joblib.load("model.pkl")

# Create a predict route that takes JSON data, makes predictions, and
# returns them
@app.route("/predict", methods = ["POST"])
def predict():
    print(request.json)
    inputs = request.json["inputs"]
    prediction = model.predict(inputs)
    return {
        "prediction" : prediction.tolist()
    }

 # Run the app
if __name__ == "__main__":
    app.run()
```

Make sure you have Flask installed:

```
python3 -m pip install flask==2.2.3 joblib==1.2.0 scikit-learn==1.2.0
```

And then run the application:

```
python3 app.py
 * Serving Flask app 'app'
 * Debug mode: off
WARNING: This is a development server. Do not use it in a production deployment.
    Use a production WSGI server instead.
 * Running on http://127.0.0.1:5000
Press CTRL+C to quit
```

Now, we can make predictions to the application and get results by submitting data points to the endpoints using curl:

```
curl -X POST http://127.0.0.1:5000/predict  -H 'Content-Type: application/json'
    -d '{"inputs":[[5.1, 3.5, 1.4, 0.2]]}'
{"prediction":[0]}
```

Discussion

In this example, we used Flask, a popular open source library for building web
frameworks in Python. We define one route, /predict, that takes JSON data in
a POST request and returns a dictionary containing the predictions. Though this
server is not production-ready (see the Flask warning about using a development
server), we can easily extend and serve this code with a more production-ready web
framework to move it to production.

23.5 Serving TensorFlow Models

Problem

You want to serve your trained TensorFlow model using a web server.

Solution

Use the open source TensorFlow Serving framework and Docker:

```
docker run -p 8501:8501 -p 8500:8500 \
--mount type=bind,source=$(pwd)/saved_model,target=/models/saved_model/1 \
-e MODEL_NAME=saved_model -t tensorflow/serving
```

Discussion

TensorFlow Serving is an open source serving solution optimized for TensorFlow
models. By simply providing the model path, we get an HTTP and gRPC server out
of the box with additional useful features for developers.

The docker run command runs a container using the public tensorflow/serving
image and mounts the saved_model path of our current working directory ($(pwd)/
saved_model) to /models/saved_model/1 inside our container. This automatically
loads the model we saved earlier in this chapter into a running Docker container we
can send prediction queries to.

If you go to *http://localhost:8501/v1/models/saved_model* in your web browser, you
should see the JSON result shown here:

```
{
    "model_version_status": [
        {
            "version": "1",
            "state": "AVAILABLE",
```

```
                "status": {
                    "error_code": "OK",
                    "error_message": ""
                }
            }
        ]
    }
```

The /metadata route at *http://localhost:8501/v1/models/saved_model/metadata* will return more information about the model:

```
{
"model_spec":{
 "name": "saved_model",
 "signature_name": "",
 "version": "1"
}
,
"metadata": {"signature_def": {
 "signature_def": {
  "serving_default": {
   "inputs": {
    "input_8": {
     "dtype": "DT_FLOAT",
     "tensor_shape": {
      "dim": [
       {
        "size": "-1",
        "name": ""
       },
       {
        "size": "10",
        "name": ""
       }
      ],
      "unknown_rank": false
     },
     "name": "serving_default_input_8:0"
    }
   },
   "outputs": {
    "dense_11": {
     "dtype": "DT_FLOAT",
     "tensor_shape": {
      "dim": [
       {
        "size": "-1",
        "name": ""
       },
       {
        "size": "1",
        "name": ""
       }
      }
```

```
    ],
      "unknown_rank": false
    },
    "name": "StatefulPartitionedCall:0"
   }
  },
  "method_name": "tensorflow/serving/predict"
 },
 "__saved_model_init_op": {
  "inputs": {},
  "outputs": {
   "__saved_model_init_op": {
    "dtype": "DT_INVALID",
    "tensor_shape": {
     "dim": [],
     "unknown_rank": true
    },
    "name": "NoOp"
   }
  },
  "method_name": ""
 }
}
}
}
}
```

We can make predictions to the REST endpoint using `curl` and passing the variables (this neural network takes 10 features):

```
curl -X POST http://localhost:8501/v1/models/saved_model:predict
   -d '{"inputs":[[1,2,3,4,5,6,7,8,9,10]]}'

{
    "outputs": [
        [
            5.59353495
        ]
    ]
}
```

See Also

- TensorFlow documentation: Serving Models (*https://oreil.ly/5ZEQo*)

23.6 Serving PyTorch Models in Seldon

Problem

You want to serve a trained PyTorch model for real-time predictions.

Solution

Serve the model using the Seldon Core Python wrapper:

```python
# Import libraries
import torch
import torch.nn as nn
import logging

# Create a PyTorch model class
class SimpleNeuralNet(nn.Module):
    def __init__(self):
        super(SimpleNeuralNet, self).__init__()
        self.sequential = torch.nn.Sequential(
            torch.nn.Linear(10, 16),
            torch.nn.ReLU(),
            torch.nn.Linear(16,16),
            torch.nn.ReLU(),
            torch.nn.Linear(16, 1),
            torch.nn.Dropout(0.1), # Drop 10% of neurons
            torch.nn.Sigmoid(),

        )
# Create a Seldon model object with the name `MyModel`
class MyModel(object):

    # Loads the model
    def __init__(self):
        self.network = SimpleNeuralNet()
        self.network.load_state_dict(
            torch.load("model.pt")["model_state_dict"],
            strict=False
        )
        logging.info(self.network.eval())

    # Makes a prediction
    def predict(self, X, features_names=None):
        return self.network.forward(X)
```

And run it with Docker:

```
docker run -it -v $(pwd):/app -p 9000:9000 kylegallatin/seldon-example
    seldon-core-microservice MyModel --service-type MODEL

2023-03-11 14:40:52,277 - seldon_core.microservice:main:578 -
    INFO:  Starting microservice.py:main
2023-03-11 14:40:52,277 - seldon_core.microservice:main:579 -
    INFO:  Seldon Core version: 1.15.0
2023-03-11 14:40:52,279 - seldon_core.microservice:main:602 -
    INFO:  Parse JAEGER_EXTRA_TAGS []
2023-03-11 14:40:52,287 - seldon_core.microservice:main:605 -
    INFO:  Annotations: {}
2023-03-11 14:40:52,287 - seldon_core.microservice:main:609 -
```

```
INFO:  Importing MyModel
2023-03-11 14:40:55,901 - root:__init__:25 - INFO:  SimpleNeuralNet(
  (sequential): Sequential(
    (0): Linear(in_features=10, out_features=16, bias=True)
    (1): ReLU()
    (2): Linear(in_features=16, out_features=16, bias=True)
    (3): ReLU()
    (4): Linear(in_features=16, out_features=1, bias=True)
    (5): Dropout(p=0.1, inplace=False)
    (6): Sigmoid()
  )
)
2023-03-11 14:40:56,024 - seldon_core.microservice:main:640 -
  INFO:  REST gunicorn microservice running on port 9000
2023-03-11 14:40:56,028 - seldon_core.microservice:main:655 -
  INFO:  REST metrics microservice running on port 6000
2023-03-11 14:40:56,029 - seldon_core.microservice:main:665 -
  INFO:  Starting servers
2023-03-11 14:40:56,029 - seldon_core.microservice:start_servers:80 -
  INFO:  Using standard multiprocessing library
2023-03-11 14:40:56,049 - seldon_core.microservice:server:432 -
  INFO:  Gunicorn Config:  {'bind': '0.0.0.0:9000', 'accesslog': None,
  'loglevel': 'info', 'timeout': 5000, 'threads': 1, 'workers': 1,
  'max_requests': 0, 'max_requests_jitter': 0, 'post_worker_init':
  <function post_worker_init at 0x7f5aee2c89d0>, 'worker_exit':
  functools.partial(<function worker_exit at 0x7f5aee2ca170>,
  seldon_metrics=<seldon_core.metrics.SeldonMetrics object at
  0x7f5a769f0b20>), 'keepalive': 2}
2023-03-11 14:40:56,055 - seldon_core.microservice:server:504 -
  INFO:  GRPC Server Binding to 0.0.0.0:5000 with 1 processes.
2023-03-11 14:40:56,090 - seldon_core.wrapper:_set_flask_app_configs:225 -
  INFO:  App Config:  <Config {'ENV': 'production', 'DEBUG': False,
  'TESTING': False, 'PROPAGATE_EXCEPTIONS': None, 'SECRET_KEY': None,
  'PERMANENT_SESSION_LIFETIME': datetime.timedelta(days=31),
  'USE_X_SENDFILE': False, 'SERVER_NAME': None, 'APPLICATION_ROOT': '/',
  'SESSION_COOKIE_NAME': 'session', 'SESSION_COOKIE_DOMAIN': None,
  'SESSION_COOKIE_PATH': None, 'SESSION_COOKIE_HTTPONLY': True,
  'SESSION_COOKIE_SECURE': False, 'SESSION_COOKIE_SAMESITE': None,
  'SESSION_REFRESH_EACH_REQUEST': True, 'MAX_CONTENT_LENGTH': None,
  'SEND_FILE_MAX_AGE_DEFAULT': None, 'TRAP_BAD_REQUEST_ERRORS': None,
  'TRAP_HTTP_EXCEPTIONS': False, 'EXPLAIN_TEMPLATE_LOADING': False,
  'PREFERRED_URL_SCHEME': 'http', 'JSON_AS_ASCII': None,
  'JSON_SORT_KEYS': None, 'JSONIFY_PRETTYPRINT_REGULAR': None,
  'JSONIFY_MIMETYPE': None, 'TEMPLATES_AUTO_RELOAD': None,
  'MAX_COOKIE_SIZE': 4093}>
2023-03-11 14:40:56,091 - seldon_core.wrapper:_set_flask_app_configs:225 -
  INFO:  App Config:  <Config {'ENV': 'production', 'DEBUG': False,
  'TESTING': False, 'PROPAGATE_EXCEPTIONS': None, 'SECRET_KEY': None,
  'PERMANENT_SESSION_LIFETIME': datetime.timedelta(days=31),
  'USE_X_SENDFILE': False, 'SERVER_NAME': None, 'APPLICATION_ROOT': '/',
  'SESSION_COOKIE_NAME': 'session', 'SESSION_COOKIE_DOMAIN': None,
  'SESSION_COOKIE_PATH': None, 'SESSION_COOKIE_HTTPONLY': True,
```

```
'SESSION_COOKIE_SECURE': False, 'SESSION_COOKIE_SAMESITE': None,
'SESSION_REFRESH_EACH_REQUEST': True, 'MAX_CONTENT_LENGTH': None,
'SEND_FILE_MAX_AGE_DEFAULT': None, 'TRAP_BAD_REQUEST_ERRORS': None,
'TRAP_HTTP_EXCEPTIONS': False, 'EXPLAIN_TEMPLATE_LOADING': False,
'PREFERRED_URL_SCHEME': 'http', 'JSON_AS_ASCII': None,
'JSON_SORT_KEYS': None, 'JSONIFY_PRETTYPRINT_REGULAR': None,
'JSONIFY_MIMETYPE': None, 'TEMPLATES_AUTO_RELOAD': None,
'MAX_COOKIE_SIZE': 4093}>
2023-03-11 14:40:56,096 - seldon_core.microservice:_run_grpc_server:466 - INFO:
    Starting new GRPC server with 1 threads.
[2023-03-11 14:40:56 +0000] [23] [INFO] Starting gunicorn 20.1.0
[2023-03-11 14:40:56 +0000] [23] [INFO] Listening at: http://0.0.0.0:6000 (23)
[2023-03-11 14:40:56 +0000] [23] [INFO] Using worker: sync
[2023-03-11 14:40:56 +0000] [30] [INFO] Booting worker with pid: 30
[2023-03-11 14:40:56 +0000] [1] [INFO] Starting gunicorn 20.1.0
[2023-03-11 14:40:56 +0000] [1] [INFO] Listening at: http://0.0.0.0:9000 (1)
[2023-03-11 14:40:56 +0000] [1] [INFO] Using worker: sync
[2023-03-11 14:40:56 +0000] [34] [INFO] Booting worker with pid: 34
2023-03-11 14:40:56,217 - seldon_core.gunicorn_utils:load:103 - INFO:
    Tracing not active
```

Discussion

While there are many different ways we can serve a PyTorch model, here we choose the Seldon Core Python wrapper. Seldon Core is a popular framework for serving models in production and has a number of useful features that make it easier to use and more scalable than a Flask application. It allows us to write a simple class (above we use MyModel), while the Python library takes care of all the server components and endpoints. We can then run the service using the seldon-core-microservice command, which starts a REST server, gRPC server, and even exposes a metrics endpoint. To make a prediction to the service, we can call the service with the following endpoint on port 9000:

```
curl -X POST http://127.0.0.1:9000/predict  -H 'Content-Type: application/json'
    -d '{"data": {"ndarray":[[0, 0, 0, 0, 0, 0, 0, 0, 0]]}}'
```

You should see the following output:

```
{"data":{"names":["t:0","t:1","t:2","t:3","t:4","t:5","t:6","t:7","t:8"],
    "ndarray":[[0,0,0,0,0,0,0,0,0]]},"meta":{}}
```

See Also

- Seldon Core Python Package (*https://oreil.ly/FTofY*)
- TorchServe documentation (*https://oreil.ly/fjmrE*)

Index

Symbols

+ (plus) operator, 17
- (subtract) operation, 17
: (colon), slicing a DataFrame, 42
@ operator, 18
× (multiply) operator, 18
χ^2 (chi-square) statistic, feature selection, 182, 183

A

accuracy metric, 194-195, 201, 213-215
activation functions, neural network, 331, 336-338, 340
AdaBoostClassifier, 258-260
AdaBoostRegressor, 258-260
adaptive thresholding, 145-147
add method, 16
agg method, 59-60
agglomerative clustering, 310
algorithm-specific methods, speeding up model selection, 228
ANN (approximate nearest neighbors), 270-274
ANOVA F-value, feature selection, 182, 184
Apache Avro, 29
Apache Parquet, 28
apply method, 61, 62, 76
approximate nearest neighbors (ANN), 270-274
area under the ROC curve (AUC ROC), 200
arithmetic operators, for multiplying tensors, 323

arrays (see matrices; NumPy arrays; vectors)
autograd, 326-327
average pooling, 364
Avro file, loading data from, 29

B

back propagation, 326
backfilling missing values, 131
background removal, images, 147-149
bag-of-words model, 113-115
baseline classification model, 193-194
baseline regression model, 191-192
batch of observations, neural network, 326
Bayes' theorem, 295
Beautiful Soup library, 106
BernouilliNB, 299
bias or intercept, linear regression, 232, 235
Binarizer, 81, 82
binarizing images, 145-147
binary classifiers
    logistic regression, 275-276
    neural networks, 333-335
    prediction evaluation, 194-197
    thresholding, 197-200
binary feature data
    naive Bayes classifier training with, 299
    thresholding variance, 179
blurring images, 138-140
boolean conditions
    deleting DataFrame row, 53
    selecting dates and times, 125

dummying (one-hot encoding), 92
DummyRegressor, 191-192
duplicate rows, dropping in dataframes, 54-55
duplicated method, 55

E

early stopping, reducing overfitting with, 347-349
edge detection, images, 149-150
effect in linear regression, 232
elastic net, 239
EllipticEnvelope, 77
embedded methods, feature selection, 177
embeddings, 103, 159-160
epoch, in neural network, 326
equalizeHist method, 142
error handling
    converting strings to dates, 122
    mean squared error, 205
    outliers, 80
Excel file, loading data from, 27
exhaustive search method, model selection, 218-220
Extreme Gradient Boosting (XGBoost), 261

F

factorization, 173
faiss library, 270
false positive rate (FPR), 199
feature extraction, 165-175
    with lasso regression, 240
    linearly inseparable data, 168-170
    matrix factorization, 173-174
    maximizing class separability, 170-172
    principal component approach, 166-167
    sparse data, 174-175
feature selection, 165, 177-186
    highly correlated features in matrix, 180-182
    on random forest, 254
    recursively eliminating features, 184-186
    removing irrelevant features for classification, 182-184
    thresholding binary feature variance, 179
    thresholding numerical feature variance, 178-179
FeatureUnion, 225
feature_importances_ method, 252-254

feedforward neural networks, 325, 333-340
fillna function, 51
filter methods
    binarizing images, 145-147
    binary classifier threshold evaluation, 197-200
    feature selection, 177-184
filter2d method, 141
fit operation, 70
fitting of data to a line
    linear regression, 231-233, 235-237
    reducing overfitting in neural networks, 345-352
fit_transform function, 70
Flask application, 380
flatten method
    NumPy array, 12, 154-156
    PyTorch, 322
for loops, 61
forward filling missing values, 131
forward method, 340
forward propagation, 326
FPR (false positive rate), 199
from_numpy function, 314
fully connected layer, 364
FunctionTransformer, 76
F_1 score, 196, 201

G

GaussianNB, 296-298
Gini impurity, 244
GitHub, xii
goodFeaturesToTrack, 152
Google Sheet, loading data from, 32
Google ViT (Vision Transformer) model, 369
GrabCut algorithm, 147-149
gradient descent, in neural network, 326
GridSearchCV, 218-220, 222-226
groupby function, 56-57, 62
grouping observations with clustering, 83-84
grouping rows in dataframes
    by time, 57-59
    by values, 56-57

H

Haar cascade classifiers, 161-163
harmonic mean, 196

About the Authors

Kyle Gallatin is a software engineer for machine learning infrastructure with years of experience as a data analyst, data scientist, and machine learning engineer. He is also a professional data science mentor and volunteer computer science teacher and frequently publishes articles at the intersection of software engineering and machine learning. Currently, Kyle is a software engineer on the machine learning platform team at Etsy.

Chris Albon is the Director of Machine Learning at the Wikimedia Foundation, the nonprofit that hosts Wikipedia.

Colophon

The animal on the cover of *Machine Learning with Python Cookbook* is the Narina trogon (*Apaloderma narina*). It is named for the mistress of French ornithologist François Levaillant, who derived the name from a Khoikhoi word for "flower," as his mistress's name was difficult to pronounce. The Narina trogon is largely found in Africa, inhabiting both lowlands and highlands, and tropical and temperate climates, usually nesting in the hollows of trees. Its diverse range of habitats makes it a species of least conservation concern.

The Narina trogon eats mostly insects and small invertebrates as well as small rodents and reptiles. Males, which are more brightly colored, give off a grating, low, repeated hoot to defend territory and attract mates. Both sexes have green upper plumage and metallic blue-green tail feathers. Female faces and chest plumages are brown, while males have bright red undersides. Immature birds have similar coloring to females with distinct white tips on their inner wings.

The current conservation status (IUCN) of the Narina trogon is Least Concern. Many of the animals on O'Reilly covers are endangered; all of them are important to the world.

The cover illustration is by Karen Montgomery, based on an image from *Wood's Animate Creation*. The cover fonts are Gilroy Semibold and Guardian Sans. The text fonts are Adobe Minion Pro and Symbola; the heading font is Adobe Myriad Condensed; and the code font is Dalton Maag's Ubuntu Mono.

O'REILLY®

Learn from experts.
Become one yourself.

Books | Live online courses
Instant answers | Virtual events
Videos | Interactive learning

Get started at oreilly.com.

Printed in the USA
CPSIA information can be obtained
at www.ICGtesting.com
JSHW061440010424
60353JS00007B/109